STRATEGIC SERVICE MANAGEMENT

BEYOND THE MOMENT OF TRUTH

THE BEST OF LONG RANGE PLANNING

Series Editor: Professor Bernard Taylor, Henley Management College

The aim of this series is to bring together in each volume the best articles on a particular topic previously published in *Long Range Planning* so that readers wishing to study a specific aspect of planning can find an authoritative and comprehensive view of the subject, conveniently in one volume.

Whereas each issue of *Long Range Planning* normally contains a 'horizontal slice' of Long Range Planning at a particular time, in different fields and in various kinds of organizations across the world, each volume in the new series will take a 'vertical slice' through more than a hundred issues, pulling out the outstanding articles on a given subject.

Titles in *The Best of Long Range Planning* Series:

Strategic Planning — The Chief Executive and the Board (Number 1)
Edited by Bernard Taylor

Entrepreneurship — Creating and Managing New Ventures (Number 2)
Edited by Bruce Lloyd

Making Strategic Planning Work in Practice (Number 3)
Edited by Basil Denning

Planning for Information as a Corporate Resource (Number 4)
Edited by Alfred Collins

Developing Strategies for Competitive Advantage (Number 5)
Edited by Patrick McNamee

Strategic Planning for Human Resources (Number 6)
Edited by Sheila Rothwell

Strategic Service Management (Number 7)
Edited by Denis Boyle

Forthcoming volumes will deal with other topical themes:

Strategic Management in Major Multinational Companies (Number 8)
Edited by Nigel Freedman

Each volume will contain 10–12 articles, and about 120 pages. In due course they will provide a comprehensive and authoritative reference library, covering all important aspects of Strategic Planning.

A Related Journal

LONG RANGE PLANNING★

The Journal of the Strategic Planning Society and of the European Strategic Planning Federation.

Editor: Professor Bernard Taylor, Henley Management College, Greenlands, Henley-on-Thames, Oxon RG9 3AU, UK.

> The leading international journal in the field of strategic planning, which provides authoritative information to senior managers, administrators, and academics on the concepts and techniques involved in the development and implementation of strategy and plans.

★Free sample copy gladly sent on request to the Publisher.

STRATEGIC SERVICE MANAGEMENT

BEYOND THE MOMENT OF TRUTH

Edited by

DENIS BOYLE
The Service Management Group Limited, London

PERGAMON PRESS

Member of Maxwell Macmillan Pergamon Publishing Corporation

OXFORD · NEW YORK · BEIJING · FRANKFURT
SÃO PAULO · SYDNEY · TOKYO · TORONTO

U.K.   Pergamon Press plc, Headington Hill Hall,
                            Oxford OX3 0BW, England

U.S.A.   Pergamon Press, Inc., Maxwell House, Fairview Park,
                            Elmsford, New York 10523, U.S.A.

PEOPLE'S REPUBLIC   Pergamon Press, Room 4037, Qianmen Hotel, Beijing,
OF CHINA   People's Republic of China

FEDERAL REPUBLIC   Pergamon Press GmbH, Hammerweg 6,
OF GERMANY   D-6242 Kronberg, Federal Republic of Germany

BRAZIL   Pergamon Editora Ltda, Rua Eça de Queiros, 346,
                            CEP 04011, Paraiso, São Paulo, Brazil

AUSTRALIA   Pergamon Press Australia Pty Ltd., P.O. Box 544,
                            Potts Point, N.S.W. 2011, Australia

JAPAN   Pergamon Press, 5th Floor, Matsuoka Central Building,
                            1-7-1 Nishishinjuku, Shinjuku-ku, Tokyo 160, Japan

CANADA   Pergamon Press Canada Ltd., Suite No. 271,
                            253 College Street, Toronto, Ontario, Canada M5T 1R5

First edition 1990

Library of Congress Cataloging in Publication Data

Strategic service management: beyond the moment of truth/
edited by
Denis Boyle
p.   cm.—(The Best of long range planning: no. 7)
1. Service industries—Management.
2. Strategic planning.
I. Boyle, Denis   II. Series.
HD9980.5.S765   1990   658.4′012—dc20   90-40614

British Library Cataloguing in Publication Data

Strategic service management: beyond the moment of truth.
1. Service industries. Management. Planning
I. Boyle, Denis   II. Series
338.4

ISBN 0-08-037752-1 Hardcover
ISBN 0-08-037751-3 Flexicover

Printed in Great Britain by BPCC Wheatons Ltd, Exeter

Contents

Strategic Service Management:
Beyond the Moment of Truth

Denis Boyle, The Service Management Group Limited, London

This volume of *The Best of Long Range Planning* is about Strategic Service Management. The authors focus on two main themes:

(1) Creating competitive strategies for a service oriented business.

(2) The process of successful implementation both short and long term.

Most of the research papers, reports and cases are drawn from the world of business. But in response to the growing interest of public services in Strategic Service Management, three contributions are included which deal specifically with experiences of 'non-profit' organizations

Beyond the Moment of Truth

When my colleagues and I first began to study the unique aspects of the strategic management of service businesses we coined the expression 'The Moment of Truth'[1] to characterize the critically important interaction between employees and customers, which takes place in service operations often many thousands of times every working day. The outcome of these 'events' greatly influences perceptions of value — for better or worse — and has been the focal point of most 'customer care' programmes.

The phrase 'the Moment of Truth' has entered the management vocabulary and was used as the title of a book describing one of Europe's Strategic Service Management success stories — the turn-around of Scandinavian Airlines.[2]

Today exploiting the 'Moment of Truth' still offers enormous gains in competitive advantage

and several of the authors in this volume eloquently explain their own exciting experiences. But Strategic Service Management goes way beyond this. It is a new approach to competing and winning in the fast changing and unpredictable environment of the 1990s. Strategic Service Management is a new world view — about what it takes for a business to be No. 1.

As an approach, the concept of Strategic Service Management makes explicit the implicit ideas and techniques behind the revolution in service management thinking which occurred during the 1980s. It focuses on two main areas:

(1) Powerful new ideas for developing customer driven competitive strategies for market leadership and profit growth.

(2) Systematic processes for successful and accelerated strategy implementation.

Surprisingly, the idea of Strategic Service Management has been embraced not only by airlines, banks and insurance firms but also by a large number and a growing variety of manufacturing companies. There are two reasons for this:

(1) *Adding Value With Service*
   Product based companies are dramatically increasing their value added through the service and information content of their products, as they battle to differentiate themselves and maximize profits in low growth, highly competitive markets.

(2) *Success With People*
   In a service organization there is no escaping the necessity to communicate, motivate and involve people as the key to productivity and profits. But as the reduction in the number of school leavers and graduates gives employees

1

a greater choice for whom they work, the lessons of 'social technology'* derived from the service oriented businesses come into their own.

The Service Management System — A Logic of Success

The authors in this volume discuss Strategic Service Management based on a wide variety of experiences and different perspectives. It may therefore be helpful to the reader to bear in mind the common 'pattern of excellence' which characterizes successful service businesses. What in reality is extremely complex can be simplified to its elements — what we in the Service Management Group have called the Service Management System (see Figure 1).

FOCUS & FIT

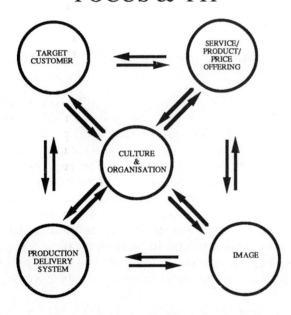

THE BUSINESS LOGIC OF SUCCESS

Figure 1. The Service Management System.
Source: Richard Normann, *Service Management*, p. 20, Wiley, (1984).

The Service Management System is unique to every service business, and is the result of a historical learning process. In times of fundamental change some of the elements tend to get out of step with the needs of the environment and misfits — perceived as strategic problems or opportu-

nities — arise. Strategic Service Management is the process of understanding the traditional pattern of excellence, identifying the main structural environmental changes, interpreting strategic problems and opportunities as misfits, developing an innovative new service strategy and carrying through accelerated change to once again put the business in a position of profitable market leadership.

While Strategic Service Management demands a tight focus on the Service Management System of the business, understanding the competitive environment, the 'big picture' is critically important.

Several of the authors in this volume stress this point and give practical examples of how the most dangerous competitors are the 'invaders' who are not even on the traditional industry map.

Accelerated Implementation

The process of successful implementation follows a number of principles. The following are some of the main emerging themes uncovered by the authors of this volume.

(1) *The strategy must be made sufficiently explicit* so that it can be communicated to everyone across the organization. This does not mean a bland mission statement but rather the essence of the 'Superordinate Goal'* and *how* it can be achieved.

(2) *Implementation must combine two approaches*:
a) *top down* initiatives based on tackling relatively few, but 'high leverage' strategic issues should be started.
b) Sumultaneously a *bottom up* mass involvement programme should be promoted. The process is interactive not sequential.

(3) *Measurement systems must make performance visible*, in agreed key areas. This enables priorities to be set in line with the strategic business goals.

(4) *Organizational blockages must be identified and removed*. Redesign of the structure is a powerful management instrument. Building in customer orientation and eliminating layers of hierarchy are priority tasks.

(5) *Providing mass training* is a concrete expression that individuals are the company's greatest asset. It also helps in communicating across functions and up and down the organization. Service training should combine personal and business development.

---

*'social technology' is the means of influencing people's behaviour so that it fits business goals.

*A Superordinate Goal represents the core mission of the organization, e.g. 'we will be the best airline for businessmen'.

(6) *Problem solving by project teams* is the heart of the implementation process. Such activities will generally be both within and across functions, with defined measurable objectives.

(7) *The mechanisms of reward and recognition are incredibly powerful.* Money is often a hygiene factor. Finding other ways to meet employees' 'life needs' in a manner which helps the business achieve its goals, is a gold mine of opportunity.

(8) *Implement right away.* This is the good news. The even better news is, you are never finished. Implementation is best phased, not least for motivational reasons. But once started, it is a one way road. This demands that leaders balance, on the one hand, the motivating challenge and on the other the celebration of successes.

Fifteen Key Articles

The articles in this volume represent experiences from Europe, South East Asia and North America. They span a variety of industries as well as the public and private sector.

The highlights of each article and its contribution to our theme, Strategic Service Management, are set out below, both to focus on points of particular interest and to enable readers to turn quickly to the articles of most interest to them.

Creating Service Business Strategies

Creating a Successful Marketing Strategy for UNI Insurance

Thorstein Øverland, the Chief Executive, describes how he created and implemented a marketing strategy; he stresses the strategic role of the personnel function.

The target customer groups were divided into three segments.

(1) People who want to insure against everything;

(2) Those who want to be covered for most things;

(3) Individuals who want to take most of the risks themselves — except the most serious losses.

The offer to each of the customer groups consisted essentially of the same basic insurance policies but there were differences in the scope of cover and the level of customer service. For the most expensive product, UNI's staff would do everything when the customer made a phone call. For the lowest priced product the customer had to provide a significant amount of self service, for example by filling out their claim forms.

In creating an offer which was perceived good value by each customer group, UNI used the principle that *in the marketing of services, it is better to design a strategy which focuses on the transactions, rather than the core products.* The reason was that most insurance policies are the same. Value in the eyes of customers is very much associated with a 'no hassle service'. Therefore, the points of interaction between UNI's sales staff and customers represented significant opportunities for adding value. There was also an economic benefit in costs since customers contacted UNI and the company could assess the risks better and minimize its average claims per customer.

The component which was particularly critical in the service delivery system was the personnel. Steps were taken to improve their quality, focusing on such areas as recruitment, training, career planning and reward systems. UNI went to great lengths to design its offering to each target customer group so that it ideally fitted the needs of its sales force.

To make their staff more responsive to the needs of their customers, the organization was decentralized and profit responsibility was pushed down to the local levels. The number of organizational levels was reduced particularly in relations with the customers. Workshops were organized to strengthen the concern for customers and to improve communication within the business. The importance of UNI staff providing good customer service was stressed in company advertising to exploit the contrast with their main competitor, who sold on the basis of product advantages.

This new marketing and personnel approach led to a substantial increase in UNI's market share.

Building a Competitive Advantage Through Information Technology

Information technology is no longer just a tool for reducing cost. It is also a mechanism for radically rethinking products, companies and even whole industries. Colin Jackson's article is a stimulating reminder with lots of interesting examples. He identifies four main areas.

(1) *Ensuring IT–led changes are in your favour*
He examines the two-edged nature of information technology–led changes by discussing the way Eddie Shah hoped to create a new competitive edge based on text processing. This failed

because in the newspaper business editorial content also matters. Having broken the traditional stranglehold of the Unions, a competitor was able to take him over and benefit from the revolution he had pioneered.

(2) *Decreasing the bargaining power of buyers and suppliers*

In America they say 'get your customers and suppliers by their terminals'. Mr. Jackson explains how in backwards integration by having direct computerlinks with its ball bearing supplier, Toyota regulates its shipments to the demands of the production line, thus eliminating unnecessary stock. In forward integration, as in the case of McKesson, the over the counter pharmaceutical supplier, information technology is used to facilitate the process of shelf stocking for chemist shops. By adding value this way, the supplier becomes indispensable to his customer. Both forwards and backwards integration are effective lock-in mechanisms.

(3) *Jumping or building entry barriers into your market*

One example is how without 'home banking' customers prefer to deal with their local branch for the sake of convenience. With a home terminal the rules of the game are changed. Not only can competitors enter the field without investing in heavy high street assets, but the individual customer can switch more easily.

(4) *Creating new value added products or even whole markets*

His final examples are about using information technology to create radically new products and markets. BMW have put computers in their cars which tell you when they need servicing. The sting is that if you do not have the work done at a registered BMW garage, the computer registers alert even when you have had the job done, thus protecting their own service.

The Transformation of AT & T

Journalists often write the best cases since their views are not clouded by theories. Carol Kennedy in describing the transformation of AT & T provides an excellent example of this.

She begins 'No U.S. corporation was prouder than mighty American Telephone and Telegraph or had a greater sense of its own destiny, which may have been partly to blame for the fate that overtook it in 1981–84 when a Federal anti trust suit forced the break-up of the entire Bell system.'

At divestiture after nearly a century of existence, the company boasted assets of $150 billion, revenues in excess of $40 billion, profits in excess of $7 billion, and more than one million employees. This institution was built on the original business concept laid down by Theodore Vail in 1909 'one system, one policy, universal service', a paradigm for the now out-dated old 'concept of service'.

The old corporate philosophy had been justified on the grounds that more wealthy consumers should subsidize the others. This, in addition to a 'cost-plus mentality', led to growing inefficiencies as this vast corporation became out of step with the demands of a competitive new age.

In 1969 fledgling Microwave Communications International entered the lucrative private line business between major industrial cities. Companies could save enormously by using MCI's direct line service. In 1972 MCI announced plans to extend its service to 165 cities from coast to coast. Today the 'invader' goes from strength to strength with its president running on a transplant heart.

One of IBM's top marketing experts, Archibald McGill, was brought in to steer the strategic direction of the company away from being technologically-led to being financially and customer driven.

To accomplish this change

☆ the structure was reshaped,

☆ the planning process redesigned,

☆ new people were brought in from outside,

☆ corporate training programmes were revised,

☆ new compensation reward schemes were set up,

☆ and international alliances were established.

Stockholders were told in 1980 of the new mission 'no longer do we perceive that our business will be limited to telephonic or for that matter telecommunications. Ours is the business of information handling, the knowledge business, and the market that we seek is global.'

As the old Chief Executive approaches retirement, he summarizes the situation when he says 'the principle issue now is how we execute the strategy'.

This is a large classic case of customer targeting and service unbundling with the industry revolution being promoted by 'invaders'.

Successful Strategies — The Story of Singapore Airlines (SIA)

The image of the 'Singapore girl' is now known across the world. Karmjit Singh tells the story of how a once small national carrier has grown rapidly to become an international airline with a network extending to 27 countries.

His report begins with a brief review of SIA's history, outlining the external and internal factors behind the success. He points to the main driving force — location. Singapore straddles the Equator and is strategically located at the crossroads of one of the world's busiest sea and air routes and the airline's home base is increasingly becoming the hub of the ASEAN hinterland with its thriving economies.

But this only provided the context for growth. How was such a successful business created?

Fleet Procurement Strategy
A critical strategic decision has always been that of fleet procurement. This has always focused on buying the best aircraft technology to minimize operating costs. The two fuel crises of 1973 and 1979 vindicated these bold decisions. Investment in aircraft also provided a hedge against inflation, as clever buying and selling was timed with the business cycle.

Service Quality as a Strategic Competitive Weapon
From the outset service quality was seen as an essential competitive edge, particularly in the highly visible arena of inflight experience. To achieve a service that 'even other airlines talk about' became the unofficial motto for employees.

Strategy Through People
Singapore is a small island economy and human resources are the only real national resource asset. SIA, a government owned firm, has invested heavily in its personnel. Recruitment procedures are some of the toughest in the industry and amounts spent on training some of the largest. The continuous involvement and motivation of staff is deep in their culture. Not long ago one person received $50,000 for an idea which saves the company about $1.5 million a year on fuel.

Unceasing Motivation
Continuously innovating to deliver even greater perceived value for customers has taken firm root. SIA were one of the first airlines to give the travelling public 'slumberettes' on B747 upper decks, as well as jackpot machines to relieve flight boredom.

Team Based Organization
The organization functions through small teams with delegation down to the lowest levels consistent with accountability and efficiency.

In the next era of development market growth is now expected to slow down. To maintain profitability in this new environment SIA will continue to pursue service quality as its Strategic Competitive Weapon.

Information Systems for Competitive Advantage at Merrill Lynch

The financial services industry makes vast investments in computer technology. Merrill Lynch is an example of such a corporation with an annual investment of more than a billion dollars in operation systems and telecommunications activities. In her paper, Elaine Koerner provides a fascinating window on current thinking inside this multinational giant as it fights to create its competitive cutting edge.

While demands for improved quality rise consistently, productivity according to Merrill Lynch will be the password of the 1990s for itself and the entire financial services business.

In coming to grips with the mounting competitive pressures, at home from commercial banks and abroad from the European Community and the Japanese, revolutionary innovation is giving way to incremental systematic productivity gains. In pursuing this strategy the focus is on integrating and simplifying a diverse collection of information systems. This is a mammoth undertaking, which affects every aspect of the business.

Attaining the status of low cost producer and distributor, has meant the establishment of a special productivity project. Expert systems are being used both by analysts in credit administration to improve turnaround times and to standardize decisions, as well as providing a powerful tool for training.

Since success depends so much on the company's systems, considerable thought is given to minimizing the business risk in choice of vendors. Three questions in particular are being addressed:

☆ Will the firm stay in business?

☆ Is the technology something that can be built on?

☆ Can we understand the growth part?

In the past the application of advanced computer technology has not enabled the firm of achieve a sustainable competitive advantage. As a consequence, today efforts are being placed on implementing state of the art technology but not pioneering it.

The company, whose goal in the early days was 'to bring Wall Street to Main Street', must now not only maintain its prominent position on Main Street but also establish a powerful global presence. To survive and prosper in this new arena it intends to demonstrate its ability to match the Japanese in their traditional strategy of 'quality up, cost down', but unlike the 1980s now through system integration rather than radical innovation.

Accelerating Successful Implementation

Building a Customer-oriented Organization at Citibank

The expression 'the difference in money is people' was coined by Citibank in the United States. In his article about developments in the U.K., Frank Cornish sets out some of the pioneering efforts made by his corporation in creating a customer-driven organization. Their success is clearly indicated by their profitable penetration of the U.K. financial services industry.

He begins by pointing out that while technology and productivity must at least match competitors, it is not feasible in the long run to sustain major advantages in this area. To be a true industry leader, therefore, Citibank has decided to focus on the service quality of their offering.

The idea that 'quality costs money' is a myth for Citibank. Getting things right first time cuts the cost base by

(1) eliminating the waste created by the error

(2) saving the extra cost in putting it right.

Citibank appreciates that the target customer for people in large organizations is not only the person who signs the cheque but the multitude of individuals at different levels in the customer's organization for all of whom they must create value. To achieve this they encourage staff at all levels to interact with their opposite numbers in the client organizations.

To find the time to make this possible in a cost effective manner, routine tasks are handled in the main by temporary or part time staff, leaving core personnel free to devote more of their energies to value creating interaction.

Service quality goals are built into every person's job description to reinforce the customer oriented culture and the reward system clearly distinguishes between good, average and poor performers.

Full use is made of non financial recognition; for example, in the form of award ceremonies and desk top plaques to promote role models of the ideal employee.

A whole gamut of techniques is used for listening and responding to customers and staff alike on a regular basis and performance expectations are made explicit by internal contracts which ensure that the 'internal customer' chain delivers high perceived value to the end customers.

Training and personnel development is taken very seriously with their in-house programme 'New Age Thinking'. This combines job satisfaction for participants and productivity for the bank.

Bridging the Awful Gap Between Strategy and Action — British Telecom

Dr. Wernham's thesis provides a unique insight into the process of strategy implementation in a large organization.

The background is set by identifying that, like so many other large organizations, the results of plans were not always as their authors had intended. To develop practical ideas about how to improve the process the research sought to identify factors influencing the implementation of strategy within British Telecom (B.T.) and to assess their relative importance. Three strategic implementation initiatives were examined:

(1) *MAC* (Measurement and Analysis Centres), a system for generating and tracing the progress of test calls throughout the network, to measure the quality of service being provided and to identify faults.

(2) *Radiopaging*, a service whereby a person who is out of the office but carrying a pocket bleeper can be alerted.

(3) *SRT* (Special Range Telephone), a new range of decorative or fashionable telephones for customers wanting a distinctive appearance.

One of the first observations was that *when things get done there is always a champion*. As one of those interviewed commented, 'I have used every method in the book or out of the book, dirty or otherwise, in order to get more than my share (of resources) because I think the unit needs it'.

Dr. Wernham found that in a large organization the headquarters, regions and individual operating units all have their own sources of power. Understanding these and the related political processes is therefore an essential part of the leader's art in getting things done.

He then analyses the reasons why implementation was more or less successful for each of the three strategic initiatives chosen. Based on these conclusions, he develops proposals for how implementation can be made more effective. His advice covers:

(1) *Have a Superordinate Goal*
The initiative must be perceived by all members of the organization to contribute in a significant way to the attainment of the shared strategic objectives.

(2) *Make sure the resources are available*
In complex organizations this means choosing between two or more priorities which comes back to the choice of the correct superordinate goal as a basis for priority setting.

(3) *The technical aspects must work*
It is irrational to expect intelligent people to try wholeheartedly to implement something which they know will not work. Dr. Wernham points out that managers do however distinguish between teething troubles and much more fundamental problems.

(4) *An early positive response from customers*
This was the case with Radiopaging, where one individual said 'we have got several hundreds of customers lined up — spontaneous demand'.

(5) *Information must be available and credible*
This is closely linked with the creation of staff enthusiasm and confidence that what is promised will be delivered.

(6) *Top management support . . . but*
Perhaps somewhat surprisingly top management backing was rated as important but not as much as the other factors. He warns 'it helps but it probably will not pull a bad scheme from the fire'.

Based on these results, Dr. Wernham proposes an alternative view to the traditional strategic management model. This is one which is much more interactive with communication both up, down and across the organization. His is the model of the 'fast-learning structure'.

Woolworth's Drive for Excellence

Personnel is a strategic function in any service oriented business. Don Rose in his description of Woolworth's turnaround is a classic example. In late 1982 a consortium of city financiers acquired F. W. Woolworth from its American parent when the giant company was regarded as the sick man of British retailing. As a result of fundamental changes which had taken place in its industry, Woolworth's 'Service Management System' had developed many misfits.

The new Management decided on a rescue mission which was launched in 1986 under the banner 'Operation Focus'. It consisted of:

(1) The creation of a new trading concept focused on six areas of strength in order to position the chain as a specialist in key areas.

(2) Disposing of low profit sites and redeveloping in more appropriate areas and a multi million pound refurbishment programme.

(3) The number of suppliers was reduced from around 8,000 to just over 1,000.

This still left a fundamental strategic issue of how to tackle the 30,000 demotivated staff who had become the benchmark for poor service.

Reorganization and cultural change
The answer was a significant reorganization and culture change through a specially designed multi million pound staff training and development programme.

The process was begun with an attitude survey of staff and store managers. A response rate of 85% was achieved. The results showed that

☆ Managers were not communicating with staff.

☆ Staff were frightened to express their views openly because of the likely reaction.

☆ Staff were afraid of customers and lacked pride.

The line managers also saw customer care and improved company performance as the basis for excellence in personnel management. To achieve this, radical changes were necessary within the personnel function. A new philosophy was adopted called 'People serving People'. This was intended to capture the new customer care philosophy by demonstrating the importance of

(1) *Concern for the customer*
    ☆ creating a friendly environment in stores,

        ☆ and making customers feel welcome so that they would continue to come back.

(2) *Concern for staff*
  ☆ recognizing the role of the sales assistant as the most important member of the team because they are the vital point of contact with customers.

(3) *Concern for the community*
  ☆ a commitment to prove that Woolworth had an important role to play in local communities.

To make this possible, the personnel structure was reorganized, following the appointment of a new Personnel Director in 1985. As part of implementing 'Operation Focus', Woolworth reorganized its management structure at the store level to put more emphasis on personal responsibility, the development of teams and freer and more open communications.

A management training programme was implemented which sent a clear signal across the company: 'management means doing things right, but leadership means doing the right things'. Woolworth was putting the main emphasis on leadership in the team, with the customer, and in the market.

A new approach to recruitment and induction was introduced in which store and section managers were made responsible for recruitment and trained in the task.

Maintaining Momentum
The Excellence Programme was introduced in 1987, designed to motivate and offer rewards to staff in recognition of their achievements and progress towards standards of personal and team excellence.

Success through People
The results have also been excellent. 30,000 motivated staff helped Woolworth raise pre-tax profits from a loss of £5 million in 1985 to £45 million in 1988. The sales per square foot, a key indicator in retailing, increased on average by 15% each year.

Controlling Overseas Insurance Subsidiaries

Professor Giorgio Petroni's well researched paper provides insights into the different kinds of control systems appropriate to the international operations of an insurance company. However, his report has a general appeal to any organization concerned with controlling its international development. The stress is on fitting the control mechanism to the needs of the business strategy.

He begins with an overview of the international insurance industry and the driving forces which are shaping it:

☆ The globalization of industrial firms means a wide range of financial and insurance services are being demanded internationally.

☆ The modern firm is subject to more and larger risks than in the past.

☆ Information technology has linked financial centres, and deregulation has spurred competition.

☆ The old, large U.S. and European firms have relatively cheap funds to invest abroad.

Following an outline of the research method, some peculiarities of the insurance business are pointed out such as:

☆ In the past there was essentially no risk of making a loss since the companies collected premiums and paid out only enough to ensure that they maintained adequate reserves and profits.

☆ Today most profits are generated from investment income and many firms make losses on the insurance element.

☆ Customers need cover over a range of risks. Traditionally the business has been run on product lines, e.g. fire insurance. The move to customer orientation is causing major planning problems.

☆ It takes a long time to establish an insurance company or for one to go out of business even if it is sick.

Professor Petroni then examines the logic of expanding abroad and finds three main reasons:

(1) *Following the flag*, such as Commercial Union moving to different parts of the Commonwealth.

(2) *Saturation in the home markets*. This is true for the large Swiss multinationals.

(3) *Exploiting the possibilities of earning attractive returns on investment*. For example, Legal and General in life insurance and the personal line area or the large American companies in their growth in the Far East.

Different mechanisms of guidance and control are then identified:

☆ Equity structure,

☆ Technical and financial control,

☆ Investments,

☆ Reinsurance,

☆ Human resources ('your man on the spot'),

☆ Assistance and services.

Professor Petroni proposes that the mix of these various instruments is adjusted according to the kind of business a company has set up in a particular country and its stage of development and he identifies three general models or strategies and the type of control system most appropriate for each.

Towards 1992: A Strategy for Training

It is a truism that in a service business people are a company's most important competitive asset. However, the shifting demographic trends and the rapidly changing demands of the insurance industry makes training an issue of major strategic importance. In his article, Derek Day outlines both the challenges and action implications, not only for his own industry, but for any facing the fundamental changes of deregulation and globalization.

He points out that from a practical viewpoint, though 1992 is more symbolic of a trend, it nevertheless demands urgency in developing training plans. He warns that the complexity in legislation will be the focal point of much training effort but at the same time this should not detract from the equally important need to develop business marketing and people skills for the new countries of operation.

Language is an obvious issue but one which is not given the attention it deserves. This is particularly so, since though we are moving towards an integrated market, it will not be at all like the U.S.A. Each country will maintain its own unique language and culture and any company developing a successful European presence must be able to operate effectively in the local language.

While 1992 and deregulation present major business opportunities, equally the opening of our traditional markets to foreign competitors will greatly increase the level of competition we face. In the 1990s, Mr. Day points out, training efforts must therefore be geared to making our own business even more competitive.

As training budgets begin to feel the squeeze for resources, it is critically important that training initiatives are clearly linked to strategic business goals.

He therefore suggests two immediate areas for action. The first includes:

☆ Development of training plans more closely wedded to business planning.

☆ Audit of current staff to identify their full range of existing and potential skills, talents and abilities.

☆ Broadening the scope of training to include the development of key non-technical skills.

☆ Examination of methodologies to determine ways of increasing the coverage and cost effectiveness of training.

A second is effectively selling the benefits of training to business leaders. Mr. Day highlights two critically important messages to be communicated through a process of internal marketing:

☆ Training has to broaden beyond technical skills.

☆ Training and development expenditure is not icing on the cake. It is an investment which, if properly managed, is vital to the continued growth and success of the business.

Experiences from the Public Sector

Corporate Strategic Planning in a University

In a pioneering paper, Professor Raymond Thomas demonstrates the applicability of Strategic Service Management to a university.

He begins 'given the changed scale and context of higher education, universities and other semi advanced institutions need to make their own choices as to other activities and uses of resources, whatever negotiating frameworks through which these choices have to be implemented'.

He argues the relevance of this technique to universities which after almost 40 years of expansion now find themselves with falling demand and pressures for economy. By applying the language of business to the problem, using such concepts as 'the offering' and 'price', he makes a creative leap in suggesting how current problems may be analysed and addressed.

To further provide a strategic background he discusses universities as autonomous enterprises. Because of their dependence on central Government funds, managing this 'negotiated environment' is in his view a key role. Also the attainment of student numbers within the constraints of a given financing arrangement becomes a key element of university strategy.

Strategic planning within a university is then considered and he discusses, for example, the interdependence between teaching and research; also the selection of the mix of disciplines to be offered in the face of financial and other constraints and the need to face the hard choices which arrive when growth stops.

In conclusion he states:

(1) There should be a long term policy review body concerned with academic development and the academics should play a major role in this.

(2) Universities need an appraisal of their own activities in which a strategic process would be as much value as any particular plan it produces.

(3) There is a need to develop and sustain these processes at all levels of the university hierarchy.

(4) The environment is not simply there to be monitored but should be influenced by advice and continual interaction.

Participative Planning for a Public Service

In public administration Strategic Service Management continues to receive increasing attention according to the authors Timothy Grewe, James Marshall and Daniel E. O'Toole. They point to two main reasons:

(1) Agencies face continuing physical stringency,

(2) There is unabated if not expanding demand for quality.

They describe how strategic planning promotes an examination of the fit between the agency's goals and the environment and it promotes potential improvement. The use of the planning process can also greatly increase participation, which the Japanese have demonstrated to be a powerful motivator in a resource scarce environment.

The article aims to provide those in public administration with a tool to assist them in managing a strategic planning process, particularly one which involves the participation of more than just the top managers.

The authors describe the importance of preparation and the role of the facilitator. They point out

the top management risk which should be accepted at the outset, namely that the participants in the process and others in the organization will assume that the final product of the process, i.e. the plan, will be implemented. Management must be prepared to stand by this.

Their experience led them to a number of insights:

☆ Strategic planning underscores the importance of the conceptual skills to enable management to understand the complexities of the overall organization and where their own operation fits in.

☆ Strategic planning provides a forum for, and helps cultivate strategic thinking in the organization's line managers.

☆ Vagueness or difficulty in quantifying goals for many public organizations requires the strategic planning process to spend more time in this area.

☆ Participation in the process may be at least as important as the contents of the plan. It promotes:

● a common vision of the future and its implications for the organization including any necessary changes

● more effective group problem solving skills

● recognition that continuous planning is a management necessity.

A Strategic Planning Process for Public and Non–profit Organizations

This recent contribution by John M. Bryson puts a number of the major issues in focus. We are told, Wayne Gretzky — perhaps the world's greatest offensive player in professional ice hockey — says 'I skate to where I think the puck will be'. This analogy is used to emphasize the critically important point that Strategic Service Management is about strategic thinking and acting. The strategic planner is in reality a facilitator for the process and a support to the organization's leaders.

He describes the process itself in terms of eight steps:

(1) development of an initial agreement concerning the strategic planning effort,

(2) identification and clarification of the mandate,

(3) development and clarification of the mission and values,

(4) external environment assessment,

(5) internal environment assessment,

(6) strategic issue identification,

(7) strategy development and

(8) description of the organization in the future.

The benefits of the process are highlighted as:

☆ helping the management to think strategically,

☆ clarifying the future direction,

☆ making today's decisions in the light of their future consequences,

☆ developing a coherent and defensible basis for decision making,

☆ exercising maximum discretion in the areas under the organization's control,

☆ solving major organizational problems,

☆ improving group performance,

☆ dealing effectively with rapidly changing circumstances and

☆ building teamwork and expertise.

In two interesting case studies, one a suburban city and the other a public health nursing service, he shows how these steps are put into practice and from experience within the public sector, he draws a number of implications about what it takes for a strategic planning programme to be initiated and to succeed. These are:

☆ a sponsor in a position of power to legitimize the process,

☆ a champion to push the process along,

☆ a strategic planning team,

☆ an expectation that there will be disruptions and delays,

☆ a willingness to be flexible about what constitutes a strategic plan,

☆ an ability to pull information and people together at key points for important discussions and decisions,

☆ a willingness to construct and to consider arguments geared to fit different demands from different stakeholders.

While seeing strategic planning as a powerful instrument, he identifies a number of issues which require careful consideration to adapt and develop traditional approaches to the specific requirements of the Public Service.

Performance Review: Key to Effective Planning

When Stan Berry wrote this paper, he was Chief Executive of a public education board in Ottawa. He wrote the article to emphasize the importance in the Public Service of performance measurement and performance review.

A performance review is defined by Mr. Berry as a disciplined communications process, relying heavily on the interview process, in which people in the organization cooperatively express their hopes and aspirations for a stated period, and rationalize them within the context of the overall goals of the corporation as stated by the Trustees (or Board of Directors or whatever).

The author describes how such a process has been working for over a decade in a particular school system in Canada.

The process was begun through the efforts of the author and a very energetic first Chairman. The most significant change has been the evolution from a strictly individual goal setting process to one in which the individuals set goals within the context of the objectives of the total management team.

The Board adopted a series of broad aims and objectives which set the overall tone of the organization. However, it was much later that the Board as a whole set annual corporate goals for the whole school system.

Strategic Planning for the World Wildlife Fund

Successful leaders help their organizations create a clear vision of what they would like to become and then proceed to focus people's energy so as to make the desired situation a reality. George Medley, Director of the World Wildlife Fund (U.K.), provides a precise and well documented account of how this can be achieved in practice. The case is particularly interesting since the results have been achieved in a 'not for profit' organization.

An important prerequisite was to carry out a structural reorganization to ensure that sufficient business oriented individuals were appointed in the fund raising areas which required a wholly professional approach.

Under the umbrella of a strategic planning workshop the heads of all departments met for two days to formulate the basic purpose of the organization. This was defined, after some considerable discussion, as one of fund raising then ensuring the proper spending of the money so generated. This broad purpose was then translated into nine key result areas.

The process of strategic thinking was further deepened by considering the particular strengths, weaknesses, opportunities and threats posed under each heading. This traditional framework in no way inhibited the creation of unique new insights. It was interesting, for example, to see how other charities were, as part of the process, viewed as 'competitors'.

The use of frameworks transferred from a commercial environment was made considerably easier when it was realized that net funds produced could usefully be equated to profitability.

In pointing out that a strategy is simply a guideline for action, Mr. Medley involved all of his departments in determining what they, themselves, would do to contribute to the objectives which had been agreed by the whole group. In this way the fundamental principle of involvement to gain commitment was used to the full.

The resulting action plans were stated as a series of 'we will —' statements and following the fundamental tenet that for a strategy to be successfully implemented, it must be tracked, performance measurement systems were suitably strengthened.

These initiatives produced a fast and dramatic success. *The process has been repeated every year since 1978 resulting in a five-fold increase in net funds and an even greater improvement in productivity*. Currently, actual performance appears to be running ahead of projections, which hints that the organization is ready for a new quantum jump in its ambition level.

Conclusion

These articles illustrate the major changes which have taken place in thinking and practice during the 1980s in some of the world's leading service businesses. Though each is a unique case, individually and collectively they deepen our knowledge and understanding of the new kind of business management which is evolving in response to the challenges of the 1990s. An approach which we have called Strategic Service Management.

References

(1) Denis Boyle is Managing Director of The Service Management Group Limited, a unique international consulting and research organization which specializes in the development problems of service oriented businesses. The Group was founded in 1982 by Denis Boyle and Richard Normann, a leading Swedish consultant and writer. Normann's book *Service Management*, John Wiley, Chichester (1984) is a key reference source for management.

(2) Jan Carlzon, *Moments of Truth*, Ballinger, Cambridge, Mass. (1987).

PART ONE

Creating Service Business Strategies

Creating a Successful Marketing Strategy for UNI Insurance

Thorstein Øverland

There are a number of obvious differences between marketing consumer goods and marketing services. The author, having spent half his career in the consumer market, in this article describes how he came to devise a marketing strategy for a service industry i.e. insurance, and the vital role that the personnel function played in this.

The basic principles of marketing are the same regardless of the kind of business you are in. Nevertheless, there are some important differences between service products and manufactured products. For example a service is intangible, cannot be demonstrated, cannot be stored, and cannot be transported. From a marketing viewpoint also there are two aspects, unique to services, which are crucial:

☆ The customer takes an active part in the production of a service; in fact the final stages of production and consumption take place at the same time, and

☆ The role of the supplier's staff is of vital importance, often as a visible part of the service.

I will illustrate the role of the staff by an example. If someone mentions the name Ford, the chances are high that the image that comes to the mind is that of one or several cars. Even if staff are an important factor in selling and servicing Ford cars, most people will look upon the car itself as the most important part of the Ford product.

This would not be the case for a car rental company. If the customer hears the name Hertz, he or she will probably not think about a Hertz car they have rented, but associate the name with Hertz personnel who they have been in contact with. Probably they will not think about how Hertz personnel behave in

general, but how they dealt with this particular customer.

In other words, the car itself is the most important part of your product when you sell cars, and personnel are the most important part of the service if you rent cars.

Modern marketing techniques were first developed for consumer goods. The basic idea is to create a product which covers specific needs in specific customer segments, and then make sure that all elements in the marketing mix are chosen in order to fit the product: design/formula, packaging, price, distribution, advertising, promotion etc.

Quite often marketeers of service products adopt the same technique, which is to build all the elements in the marketing mix around the core product. However, a service is not something which can just be handed over to a passive customer. A service can only be delivered through one or several transactions, where the customer's behaviour will influence the nature or quality of the service. Furthermore, as will be seen from the Ford/Hertz example, in a service industry, customers will often not regard the core product as the most important part of the transaction. The role of the staff will often be the decisive part of the product.

So, the most important difference between marketing of goods and services is the following:

> In the marketing of services, it is better to design a marketing strategy and develop a marketing mix which focuses on the *transaction*(s) instead of the core product. The core product will be only one of several elements which will influence the outcome of the transaction.

The elements in the marketing mix should be developed with the objective of making all transactions as successful as possible. As personnel are quite often the most important part of a service product, the transactions are mostly in the form of *interaction* between customers and staff.

Thorstein Øverland is Deputy Managing Director of UNI Insurance in Oslo.

A Case Story: Creating a Marketing Strategy for a Service Company

In UNI Insurance we have developed a marketing strategy which has taken account of these important differences. This strategy was developed in 1985, and was later improved, but still remains the basis of our business. The strategy was developed in co-operation with the consulting group, KIA, who have developed a model specifically for this purpose—the Service Star (Figure 1). The Service Star takes as a focus the transaction i.e. what you want to achieve at the most crucial interactions or meeting with the customer—and is used to build a 'business mix' for the particular service being developed.

The Service Star indicates the five elements of the 'service mix'; the elements which need to be balanced one-with-another and with the defined market.

UNI's Business Purpose

UNI's mission is to provide security to its customers. In principle, insurance is only one of several ways of creating security.

The Focus on the Transaction

Figure 2 illustrates a common view of the relationship between an insurance company and the customer. Drawing a parallel with industrial products, insurance companies often see their products as being made of paper, in the form of policies, claims settlements etc. The role of the staff is to help in delivering the product and assisting the customers

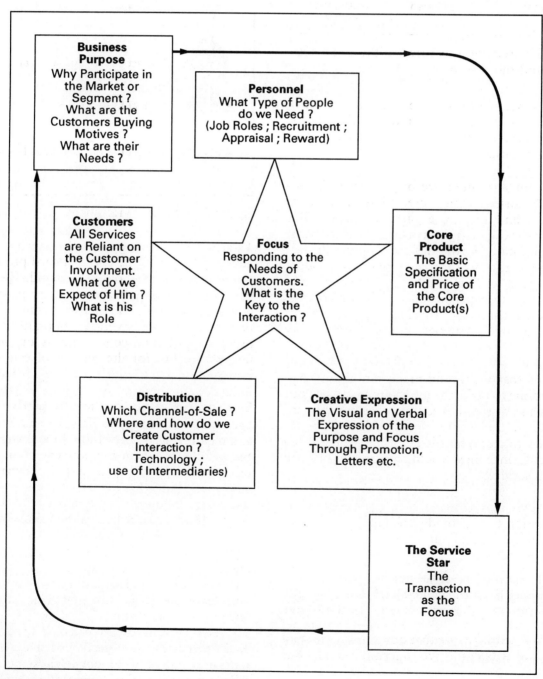

© *Ken Irons Associates*, 1985.

Figure 1. The service star

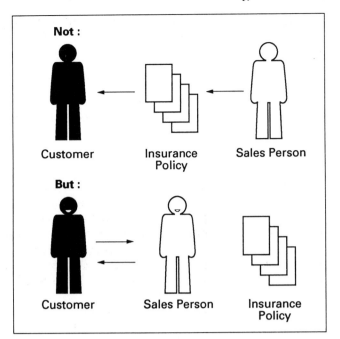

Figure 2. The relationship between the insurance company and the customer

in various ways. Most people realize that the role of the staff is important, but not more so than in the case of industrial products supported by a first class service organization.

However, our customers are buying security, not insurance. Security is mainly created by a number of transactions, and not by a piece of paper. The outcome of the transactions is mainly decided by the actions of our staff. We decided to recognize the fact that our staff constitute the main part of our product and to assign a leading role to our personnel and secondary role to paper products. The function of the policies, technology, routines etc. is to be of assistance to our personnel, not the other way around.

We decided that we should make sure that everything was done to make the interaction between our customers and our staff as successful as possible. By being better at 'the decisive point', we have a better opportunity to create satisfied customers, and more satisfied staff, since they would take greater pride in giving this service.

The Key to the Interaction

As our mission is to provide financial security, we decided that the focus of our marketing strategy was expressed as follows:

> 'The main difference between UNI and other insurance companies shall be the extra value—extra security—which our employees can create in interaction with our customers.'

Our task was to make sure that our employees were both *able* and *willing* to give superior value to our clients.

The Core Products

Having defined the key to the interaction, the next step was to look at our core products. Our products should be an aid to our employees, and not the other way round. This meant a radical change in our product development programme. We did not need any product 'stars', but we needed enough variants to be able to satisfy various customers with different needs. We therefore developed what we called 'security pyramids'. From now on our customers could choose from *three different security levels*: To be insured against everything, to be insured against most risks, or to be insured against only the most serious losses. (Figure 3.)

Figure 3. Security pyramids

To achieve this strategy, we developed a number of new product variants. Our standard products were on the medium level of the pyramid. We therefore had to introduce a cheaper, simpler product and a new top product in our security pyramid, which we named 'UNIversal coverage'. This top product has a premium price and covers almost any sudden and unexpected loss for the owners of cars, houses or homes.

Our advertisements for the new UNIversal coverage reflected this policy. The products are intended as a tool for our sales people. In keeping with this, the people shown in the advertisement belong to our sales staff. This is not important to our customers, but it has a symbolic value internally.

A year later we launched a new campaign based on the theme 'I will do it for you.' We showed in our advertisements our sales staff business cards with photographs, and the copy of the advertisements is written so that the message goes from our staff to our customers. It is about what '*I* can do for you', not just what UNI can do.

At the same time our main competitor, Storebrand, ran a new publicity campaign, showing a customer who was anxious about having bought the wrong kind of policy. The message was: Buy the new policy and get rid of any doubts. Storebrand's advertisements stresses the core product. UNI stresses the importance of getting in contact with the right kind of person.

Distribution

At a time when most other insurance companies are working hard to find new distribution channels, we decided that the natural consequence of our strategy was to concentrate on selling through our own sales force, working in, or out of, 225 offices. Our office network is the most extensive in Norway, and this gives us a strong basis for customer contact.

We still use direct marketing and agents. However, these approaches are not regarded as alternatives to our own sales force, but as a support to the sales force. Direct marketing activities are organized from each of our offices, not only in Head Office.

Our distribution strategy fits the needs of the main segments of the market where UNI Insurance gets most of its business. However, in order to exploit new and small segments of the market which may be growing, we started a new subsidiary company: Plus Insurance. The business idea of this company is to sell low priced insurance products without personal service. Distribution is arranged through direct marketing or by selling through banks. This company is selling only the core product without any extras. We are able to go more wholeheartedly for the quality-service concept in UNI, leaving the low price end of the market to Plus.

The policies of Plus Insurance are more or less the same as the medium level policies sold by UNI. Some people are surprised to find that we can sell the 'same product at a lower price' through Plus. However Plus does not sell the same product as UNI. The difference is the same as the difference between a ready-made product and a 'do-it-yourself' kit.

Customers

The role of the customer is most easily described by pointing at the difference between UNI and Plus. In UNI it is enough that the customer should contact our personnel by telephone or by visiting our office. The rest will be taken care of by our staff. A customer in Plus has to fill out the forms and assess various alternatives for themselves.

Another benefit of our focus on 'the interaction' is that this enables our people to make a judgement on the risks involved with each individual customer. This is of vital importance in insurance.

Personnel

UNI's new strategy led to a reappraisal of the personnel function. Clearly this function is the key to our success in carrying out the strategy. So, a number of measures were taken to improve the quality of our personnel:

☆ Recruitment guidelines: all new personnel must be serviceminded and have a growth potential.

☆ Improved internal education.

☆ An improved internal career system, both for managers and specialists.

☆ A bonus system for all personnel.

☆ Organizational changes based on the following principles:

—Decentralization.

—Each office is a profit centre.

—Never more than two steps in decision-making about customers.

Carrying out the Strategy

Many of our actions were aimed at improving the *ability* of our staff to give added value to our customers. It is a more long term task to make sure that our staff also is *willing* to give superior service. Some of our best sales people were already aware of their importance in creating customer satisfaction, but most of our staff, nevertheless, looked upon themselves as having a secondary role. Their attitude could be described in this way: 'I am just as good or as bad as my colleagues in other companies. People will buy our products only if UNI has better products, lower premiums, more money to lend.' In the future the employees attitude had to be: 'UNI has products which are just as good as the products of other insurance companies, and in the long run it is no more expensive to be insured with UNI than with anyone else. But with UNI I and my colleagues will give better service than our competitors, and that is the main reason why people should choose UNI.'

In order to make sure that we really brought about change, where it matters, the transaction with the customer, we ran a series of workshops in each region. To enable our staff to get acquainted with the thinking behind our strategy, and to find out what changes they themselves could make in order to make the strategy work. This meant that they could be confident in the vital role they played in turning the strategy into reality.

Summary

To UNI Insurance, building a marketing strategy with a focus on the transaction had a positive effect on our market performance from the start in 1985. Making our personnel the most important part of our insurance products is now one of the foundations of the strategy of UNI Insurance.

Building a Competitive Advantage Through Information Technology

Colin Jackson

The two terms 'Competitive Advantage' and 'Information Technology' have recently been combined in the minds of many businessmen as representing a new, sophisticated way of taking a quantum leap ahead of their competitors. Some executives, however, are not quite so sure. There is more than a nagging suspicion in their minds that this is just another craze. Others have moved so swiftly and decisively that the ensuing reorganizations have left both managers and personnel completely stunned. The majority of executives are uncertain. In an attempt to provide a pathway forward, we have examined two areas:

(1) out of the many strategy concepts discussed, what works best in practice?

(2) how can a company best organize for competitive advantage?

In this article, we examine concepts which work in practice in developing competitive advantage through information technology.

In our investigation of current practice we have found that the following concepts can be used to obtain a significant edge over competitors. The list is not exhaustive but these are some of the most powerful concepts where information technology has a significant role to play:

(1) ensuring either that the industry structure changes in your favour or that steps are taken to reduce the effects of it moving against you,

(2) deliberately decreasing the bargaining power of buyers of your goods or services and, in a similar fashion, the power of your suppliers,

(3) ensuring that entry barriers to your markets are raised in your favour, thereby discouraging the entry of new competitors,

(4) using information technology to create new

Dr Colin Jackson is Managing Director of Organisation and Technology Research Ltd.

products out of old ones and to build new markets that were previously not available.

We illustrate the use of these concepts in the following section.

Changing the Industry Structure

Most non-marketeers are surprised to learn that industry structure can be deliberately manipulated by the competing companies. Most non-information technologists are equally surprised to discover just how powerful information technology can be in triggering and sustaining such changes. The following examples illustrate two points. Firstly, they demonstrate just how devastating an information technology-provoked change in industry structure can be to the unprepared. Secondly, they demonstrate the pre-emptive nature of many of the initiatives taken. Figure 1 shows how information technology can make industrialized countries competitive with developing countries on labour costs.

The overall moral is that you do not need to be a giant corporation to trigger a change in industry structure. The following examples demonstrate the principles involved covering both large and small protagonists: the typewriter industry, the U.K. newspaper industry, EFTPOS—The Anglia Building Society, SNA and IBM, Barclays 'Connect' card, IBM and PS/2.

The typewriter industry. For most of this century, the manufacturers of mechanical typewriters lived in a fairly predictable and stable industry. Manufacturing took place in factories containing specialists in the assembly of parts, such as type-bars, keyboards, etc. Surrounding these factories were secondary

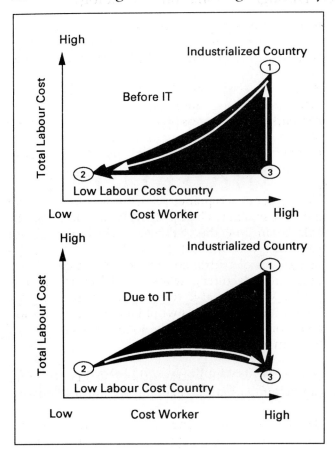

Figure 1. Labour-intensive production in an industrialized country 1 is moved to a low labour cost country 2. Production is moved back to the industrialized country 3 when the substitution of information technology for labour makes repatriation of production economically attractive

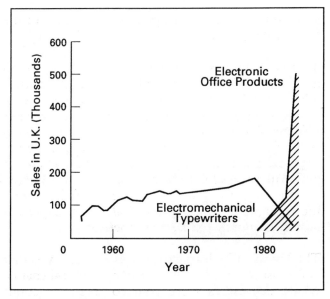

Figure 2. Almost overnight, the highly-developed skills of the electromechanical typewriter manufacturers were made obsolete by the application of electronics

industries which supplied them with parts and materials.

The advent of the electric typewriter simply meant that this process continued. In other words, the structure of the industry remained basically unchanged.

In 1978 Olivetti launched one of the world's first electronic typewriters. Each machine consisted of about 10 electronic modules. Apart from a daisy wheel printer, its most important attribute was the use of a microprocessor and associated electronics.

Any company that could assemble the few electronic modules required to make an electronic typewriter could enter the industry. In a very short space of time, the skills in metallurgy and manufacturing related to the original industry became virtually redundant. Companies such as Triumph Adler, Olympia, and even IBM's Office Products Division found that their markets for electrical and mechanical typewriters had collapsed (see Figure 2). In their place, new markets emerged for a new generation of electronic office products, including electronic typewriters and word processors. These products

required a completely differently structured industry.

Olivetti had precipitated a change in the structure of the typewriter industry, by the use of information technology. Our research showed that they did this unwittingly.

The newspaper industry. In the United Kingdom, the Trades Unions had successfully 'locked out' the use of computing equipment in the production of national newspapers. Text prepared by journalists had to be keyed in by specialist staff on machines which were universally recognized to be virtual museum-pieces. The overheads and inefficiencies incurred by such systems were obvious. Nobody, however, had succeeded in making that leap forward whereby journalists would directly key in their text, and text-processing systems would eliminate the need for re-keying.

In 1985, the *Today* newspaper was launched by Mr Eddie Shah. His idea was to obtain a massive competitive advantage by the use of information technology. Previously, Mr Shah had won a much publicized battle against Trades Unions in a similar situation concerning a provincial newspaper. This time, his intention was to create a high technology, national newspaper operation. The structure of the industry was such that Mr Shah believed he would remain a quantum leap ahead of his competitors.

And so, in a barrage of publicity, the newspaper was launched. However, within a very short space of time, one by one, all of the national newspapers individually began to make similar changes. They moved to new premises and, despite the virulent protestations of the Trades Unions, new computer technology was introduced. Eddie Shah had triggered off a dramatic change in the structure of the United Kingdom national newspaper industry.

There was, however, a sting in the tail. *Today* found itself participating in a newly structured industry where everybody was using information technology. Unfortunately, *Today* had rather less news content than its competitors. Mr Shah thus found himself in a new industry where he was competing on equal terms with everybody else but where his newspaper was of inferior quality. He had triggered off an industry structure change which rapidly moved against him, and the *Today* newspaper has now been purchased by a competitor.

The lesson to be learnt from this case study is that you must check that any industry structural change which *may* follow from your competitive actions will move in your favour and not against you.

EFTPOS—the Anglia Building Society. A Building Society is a United Kingdom institution whose original purpose was to offer a savings service and to provide loans for the purchase of housing. Recently, in the United Kingdom, their role has been greatly enhanced and they can now offer a wide range of financial services.

The Anglia Building Society (now merged with Nationwide) was a medium sized company with branches throughout the United Kingdom. It was an innovative organization and installed one of the country's first pilot EFTPOS systems called Paypoint. This system was based on ICL equipment and operated in the Northampton region of the United Kingdom.

Examination of their motives revealed that one of their reasons for having implemented Paypoint was to be able to have a negotiating voice when a national EFTPOS system was set up.

This is an example of a pre-emptive use of information technology enabling a company to safeguard itself against a potential industry structure change.

SNA and IBM. To most information technologists, SNA (Systems Network Architecture) is simply IBM's proprietary network architecture. It enables IBM computers and terminals to be connected to each other in various standardized ways. Such is the power of IBM that SNA has become a *de facto* standard. Many manufacturers competing with IBM offer SNA or SNA-compatible products to their customers. By this means, competing manufacturers' equipment may communicate with IBM hardware and systems.

To a marketeer, SNA represents a way of imposing a partial structure on an industry. It is a much more abstract structure than that concerning, for example, the typewriter industry. In practice, the marke-

teer sees SNA as a way of ensuring the continuing role of central mainframe computer departments on which a company such as IBM currently depends.

A rival concept to SNA is the much talked about OSI (Open System Interconnection) model. This is currently in the process of being fully defined. Much interest is shown in this standard by manufacturers competing against IBM and by the European Commission.

The general acceptance of OSI would mean an industry structure change. IBM would no longer be able to impose their standard which would not particularly favour IBM and, encourage the development of central computer departments. Also, other manufacturers, whose machines are incompatible would be able to interconnect their equipment more freely. This would increase competition and would also increase the long-term viability of those manufacturers.

This example demonstrates that industry structure can be influenced by changing technical standards.

Barclays 'Connect'. The VISA credit card was introduced by Barclays Bank into the United Kingdom under the name 'Barclaycard'. Barclay's VISA customers form a large customer credit card population in the United Kingdom, and Barclaycard competes against well-known rivals such as Mastercard, known as 'Access' in the United Kingdom.

For some time, Barclays has been studying and experimenting with debit cards (as opposed to credit cards) for use in EFTPOS systems. As a result, in 1987, Barclays suddenly announced the launch of a new debit card called 'Connect' and attempted to impose this on the VISA outlets. In doing so, it initially imposed conditions which many retail chains found unacceptable.

The protestations of the Barclaycard outlets simply represented the reaction to the speed at which Barclays felt obliged to move. They believed that once their intention became known, the new standard needed to be quickly put in place before competitors could enter with different standards.

This is an example of a pre-emptive change in industry structure being provoked by information technology.

IBM and PS/2. IBM launched its first personal computer (PC) in 1981 and large numbers of PCs were purchased by companies because the IBM brand label gave PC's a seal of legitimacy.

Soon after many competing PC manufacturers produced copies of IBM's PC which were much cheaper and performed essentially the same functions as IBM's product. COMPAQ and more recently Amstrad became successful, by this approach.

In marketing terms, the IBM PC had become a commodity. It had also become a standard—see Figure 3. It did not matter where the device came from; if it was IBM PC compatible, companies and individuals would simply purchase the commodity in its cheapest form.

The structure of the 'IBM PC industry' was therefore one of a series of manufacturers producing a commodity. IBM, unfortunately, was just one of these!

IBM considers that it does not trade in commodities—even the chips it produces are for its own consumption. IBM, therefore, decided to change this industry structure and to make a pre-emptive move to modify it, in its favour, back to that of a branded device industry.

The move was made by launching a new family of personal computers known as the PS/2 range. IBM heavily publicized the PS/2 as representing the future—by implication, the original PCs were out of date and defunct.

At the time of writing, this battle is still being fought. Industry observers are watching closely to see whether IBM can change the industry structure in its favour, or the commodity market of the original PCs represents too significant an investment for it to be written off.

This case study provides an example of how a major corporation can inadvertently give birth to a new industry and then find itself an unwitting victim of the structure which develops. To avoid the competitive disadvantage which results, the company is then obliged to attempt to change back the industry structure in its favour.

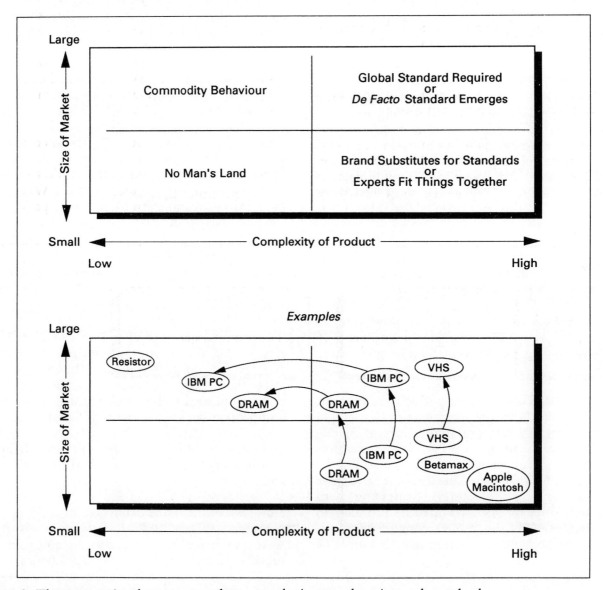

Figure 3. The connection between product complexity, market size and standards

The VHS video cassette recorder format became the global standard. The IBM PC became the *de facto* standard for professional personal computers and went on to become a commodity product.

Decreasing Buyer or Supplier Power

One of the concepts of Competitive Advantage which has received great attention is that of modifying the bargaining power of suppliers and/or buyers in a company's favour. This is usually undertaken by a process known as 'Forward or Backward Integration'.

In simple terms, Forward Integration means that an organization incorporates a value-adding activity as part of a product (or service) that the buyer would normally have to provide himself (Figure 4). In terms of value chains, this means that the company's value chain becomes extended into the buyers' value chain. Backward Integration means just the opposite and refers to the identical process with a company's suppliers.

The objective of such techniques is to reduce the bargaining power of buyers or suppliers. An enhancement of this is to 'lock in' either buyers or suppliers.

What is intriguing about this concept is that it works so well. We demonstrate this below.

Backward Integration
One example will show how a company may decrease the bargaining power of a supplier.

Toyota. Toyota makes extensive use of ball bearings in many of its products. One of its suppliers is the Japanese company Minibea. In many cases, Toyota supplies a direct link from its production control computers to Minibea and requests delivery of ball bearings 'just in time' (see Figure 5 for typical benefits provided by 'Just in Time'). Such is the power of such systems that Minibea deliver ball bearings to Toyota some five times per day!

The advantage to Toyota is the elimination of stocks of ball-bearings previously stored at the beginning of its production lines. More interestingly, the advantage to Minibea is that it no longer needs to stock huge piles of ball bearings in anticipation of orders from Toyota. It can produce to precise demand. By such a system, Toyota has taken over two of the value activities of Minibea. The first is by eliminating the need for stock and the second is by the elimination of regular visits by salesmen.

In this way, the negotiating power of Minibea is reduced. In other words, Toyota has reduced the bargaining power of this particular supplier.

Forward Integration
The following examples demonstrate how the bargaining power of buyers can be reduced by information technology. They also show how Forward Integration may 'lock in' buyers.

McKesson. At McKesson (a supplier of over the counter pharmaceuticals), they devised a novel way of providing an extra service to pharmacists who purchased their products.

The company's sales representatives noted down the layout of the products on the shelves of their customers' shops. This information was then stored in the company's computer systems. Whenever a shop ordered goods from McKesson, a package was

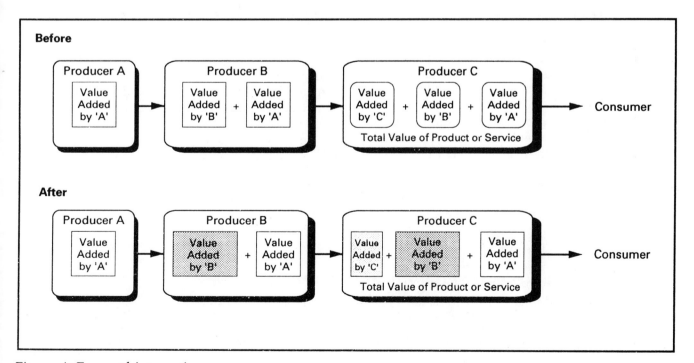

Figure 4. Forward integration

In the lower value chain, Producer B adds value to the product or service that was formerly added to Producer C. By such 'forward integration', Producer B can alter its relationship with Producer C to its own advantage.

	'Old' Factory (Man hours per ton machined)	'New' Factory with JIT (Man hours per ton machined)	Multiples of Productivity Improvement
Direct Labour	12.3	5.2	2.4
Direct Overhead and Production Control	2.6	1.1	2.4
Inventory Management and Material Handling	4.2	0.8	5.3
General Overhead at 17 per cent Loading	3.3	1.2	0.4
	10.1	3.1	3.3
Total	22.4	8.3	2.7

Figure 5. Estimated labour productivity improvements for a factory with JIT

made up in the correct order for the recipient to place the items directly onto the shelves. Thus, a pharmacy would prefer to place an order with McKesson because the goods would arrive in a particularly convenient way.

McKesson had taken over a specific value activity from its buyers. Although small in real terms, its perceived value was great enough to give McKesson a competitive edge.

IBM's invoicing system. Major users of IBM equipment will be familiar with the voluminous and detailed invoices covering the various items making up their computer systems. Some of these bills, for large organizations, assume legendary proportions and could be liable to error. A major retail store described to us, in convincing tones, the daunting task of wading through and checking such documents.

IBM realized that this situation needed a solution but also created an opportunity to be exploited. It tried out on-line access to data bases containing the detailed invoice information. By this means, customers could use their own terminals and check the various items, thereby avoiding being submerged in mountains of paper. Despite its simplicity, the idea is very attractive and convenient. In practice, an IBM customer would be able to evolve a whole new way of working based on this facility.

In reality, IBM are taking over activity from the customer and replacing it with a new, more convenient activity. The perceived value of this service appears far greater than the basic cost of interrogating a remote computer file by terminal. More significantly, were a company which had become accustomed to such a system to purchase some items of equipment from suppliers other than IBM, it would have to receive and process an old style invoice from those suppliers. Looked at from this point of view, IBM provide an incentive for companies to purchase all of their computer equipment from them.

BMW's in-car systems. BMW install microprocessor-driven systems in their cars. They monitor and display to the driver the state of various functions, for example, the condition of the engine oil. With such systems, a car need no longer be serviced at a fixed number of kilometres or miles. When a car is ready to be serviced, the conditions are displayed on a panel.

The advantage to the buyer of a BMW car is obvious. The careful driver is rewarded by reduced servicing costs because unnecessary garage maintenance bills are eliminated. By this means, BMW provide extra value to their customers.

These systems, however, are not quite as straightforward as they appear. They can only be reset by BMW accredited garages possessing the correct equipment. Were a customer to have his car serviced elsewhere, the panel lights would continue to indicate that the car needed servicing!

This is an example of Forward Integration where information technology has played a direct role and where the buyer's bargaining power has been considerably reduced. The customer is obliged to return to BMW garages, thereby ensuring a steady sale of BMW-made spare parts.

Perceived Value and Price
An important parameter to monitor, when contemplating the development of systems which attempt to 'lock in' customers or suppliers, is the notion of Perceived Value.

This is the value that the customer or buyer perceives when you provide or take over a value activity in the process of Forward/Backward Integration. Often the perceived values are much higher than the prices which would have to be paid for those services because the convenience which is experienced when an extra service is provided along with the product.

Entry Barriers

Our research also showed, how market entry barriers can be exploited to obtain a significant competitive edge. By raising or lowering entry barriers, companies can modify the 'rules of competition' which have hitherto applied (see Figure 6).

This concept can be a two-edged sword. Raising entry barriers to discourage new entrants to a market is not always a good thing. It may also heighten the rivalry between existing competitors to such a degree that it provokes a 'fight to the death' from which no viable survivor emerges. On the other hand, lowering entry barriers may enable a new company to enter a market but it may also unleash a flood of other new entrants which could make an attractive market unprofitable.

Just as companies can manipulate market entry barriers to achieve a competitive edge, governments may manipulate them to change their national competitive environments. They do this by changing the law.

In this section we demonstrate the power of the entry barrier concept and illustrate how they can be lowered, or raised, by using information technology.

Lowering Barriers
The following examples demonstrate how market entry barriers can be lowered, whether by intention or by chance, in the cases of home banking, IBM personal computers, and flexible manufacturing systems.

Home banking. There are several variations on the concept of home banking. The most common technique employs the combination of a user's television, telephone set and a videotex adaptor as the means of interrogating the computer system of

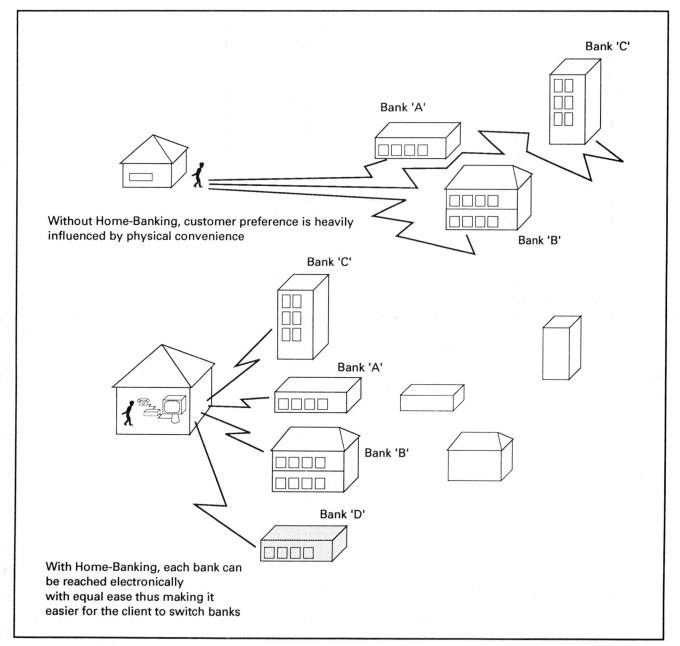

Bank 'C'

Bank 'A'

Bank 'B'

Without Home-Banking, customer preference is heavily influenced by physical convenience

Bank 'C'

Bank 'A'

Bank 'B'

Bank 'D'

With Home-Banking, each bank can be reached electronically with equal ease thus making it easier for the client to switch banks

Figure 6. Competitive disadvantage through information technology

the providing financial institution. By such means, account balances can be examined and simple fund transfers initiated. Such systems, were developed and introduced in the United Kingdom by the Nottinghamshire Building Society and the Bank of Scotland.

The fundamental characteristic of these systems is that very little specialist skill needs to be acquired in order to use them. This has a profound consequence. If several financial institutions offer such home banking facilities, there is very little to inhibit the user of one system abandoning it in favour of a rival. Setting aside the correspondence necessary to transfer an entire account from one financial institution to another, using one system is very much like using another.

This has a profound effect on the entry barriers to some of the markets being served by those institutions. Companies which initiate and promote home banking are effectively lowering the entry barriers to their markets. Any organization which offers a videotex based home banking system can enter. This is shown schematically in Figure 7. Such new entrants need not necessarily be encumbered by a large network of costly High Street branches.

Our research indicates that the pioneers of home banking services may be ultimately providing themselves with a competitive disadvantage through the lowering of market entry barriers.

Flexible manufacturing systems (FMS). FMS systems enable manufacturers to change rapidly from one

product line to another and to reduce the lead-times for new products.

There is, however, another effect which must be taken into consideration. If a company attempts to gain a significant advantage over its industry competitors by using FMS, this advantage may be only short-lived. What can happen is as follows. A company is seen to have outstanding success through rapid product change and rapid delivery of goods. Existing competitors then decide that they must follow the same route in order to remain competitive. In this way, the entire industry manufacturing process changes and the competitive process speeds up. At the same time, firms outside that industry, which have already invested in FMS, realize that now they too have the means to enter that industry, and they may enter so rapidly that the original industry competitors are taken by surprise.

In this case, FMS lowered entry barriers. Another example of this is the modern electronic typewriter industry. Even manufacturers of sewing machines such as Brother realized that they had the capability to manufacture electronic typewriters. Also, as we showed earlier, IBM by introducing a PC which established an industry standard, opened up the PC market to a large number of IBM compatible producers.

Raising Barriers
We illustrate the effect of raising entry barriers by; reference to the microwave oven industry, and Xerox Corporation.

Microwave ovens. The microwave oven industry was, to a very large extent, developed by Japanese

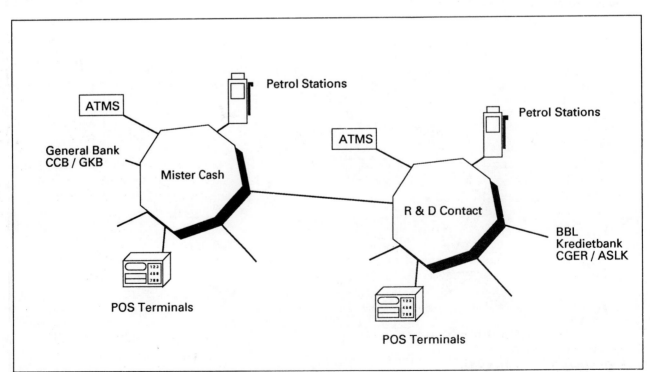

Figure 7. New services through the creative application of information technology

The Belgian advanced electronic funds transfer infrastructure led to the creation of a new service: unmanned 24-hour petrol stations.

manufacturing companies. The market has emerged since the mid 1960s, the major geographic markets being the United States, the United Kingdom and Japan.

Japanese manufacturers of microwave ovens deliberately raised entry barriers in two ways:

☆ by extremely cheap manufacture (through the production of large quantities) of the basic microwave radiation generating component called a magnetron,

☆ by using highly automated production processes incorporating information technology.

Thus, any manufacturers wishing to enter the industry had to overcome several barriers. They had to purchase magnetrons directly from Japan, obtain a licence for the manufacturing technology or, invest heavily in R & D and magnetron production facilities. Secondly, they had to invest heavily in highly automated production facilities using information technology.

This strategy worked extremely well for the Japanese manufacturers. However, it provoked a near 'fight to the death' between Japanese and Korean manufacturers of microwave ovens.

Xerox Corporation. The Xerox Corporation is well known as the pioneer of the xerographic process where images of documents are transferred onto plain paper by means of an electrostatic process. This is traditionally described as the plain paper copying process (PPC).

Xerox created two large entry barriers to their PPC markets. The first of these was provided by the legislation concerning patent protection. Xerox jealously guarded their patents and any infringements were attacked remorselessly through the courts. Furthermore, no other company was granted licenses for the basic xerographic technology.

The second entry barrier was provided by the rental regime. Xerox Corporation generated a set of financial conditions which encouraged a potential PPC purchaser to opt, instead, for the rental option. This meant that the entire PPC market was rental dominated. Any manufacturer wishing to enter into competition with Xerox, even if it had the technology, needed to have massive resources of capital in order to finance the rental of photocopiers.

The Xerox strategy was so successful that in 1975 a Consent Order in the United States obliged Xerox to release its stranglehold on the market. Until then the company had virtually a monopoly of the photocopier market.

This example illustrates just how effective the entry barrier concept can be.

Creating New Products and New Markets

Companies can obtain a significant lead over their competitors through the use of information technology to generate:

☆ new products from old ones,

☆ new markets which were previously not viable.

An example of the first category is where information is added in some way to an old product, thereby generating a new one. An example of the second is where FMS systems allow small production runs to be made on a profitable basis.

In researching where information technology had generated new products and new markets, we found it most convenient to classify the results under two headings:

☆ in the company's internal value chain,

☆ by transformation of the product.

The Company's Internal Value Chain
The following examples demonstrate how information technology has helped create a new product or market but where part of the internal value chain or process has been affected by information technology, as opposed to a direct transformation of the product. We illustrate this with the following cases:

☆ International Leisure Group,

☆ Deposit accounts,

☆ EFTPOS,

☆ International Paints.

International Leisure Group. Intasun is a holiday travel company which forms part of the International Leisure Group in the United Kingdom. The group is a market leader and uses information technology to help generate new products and markets.

A sales brochure is an essential item for any travel group because it describes in detail the elements of the product being sold. This may vary from a standard holiday package to a special product for a niche market such as Club 18/30 for younger holidaymakers.

Intasun rely on information technology to enable production of their brochure at the very last minute. This means that they can include the keenest prices and adjust to market demand right up to the last minute.

Such Intasun products would be virtually impossible without information technology.

Deposit accounts. A traditional deposit account pays a fixed rate of interest to the account holder on a regular basis. Nowadays, such calculations are obviously performed automatically by computer systems.

In order to attract customers to deposit funds, financial institutions have created many types of deposit accounts with more complex but, nevertheless, attractive rates of interest. Different sliding scales of interest varying as a function of the amounts deposited are to be found.

Another example is the 'Sweep Account' where funds are automatically transferred from a client's current account to a deposit account or vice versa.

Products such as these would be impossible without information technology. Without it, these markets would be too small to be viable. Information technology makes their administration profitable. In these cases information technology has created new viable markets.

EFTPOS—Bancontact and Mister Cash. In Belgium, there are two common cash-dispenser networks which were created by two major groupings of the country's banks. Named Bancontact and Mister Cash, they have recently been linked together to form a single joint facility. By means of a plastic card with a magnetic stripe on the reverse side, a customer can make a balance enquiry and withdraw or deposit cash through this common network of ATMs.

The system is now progressively forming the basis of a national EFTPOS network—the Bancontact/Mister Cash cards being, of course, debit cards.

For some years now, a large number of petrol pumps has been directly connected to either the Bancontact or to the Mister Cash network. This has created an entirely new service, 24-hour petrol stations. All petrol stations having their pumps linked to either of these networks offer petrol, without any supervision, throughout the night. The perceived value of the product is high because of the convenience to the customer. The system has been very successful and forms a normal part of motoring life in Belgium.

This is an example of information technology supporting the creation of both a new market and a product.

International Paints. International Paints is one of the companies making up the Courtaulds Group in the United Kingdom. One of its major product areas is marine paints. There are, however, tremendous problems of logistics associated with this area. When a ship is ready to be re-painted, a very large quantity of the correct paints in the correct colours has to be quickly supplied. Rapidly matching supply to this varying demand pattern poses huge problems.

Whereas some companies tracked ship movements

manually, International Paints created a computerized data base enabling it to follow the shipping's requirements.

By this means, International Paints increased the viability of the marine paint market whereas other competitors found it extremely difficult using old manual methods. One of the U.K.'s largest paint and chemical companies even abandoned the market.

International Paints is currently trying to interest other paint suppliers to collaborate in creating a marine data base using an expert system.

This example demonstrates how information technology can be used to increase the viability and attractiveness of a market.

Transforming the Product
This method of obtaining a competitive edge is easier to understand than the previous value chain category. Here an old product is transformed into a new product by the direct intervention of information technology. We demonstrate the principle involved with the following examples:

☆ Sensor microwave ovens,

☆ Smart credit cards,

☆ Barcode readers.

Sensor microwave ovens. In the initial type of microwave oven, food is placed in the cooking cavity and the time calculated for exposure to microwave radiation. The appropriate settings of time and power are dialled in and the cooking process started.

This basic product has now been transformed by information technology. Weight and humidity sensors are incorporated in recent generations of microwave ovens. Taking its input directly from these sensors, a microprocessor calculates the microwave radiation required and monitors the state of the cooking process. By this means, new features such as one-touch defrosting have become available and the convenience of the device has been improved.

This demonstrates how an old product can become transformed into a new product through the direct use of information technology.

Smart credit cards. Normal credit cards consist of a plastic card with a magnetically encoded stripe on the reverse side. By contrast, Smart cards have a microprocessor chip including a memory which is buried within the thickness of the card. Such systems have been pioneered over the last decade, particularly in France.

By the addition of information technology to the

old credit card product, a dramatically improved new product is formed. Such a card normally has sufficient memory to hold details of the possessor's account, credit limit, previous transaction record and a security number. Using such a card means that ATMs and EFTPOS terminals no longer need to access a financial institution's central computer system to check whether or not funds are available because this information is stored in the card.

One of the many advantages of using such a smart card is the creation of a new customer market consisting of people who would otherwise be considered an unacceptable risk for normal credit cards. The major disadvantage is, unfortunately, the high cost of the card.

Nevertheless, the addition of information technology to the card has produced a new product and has opened up a new market—those people who previously would have been unacceptable risks.

Barcode readers. Japanese manufacturers have also created a new generation of video recorders (VCRs) and domestic microwave ovens which incorporate barcode reader technology.

In the case of the VCR, the user opens a television guide and selects a programme to record. A barcode marking is printed alongside the programme. The user wipes the barcode reader over the mark and then pushes a button which transmits the information to the VCR. The machine will then automatic-ally record the programme when it is transmitted.

In a similar fashion, the user of a microwave oven equipped with a barcode reader selects a recipe from a recipe book. A barcode reader is wiped across the mark printed beside the required recipe, a button is pressed and the information transmitted directly to the microwave oven. A small display on the front of the microwave oven then gives step-by-step instructions to the user on how to prepare the selected dish. At the appropriate moment, the prepared ingredients are placed in the microwave oven, as instructed on the display. The microwave oven automatically cooks the ingredients and then gives further instructions to the cook.

These examples show how information technology has transformed two relatively mature pro-ducts—the VCR and the domestic microwave oven.

Conclusion

The concepts referred to in this article relate to the strategic use of information technology. In practice they require the collaboration of information systems specialists, and personnel involved in sales and marketing, purchasing, manufacturing, distri-bution and service operations. It emphasizes the need for information specialists to be trained in business, and for line managers to learn more about the strategic possibilities of information technology.

The Transformation of AT & T

Carol Kennedy

The oldest and largest U.S. multinationals, and those who work in their upper corporate echelons, exude a kind of pride and purpose rarely found in their European counterparts. Perhaps it has something to do with having their roots in the heroic age of American business, when enterprise and engineering were together literally pushing out the frontiers and forging the ethos immortalized in 1925 by President Calvin Coolidge: 'The business of America is business.'

No U.S. corporation was prouder than mighty American Telephone and Telegraph, or had a greater sense of its own destiny, which may have been partly to blame for the fate that overtook it in 1981–1984. A federal anti-trust action had been looming for years, but it was totally unexpected that AT & T would lose—and agree to lose—so much; nothing less than the breakup of the entire Bell system of regional telephone companies, known affectionately to generations of Americans as 'Ma Bell'.

Although the company kept its research and manufacturing core, and was freed for the first time to compete in information age markets, it is arguable—and no doubt will be argued in business school case studies for years to come—whether a less hubristic strategy on AT & T's part in the early 1970s could have delivered more from the U.S. Justice Department. After all, in 1956 the company had been promised 'no real injury' in future anti-trust cases in return for its exclusion from the then fledgling data processing industry.

AT & T is still a mighty force in U.S. industry, ranking fourth by market value in the *Forbes 500* of 1988. It retained the rights to provide a long distance telephone service, the so-called 'Long Lines'; its equipment manufacturing subsidiary, Western Electric, now renamed AT & T International, and the renowned Bell Laboratories, the world's most fertile source of electronics inventions. Bell Labs have some 20,000 patents to their credit, including such fundamentally world-changing technologies

as radio telephony, cable TV, lasers, the transistor and the silicon chip.

Since the release from its 30-year undertaking not to enter the computer market, a rich global potential lies open to it, though some of its international ventures, notably that with Olivetti, have proved troublesome.

The company is still, as Vice President John L. Segall admits, feeling the after-effects of a gigantic culture shock as the deeply imbued public service philosophy of founding president Theodore Vail has been forced to give way to aggressive competition in the marketplace. To cap a singularly difficult period in the company's history, just as its new strategy was in place and beginning to run, chairman and chief executive James Olson died unexpectedly of cancer in May 1988. In December 1988, it reported the first annual loss since its foundation in 1885, following a much larger than anticipated write-off of obsolete long distance equipment.

AT & T still, in the words of a senior international executive, has 'a high concept of its own destiny', but that destiny is not quite so clear-cut and immutable as it seemed in 1980, when AT & T was the largest corporation in the world, unquestioningly pursuing the mission laid down by Theodore Vail in 1909—'One System, One Policy, Universal Service.' That mission, known to AT & T veterans as 'POTS'—Plain Old Telephone Service—was to provide a 'universal service' at the lowest price for the average customer. Heroic myths abounded in the company of AT & T employees who kept the service running, linking America coast to coast, through blizzards, floods and all manner of natural disasters. And undeniably the mission had succeeded: the Bell System was widely acknowledged as the most technologically advanced and efficient in the world.

At divestiture, after nearly a century of existence, the company boasted assets of $150bn, revenues in excess of $40bn, profits in excess of $7bn and more than one million employees. (Today's much leaner corporation has assets of $38·4bn, sales of £33·6m,

Carol Kennedy is a journalist and Deputy Editor of *Director* magazine.

and employs 370,000.) AT & T was one of the soundest of Wall Street's blue-chip stocks, renowned as a haven for widows' savings.

When George Saunders, the chief defence lawyer at the anti-trust trial, stood up to begin his plea, he was able to declare without hyperbole that he represented 'the greatest business enterprise this world has ever produced'. And he added: 'Let there be no mistake: the government is here to destroy that enterprise.'

There was, undoubtedly, an element of hostility in Washington to a corporation widely perceived as arrogant and overconfident of its power. John DeButts, the company's patrician southern chairman in the early 1970s, spent millions of dollars fruitlessly lobbying for the so-called 'Bell Bill', which would have preserved the old single system had it got through Congress.

Deregulation

But the company could have detected the shape of its future as early as 1968, when the Federal Communications Commission (FCC) took the first steps towards deregulating the telecommunications business by opening up the terminal equipment market to competing companies. (Before 1968, AT & T owned almost every private telephone and business switchboard in the U.S., and leased them profitably to its captive customers.)

The FCC decision was known as 'Carterfone' after Thomas Carter of Carter Electronics, who pushed through a successful anti-trust suit against AT & T enabling him to 'patch' his mobile and car phones into the AT & T network. Its significance was immense for independent telephone companies, who were now free to interconnect with AT & T's switched phone network. Users could buy equipment from any supplier and simply plug it into the AT & T network.

Microwave Communications International

In 1969, another threatening marker was set down when the FCC allowed Bill McGowan's fledgling Microwave Communications International (MCI) to enter the lucrative 'private line' business between two major industrial cities, Chicago and St. Louis. Companies with offices in both centres could save enormously by using MCI's direct line service, which was bounced by microwave technology off terminals set at intervals between the two cities, instead of dialling into AT & T's switched long distance network. With supreme irony, microwave technology had been first developed in Bell Labs.

MCI prospered and began aggressively to expand.

In 1972 it announced plans to extend its service to 165 cities from coast to coast across America. AT & T could no longer ignore this pushy upstart. Many of its regional company presidents, led by Charles L. Brown of Illinois Bell (later to succeed DeButts as AT & T chairman), urged a strategy of direct confrontation by lowering prices wherever the giant corporation was in competition with MCI.

AT & T finally adopted that strategy, but at the cost of a delay that gave the rival time to develop its strength. At bottom, there was a cultural resistance: to John DeButts, AT & T's founding principles of universal service to all had been so bred in the bone of a 40-year career with the Bell system that he found it difficult to respond in entrepreneurial fashion to MCI's flagrant 'cream-skimming' tactics in high-profit business areas.

Until DeButts became chairman in 1972, indeed, AT & T had never even had a marketing department. For more than 90 years it had operated like a utility; far from having to market its products, it *was* the marketplace. The company's profit margin or 'rate of return' was fixed by the FCC and state regulators as a percentage of its costs—usually between 10 and 15 per cent. As its costs rose, so did its profits: it was hardly a system that fostered economy or the trimming of overheads.

The R & D programme was managed by a committee and was not as responsive to market pressures as it should have been. There was no mechanism for integrating marketing and research. The company was run by engineers and the overwhelming factors in determining the characteristics of new products were technical and technological. AT & T's attitude to the marketplace was epitomized by the president of one of its operating companies, New York Telephone, who remarked of his marketing director: 'We don't have anything to sell, so I don't know what he does.'

What the whole Bell System did have, however, was a service motivation second to none. DeButts believed implicitly that this was the result of the company's historic regulated monopoly status: should the corporation be cut loose upon the rough seas of competition, DeButts felt, 'we would be a different business, and I for one would feel the poorer for it'. Yet he understood the need for some internal change and hired one of IBM's top marketing experts, Archibald McGill, to set up new marketing systems.

McGill saw his task as steering the strategic direction of the company from being technologically driven to being financially and customer-driven in the IBM mould, using financial evaluations in place of technological ones and replacing the concept of a uniform telephone service by a drive to identify and appeal to discrete groups of consumers. To those long nurtured on POTS—they were said in

AT & T to have 'Bell-shaped heads'—such talk was heresy. Outside the corporation, McGill's appointment prompted suspicion that AT & T was trying to get the best of both worlds; preparing to compete while attempting to hold deregulation at bay until it was ready to handle it.

The Anti-trust Suit

When, belatedly, AT & T did hit back at MCI's challenge, cutting its prices in MCI areas and negotiating toughly on interconnection fees, McGowan riposted by filing a huge anti-trust suit in the spring of 1974. In a bitter sequence of events for AT & T, judgement was finally handed down in MCI's favour just as the federal anti-trust trial got under way in 1981. AT & T's bill was $1·8bn—the biggest anti-trust loss in U.S. history.

Well before that, however, it was clear to many at AT & T that an era was passing irrevocably into history. MCI was heading to become a billion dollar corporation by 1980 and it was estimated that between 1977 and 1980, the free-for-all in the equipment market would bite away half of Western Electric's market share, much of it going to Japanese manufacturers. Charles Brown of Illinois Bell, who succeeded DeButts on the chairman's early retirement in February 1979, was one who did clearly see the need for a more competitive stance.

In 1978, McKinsey's advised the company to change its public utility structure to that of a competitive firm. Similar proposals had been fiercely resisted in 1973, but Brown was determined to implement them. Early in 1978 he appointed a task force to recommend restructuring based on market segment rather than departmental objectives. The whole financial basis of AT & T was to be changed, from plans made largely on technical grounds to decentralized budgets from each segmented business, each competing for resources from a central management body.

The Fall of the Bell System

As Peter Temin of M.I.T. and Louis Galambos of Johns Hopkins University explain it in their lucid and scholarly study 'The Fall of the Bell System', commissioned by AT & T to record the divestiture while personal experiences remained fresh, the switch from domination by engineers to domination by marketeers was matched by a shift in basic power structures.

Ever since Vail's time, the regional company presidents had set policy and interacted with AT & T while the operating vice presidents ran the businesses—reflecting the corporate relationship of AT & T chairman and chief executive officer. Under reorganization, operating VPs would be replaced by the heads of the business segments, reporting directly to the company presidents. A whole proving ground of management succession had been wiped out.

Although management stresses were considerable (and may have influenced DeButts' decision to retire 2 years early), Brown pushed ahead, spelling out clearly what the new era would mean. In a Chicago speech entitled 'Meeting Change With Change', delivered in November 1978, Brown described how high technology businesses—the direction in which AT & T would have to expand—required advanced marketing strategies. Ma Bell, he said, was a symbol of the past. 'Today, ours is a business that knows it is not we, AT & T, but the customer who knows best. Mother Bell simply doesn't live here any more.'

Internal changes and stirring speeches were not, however, going to halt the looming federal anti-trust case. Brown faced several alternatives, all of them unpalatable. Loss to AT & T was inevitable; either vertical (from the equipment subsidiary and Bell Labs) or horizontally (from the regional telephone companies). The former would be far more damaging to AT & T as it faced the rapidly enlarging IT markets for integrated telecommunications systems.

Hopes of a limited divestiture were dashed, ironically enough, by the incoming, business-friendly Reagan administration in 1981. The new assistant attorney-general, William Baxter, was 'a man on an ideological mission', in the words of Temin and Galambos. He resisted even the arguments of defence secretary Caspar Weinberger that the anti-trust case should be dropped because the AT & T network was a national strategic asset, and declared he would 'litigate to the eyeballs'.

Brown was left with one effective option—to divest the operating companies. This would have the advantage of leaving a vertically integrated central AT & T core, well placed through Western Electric and Bell Labs to compete in information age markets. It would remove the company from the uncomfortable spotlight of public policy. But it would also mean surrendering all responsibility for a national telephone network, thus destroying forever the Bell System.

It was, as Temin and Galambos write, 'the biggest single decision that an American businessman has had to make in the last century . . . He accepted the fact that his best option was to break up the Bell System'.

The AT & T board was naturally unhappy but accepted Brown's decision without a major revolt, realizing, in Temin and Galambos' words, that 'the unthinkable had become . . . unavoidable'. Abandoning the Bell System was the only way for

AT & T to extricate itself from the massive judicial, regulatory and legislative firepower aimed at it.

The Baby Bells

Agreement was reached, the trial was stopped and on 1 January 1984, a much slimmed-down and altered AT & T opened for business. In all, it had lost three-quarters of its previous assets. Out of its 22 former operating companies were carved seven regional holding companies—the so-called Baby Bells—each with between $15bn and $20bn in assets. This had been chosen as the most financially viable size, on the model of two successful pre-divestiture companies, Pacific Telephone and Southwestern Bell. (Brown wanted AT & T to retain ownership of the Bell name and logo, but the judge awarded it to the 'Baby Bells' after Tandy Corporation objected that it would give AT & T an unfair advantage in selling phone equipment to its former subsidiaries.)

The Baby Bells have since gone from strength to strength. Between them they provide local phone service to around 80 per cent of the U.S. population and their revenues ranged in 1987 from $8bn (Southwestern Bell) to $12·3bn (BellSouth). 'They are just like cash registers', observes one Wall Street analyst. In years to come they are expected to break out of 'plain old telephone service' into all sorts of transmission facilities over the phone lines, including cable television; perhaps even competing against the remaining fiefdom of Ma Bell, long distance services. At present they are prohibited by the divestiture terms from doing this, though they have been able to squeeze some other concessions such as data base transmission, seen as a huge market.

While the Baby Bells flex their muscles in pleasurable and profitable freedom, albeit in some frustration at their remaining restraints, the cultural trauma for the management of the old 1m-strong AT & T has been enormous. Vice President Segall, who was placed in charge of divestiture planning by Charles Brown, compares it to the 'Big Bang' theory of the universe, whose experimental verification won two Bell Labs physicists the Nobel Prize in the mid-1960s. Yet job losses were minimal—nine out of ten Bell System employees stayed in the same job after divestiture, even working for the same supervisor, and shareholders did better out of the breakup than before. (All 3m shareholders retained their stock in AT & T and in addition were given proportionate values in the local companies, which have expanded so aggressively since divestiture.) As for the telephone service itself, Theodore Vail would have been proud of the seamless way it carried on over the transition, though some residential users have since found some deterioration in the repair service.

Managing the Crisis

For the skilful short-term management of crisis, indeed, much credit must go to the durability of Vail's old Bell System culture, though it acted as a drag-anchor in other respects. As Segall told a conference in Hong Kong 2 years after divestiture: 'Employees performed as if they were involved in the restoration of telephone service following a devastating hurricane, fire, flood or snowstorm . . . a company composed of 1m employees and $150bn in assets. having 3m shareholders, needed to be reorganized in 24 months! Few companies in the world could have carried out such a task with the efficiency of the Bell System.'

Yet the deeply embedded values of the system meant also that, as one manager observed: 'Employees reacted to the news much in the way they would have done if a close family member had been suddenly killed in a accident.'

It was a massive exercise in the management of change. AT & T executives, says Segall, followed the maxim of Robert Louis Stevenson: 'Keep your fears to yourself, but share your courage with others.' In briefings across the length and breadth of the land, they stressed the bright future that telecommunications could offer in the information age. 'The task that management faced', said Segall in Hong Kong, 'was nothing less than mapping out a new course for the future, and redesigning an institution to pursue that course, bringing with it an understanding and dedicated workforce'. This would involve deep changes in 'the theory or vision of the firm—and in the processes by which it would be managed'.

The Transformation

Three main transformations were required, as Segall outlined them:

☆ What had been a telephone company for nearly a century had to become a company whose business was the movement and management of information.

☆ What had been a domestic American company had to become international.

☆ What had been a government-regulated monopoly had to become a competitive company dictated by the marketplace.

To accomplish these, changes were required in six sectors:

(1) The corporate structure was reshaped into a decentralized organization of strategic business units, known in AT & T as 'Lines of Business' (LOB). Each LOB was to be a profit centre focused on a particular market or business segment, with autonomous decision-making

within operational and financial boundaries set by AT & T headquarters, which would also spot and facilitate synergies between, say, silicon chip manufacture and computer system sales.

(2) The planning process was completely redesigned. 'As recently as 1970,' recalled Segall, 'when AT & T officials were asked "Who is the Bell System's chief planner?", it was not uncommon for them to answer, in dead seriousness, "Theodore Vail".'

The Bell System was operationally oriented and run largely on management by objectives. Continuing evaluations and long range strategic planning were, for the most part, regarded as unnecessary. No planning group as such existed in the old Bell System, apart from a 'cabinet' of AT & T top officers and the presidents of Western Electric and Bell Labs. They met on alternate Mondays and in between came meetings of the so-called 'Odd Monday' group, consisting of the AT & T chairman and those reporting directly to him. This eventually became the Executive Policy Committee, responsible for long range planning, but no strategic planning system as such was set up until 1982/1983.

Post-divestiture, each LOB would be responsible for its own 5-year plan, subject to corporate review and approval to ensure compatibility with corporate strategies and priorities in the allocation of resources. There would be a strong emphasis on flexible strategies focused on markets and market segments, both corporate and LOB.

(3) People were brought in from outside the corporation at all levels to impart new perspectives and expertise, especially in marketing. An important aspect of this strategy was to 'attract individuals with a bias towards risk-taking and to make all parts of the company more sensitive to the competitive marketplace,' as Segall explained. (Management development in AT & T had, until McGill's appointment, traditionally been from 'within the ranks'.)

(4) A major revision of corporate training programmes was required at all levels, stressing the importance of understanding customers' needs and competitors' strengths and weaknesses in the fast-changing global information marketplace. 'A key objective of this refocused training is to build into the new corporate culture an acceptance of ever-changing market conditions and, more important, the ability to adapt quickly to those changes', said Segall.

(5) Incentives were encouraged by new compensation and reward schemes. Individual and organizational awards for reaching and exceeding sales and financial targets are now part of AT & T's compensation packages.

(6) International corporate alliances were actively pursued in order to gain entry and expertise in markets around the world. In just over a year, AT & T arranged with six of the top European computer companies to adopt Unix, AT & T's standard for a software operating system; went into a joint venture with Philips for the marketing of switching and transmission equipment in Europe; arranged with Wang to produce compatible computers and document standards; took a 25 per cent interest in Olivetti, manufacturer of the PC6300 computer sold by AT & T in the U.S.; went into a new computer communications company in a joint venture with several of Japan's leading electronics companies including Hitachi, Fujitsu, Mitsubishi Electric and Sony; set up a plant to manufacture telephones in Singapore and entered joint ventures with companies in Taiwan (digital switches), Korea (switches and fibre optic equipment); with Rockwell, Honeywell and Data General (swapping data between computers and switches), and with Telefonica of Spain (to design and manufacture integrated circuits).

Commenting on this in 1986, Segall said: 'We have moved significantly into the international marketplace in a shorter time, we believe, than any other company in modern times.'

The New Mission

Divestiture cost AT & T dearly in its demands on management and strategic planning time. It cost in other ways, too. In 'The Fall of the Bell System', Temin and Galambos compared the state of corporate shock to 'Vienna after World War I . . . (AT & T) has had to reduce the size of its internal bureaucracy, to develop new leadership paths and—most importantly—to define a corporate mission appropriate to its new business.'

This was done formally in 1980 in AT & T's report to stockholders: 'No longer do we perceive that our business will be limited to telephony, or, for that matter, telecommunications. Ours is the business of information handling, the knowledge business. And the market that we seek is global.' Not as boldly inspirational, perhaps, as Vail's 'One System, One Policy, Universal Service', but appropriate to a far more complex and sophisticated business environment.

Implementing the new mission has not been easy. Some of the expected new directions did not materialize—for example, the great jousting between AT & T and IBM which was predicted after deregulation. IBM remains a full-time computer manufacturer with an interest in telecommunications, while AT & T manages a national telecommunications network and sells computers principally to facilitate switching functions in that network. As Temin and Galambos explain: 'The two firms overlap to some extent—in electronic transmission of data, for example—but are almost completely in different markets.'

How far and in which directions it would go into information technology, and how much the company would continue to rely on telephony were broad strategic questions following divestiture, but there were also difficult technical matters of finance to be resolved in the change from a regulatory to a cost accounting system. One of the most complex aspects was the breakup of billing systems which had been, as Segall said in a 1988 interview, 'a bit of a black art . . . whereby we shared the benefits of a decreasing cost per unit in the technology in long distance with the exchange companies. In the Bell System they were principally our companies but also independent telephone companies. . . These were huge amounts of money, at the time of divestiture about $7bn–$8bn. The entropy level of the organization was very high.'

How then does AT & T see its strategic direction now, and the change to a new corporate culture? Visiting Vice President Segall (who has responsibility for corporate planning under Vice Chairman Morris Tanenbaum) in AT & T's headquarters building in midtown Manhattan, one gets a clear impression that this is still a company with a special sense of mission and destiny.

Until divestiture, the New York headquarters was a remarkable 1957 building at 195 Broadway, once described by the New York Times's architectural critic as 'a temple to the god of the telephone'. The roofline above its rising tiers of Ionic colonnades was crowned with a gilded sculpture known as 'The Spirit of Communication'—a naked youth bound round with coils of wire. When the company sold 195 Broadway, the statue was removed to the white marble lobby of the new AT & T Building on Madison Avenue, popularly known as the 'Chippendale Building' because of its broken-pediment skyline.

Most of AT & T's management business is now carried on at Basking Ridge, New Jersey, and the company has leased out most of the Madison Avenue building, retaining the two top floors, mainly for board meetings surveyed by the portraits of Vail and Alexander Graham Bell.

Data Networking: Everybody's Strategy

'The principal issue now is how we execute the strategy', says Segall, whose 40-year career with AT & T is approaching retirement. 'We need to do it as measured change rather than in dramatic fashion. Some things are quite clear to us. We are on

a course that will take a portion of our business into the computer business, which was clearly in its nascent state when we were formulating strategy.' AT & T is now convinced, he says, that not only will it stay in that business but will become 'a significant player' in it. Data networking is 'everyone's strategy now' as the 'building blocks of the information age' become less expensive and 'people think less of individual boxes, more of creating networks'.

'Some of us have long thought that the inherent value of an operating system like Unix would be terribly important in a world of data networking, and there is a growing understanding of this.'

(Unix, a Bell Labs invention, is widely licensed and it is estimated that it will account for nearly a quarter of the world market by 1991. In 1987 its 10·3 per cent share was worth $7·3bn. America's Unisys (the former Sperry Univac) and Britain's ICL are building computers around Unix. The richest prospect for AT & T lies not in licensing but in designing and building Unix-based computer networks, which is where its 20 per cent stake in Sun Microsystems of California—a manufacturer of brilliantly successful PCs which run on Unix—becomes crucial.

AT & T and Sun, with their U.S. and European allies Unisys, ICL and Olivetti, are now setting out to make Unix the industry standard: in May 1988 they forced the setting up of an Open Software Foundation backed by Hewlett–Packard, Digital, Apollo, IBM, Siemens, Nixdorf and Honeywell.)

Segall, speaking before the great software alliances confronted each other, went on to note that the natural concomitant of providing systems is 'how one manages those systems'. This is a field, he added, on which AT & T puts a high premium. 'Coming into being now are the first systems for network management, and I believe they will be terribly important. In some instances I would expect us certainly to be a leader in that field.'

'We have been credited with, if not inventing the term "systems engineering", then certainly bringing it into general use. And we have built wonderfully complex machine systems, almost ideally disciplined. They really gave substance to the term "user friendly". But the regal elegance of that achievement was in the systems engineering, the fact that you could take all these pieces and get them to work in practical harmony. . . To me, that was one of the principal strengths that came out of Bell Labs.'

Segall expects AT & T to be a leader in integrating those functions that exist on a customer's premises with complex networks, whether local area or worldwide. 'In the management of networks from systems integration conception to actual management, we should be one of the principal players, although it will take time because the field is only just being developed.'

Competing with IBM on mainframes is no longer seen as realistic. 'That's not a high-growth area, and you always have to be careful not to put your energies into a fading area', says Segall. 'There are compelling reasons why we should not: IBM is too well entrenched and I don't believe it's the area of great growth for the future.'

Reflecting on the huge increase in competition from the variety of businesses that now deliver financial information, such as Citibank, Segall agrees with Walter Wriston that 'information is money', and says 'everybody now is on that bandwagon. Citibank is a competitor, no question about it. 19 October 1987 (the stockmarket crash) captured everyone's attention; currency is a 24 hour business dependent on information. But one has to ask, where are the associated decision analytics that go along with all of that data to turn it into useful information?'

'If I had to pick one thing for the future that will distinguish the information systems, it would be in the areas of decision analytics, to be able to say to the user: "I will give you the tools to manage all of this stuff that is dumped on you in such huge quantities". That's one of the most exciting things for the next 10 years or so.'

How to manage the headlong pace of technological change, and how corporations should handle the tremendous demands it puts on human resources and management systems, will be a major challenge for the future, Segall believes. 'All the consultants will build new careers on managing technology', he predicts with a smile. 'There is the question of how we develop the management structures to do it, how we develop the business leaders to handle it.'

The Top Gun Program

AT & T has its own programme to meet the latter challenge. Called 'Top Gun', it is, says Segall, still in its design stage, but 'its principles are to acquaint our future business leaders with the kind of problems they are going to be facing. We want to put them into circumstances where they will work on actual problems complete with competitive responses.' He draws the analogy of pilots in wartime being trained by flying against colleagues 'who fly as if they were enemy pilots'. To do this, AT & T must develop people who can act like competitors or 'impeders' to their own corporate thinking.

'We can't give them a template, a set of rules to follow. We will force them to react to change.' While Segall says it is too early to judge the merits of

the Top Gun programme, it is clear that it will be no easy ride for those who go through it. 'Top Gun is not a place where you go to listen; it's a place where you go to succeed', says Segall firmly.

Future thinking ranges more widely throughout the management of AT & T in the wake of divestiture. After its forced change of corporate culture, strategic planning and brainstorming appears to be fast making up ground for the years of respectful adherence to missions set in 1909.

The Twenty-first Century Project

One mechanism for 'brainstorming the future' is known as the 'Twenty-first Century Project'. In Segall's words, 'this represents efforts from all our best functional and business units as well as some of the better free-thinkers and planners outside our business, such as Peter Schwartz of Royal Dutch Shell and Michael Porter of Harvard. We look for the technology drivers for the future. On a continuing basis we have a group that looks for weak signals—on the analogy of people who listen out into space—to spot things before they become obvious to everyone. Then we play with those ideas and test them.'

'I don't know a good process that ensures you are successful in forecasting. I don't personally believe that an extrapolative approach is fruitful either, because extrapolation is like steering the boat by looking at the wake. That is not to suggest', he stresses carefully, 'that one must not do extrapolative planning, but that you modulate it, you don't become captive. More businesses have gone down the drain by pathological precoccupation with what they did well for many years. . . We ask in our formal business plans that there should be sections devoted to risk and uncertainty.'

The Twenty-first Century Project had its first formal readout to senior AT & T officers in May 1988, at the end of its first year. The last 7 weeks before delivery were marked by intense activity, with groups meeting on Saturdays and Sundays. Polishing and testing went on between May and September, and elements of the report will be fed into the broad-gauge strategic plan with the 5-year financial forecasts that are prepared each May. More detailed operational plans and 2-year budget plans are then worked on between early summer and autumn.

Whatever diverse activities the information age holds for AT & T, telephony is expected to continue producing growth, a matter of some satisfaction for Segall, whose long career with New York Telephone gives him a proprietorial pride in the Manhattan panorama spread beneath his office windows. Telecommunications services produced approximately half AT & T's revenue stream in

1987, with strong volume growth. 'Telephony is not a dead end, it's a major area of evolution', says Segall.

In its bid to internationalize fast through alliances, the company acknowledges lessons learned through hard experience. 'Nothing fails like success', says Segall, quoting Britain's Dean Inge, to point up the dangers of relying too complacently on technological quality at the expense of marketing. 'We were wonderfully successful. We had some of the best technology the world has ever seen, and we still do. It was natural for us to assume that the world would come running with great enthusiasm to embrace us. But the world doesn't work that way.

'We didn't have any contact with the end-users of what we wanted to sell, whether telephone instruments, computers or whatever. We had no marketing or sales infrastructure. Larger telephone systems we could sell to the PTTs, but in every country there is big political persuasion to use its own and not to welcome foreign suppliers. There were lessons of marketing, lessons in understanding political realities, cultural sensitivities and the approach to each country. So we are re-assessing those approaches now.'

One problem with its foreign relationships may be, as the journal *International Management* suggested, that AT & T is perceived as having too American an image in the world at large. Segall concedes the criticism has a point. 'We *are* too American. I don't know how we can hurry that.'

Lessons will be drawn from the setbacks with Olivetti ('we just did not have an international product line poised to go through Olivetti') and there will be 'much closer alliances in terms of product manifestation'. In early 1989, those lessons appeared to be bearing fruit when AT & T was chosen as the foreign partner for Italy's state telecommunications equipment company. The agreement with Italtel could be a significant bridgehead into the European telecoms market as Italy gears up for a 5-year modernization plan.

If by 1992 there is a common tariff on data in Europe, Segall sees great opportunities in that area. 'I'm also a strong believer that there will be communications and commerce on a much broader scale with Eastern Europe. One of Gorbachev's main planks is to double civilian telecommunications capacity and introduce computers at every level in the U.S.S.R. We would have to plan for that.'

Part of Segall's responsibilities is to look at potential new markets, and he emphasizes the difficulties here of having part of the business still under the regulatory eye of the FCC. 'Any entry into new markets with respect to some of these complex networks must be approved by the FCC: that's terrible both in terms of what can be done for the customer and in terms of our planning. I do not want to under-estimate the penalties and burdens. I'm not the resident Pollyanna. My role is to cast doubt on the aspirations of other groups.'

In some respects, ironically, the power of the FCC is felt more after divestiture than in the days when Washington was seeking ways to cut the old monolithic AT & T down to size. This will continue through the early 1990s as the FCC decides the crucial issue of long distance equal-access payments.

In many ways, as the study by Peter Temin and Louis Galambos concludes, divestiture as an experiment in competition remains 'an enormous gamble'.

Bibliography

Peter Temin and Louis Galambos, *The Fall of the Bell System*, Cambridge University Press, Cambridge, U.K.

Steve Coll, *The Deal of the Century: The Breakup of AT & T*, Simon and Schuster, New York.

John L. Segall, *Dealing with Change: Cosmic, Corporate and Personal*, paper given at the Human Resources Conference in Hong Kong, 8 January (1986).

Successful Strategies—The Story of Singapore Airlines (SIA)

Karmjit Singh, Company Planning Manager, Singapore Airlines Limited

This case study describes the growth and development of Singapore Airlines from a small national carrier serving the Malayan States to an international airline with a network extending to 27 countries. Its strategy is simple: quality service at a competitive price, made possible by high investment in equipment and in staff training.

Introduction

SIA is the national air carrier of the island-state of Singapore. SIA's roots can be traced back to early 1947 when a twin-engined Airspeed Consul under the Malayan Airways insignia first started scheduled services between Singapore, Kuala Lumpur, Ipoh and Penang.

By 1955, international services were added using DC3s to Jakarta, Medan, Palembang, Saigon, Bangkok, North Borneo, Sarawak, Rangoon and Brunei. The airline underwent several fleet changes whilst additional destinations were added.

In 1963 it was renamed Malaysian Airways. In 1966, the governments of Malaysia and Singapore acquired joint majority control of the airline and in 1967 it was again renamed, this time to MSA (Malaysia–Singapore Airlines). MSA started to expand beyond the region with a chartered B707 operating to Sydney in the same year.

SIA was born on 1 October 1972 when MSA ceased operations and SIA took to the skies as Singapore's own national airline. The 'new' airline retained the B707s and B737s and continued to serve the entire international network formerly served by MSA. Today, SIA has grown to be among the top 10 international air carriers in the world. Its production of 18,081 million RPKs (revenue passenger kilometers) in 1982 puts SIA ahead of such well-known names as Qantas and Swissair and just behind Lufthansa and Air Canada (see Figure 1).

Over the past 10 years, total revenue has grown from S$389m to S$2,621m or more than six times (see Figure 2). Staff strength, however, has grown at a slower rate from 4906 10 years ago to 10,655 (see Figure 3)

SIA's fleet today comprises 17 B747s, eight A300s and two B727s. The average age of this fleet is less than 3 years old (as at October 1983) making it one of the most modern of any major airline.

SIA has also shown a decent profit in every year of its operations since 1972 (see Figure 4).

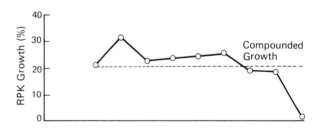

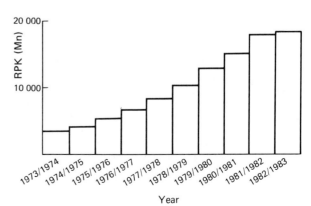

Figure 1. RPKs and growth rate

The author is Company Planning Manager with Singapore Airlines Ltd., Airmail Transit Centre, PO Box 501, Singapore 9181.

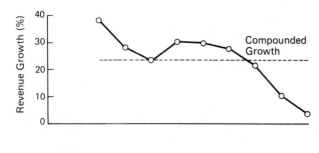

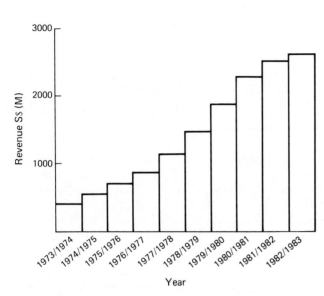

Figure 2. Revenue growth

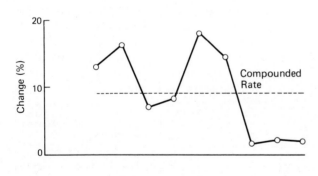

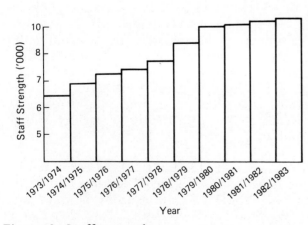

Figure 3. Staff strength

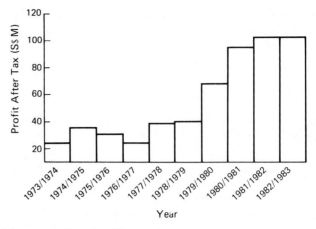

Figure 4. Profit after tax

Reasons for SIAs Success

What, one may ask, accounts for the enviable success of an air carrier from a tiny developing island-state half the size of Los Angeles with a population of only 2.5 million inhabitants and ill-endowed with natural resources other than its people?

Both external and internal factors have played equal and complementary roles in accounting for SIA's prosperity.

External Factors

Singapore straddles the Equator and is strategically located at the crossroads of one of the world's businest sea and air routes. More importantly the airline's homebase is increasingly becoming the hub of the ASEAN hinterland with its thriving economies. It is also centrally located in the fastest growing region in the world—the Intra-Orient-Pacific Basin.

Hard-work and pragmatic government policies have turned Singapore into a modern and efficient metropolis, making it the most prosperous country in Asia after Japan. Its free enterprise ideology has attracted many Fortune 500 companies to set up regional headquarters in Singapore. Singapore today is the second largest port after Rotterdam and has the third largest oil-refining centre in the world after Rotterdam and Houston.

Liberal visa rules, good hotels and infrastructure and the promotion of Singapore as a shopping paradise have also helped to attract visitors by the thousands. Singapore now handles the largest number of foreign visitors among the Asian countries including Japan and Hong Kong.

The government also welcomes airlines from all over the globe to land at Singapore either as a terminating or transit point. To entice more of them to do so, airport and ancillary activities are constantly upgraded. Consequently, SIA was able to take advantage of reciprocal traffic rights to expand. (Its current network extends to 27 countries spread over 4 continents.) Now, more than 30 scheduled international airlines call at Singapore in addition to numerous non-scheduled operators.

Internal Factors

Skillful exploitation of the opportunities created by the government was the key to SIA's success. In order to gain a better insight into the airline's ability to exploit its strategic location, and other advantages, we must return briefly to its inception stage.

Though almost wholly government-owned, the Airline does not receive any subsidies (which is taboo for all government-owned industries in Singapore). SIA is run along purely commercial lines—i.e. to make a reasonable profit for its shareholders. The airline is taxed like any other business and pays dividends yearly to its share-holders. SIA even has to pay fees to the government in return for guarantees that may be required by some banks on loans for aircraft purchases. The airline is constantly reminded that Singapore can exist without an airline since it is already well connected by air to all corners of the globe. Thus SIA fully recognizes its fate should it not make good in the marketplace.

Fleet Re-Equipment Decisions

SIA started with only five B707s and five B737s. To this were added four more B707s in 1972. After careful evaluation, the fledgling carrier decided to take a quantum leap into the jumbo league by ordering two B747s for delivery in 1973. This was not a hasty decision. Detailed studies had shown that this aircraft had the lowest unit operating cost. This was the first of many bold fleet re-equipment decisions. Thereafter the airline started to grow rapidly. More B747s were acquired in 1974, 1975, 1976 and 1977 as SIA's route network expanded to more European cities. Passenger response to the new aircraft and the inflight service was encouraging. In 1976 orders were also placed for three B727s. This order was then expanded to six in early 1977. These aircraft were needed to strengthen SIA's regional services and to replace the older B737s and B707s.

In late 1977 two more advanced versions of the B747 and five DC10s were ordered to service the TransPacific services.

In 1978 SIA shocked the world by announcing the then largest commercial aeroplane order ever placed, valued at U.S.$900m for 13 B747s and another six B727s. A few months later two more DC10s were ordered from McDonnell Douglas.

In 1979, it ordered six airbuses with options for a further six. Another huge order worth U.S.$1·6bn was placed in December 1981 comprising eight B747-300s with the stretched upper deck and eight more A300s. May 1983 saw yet another large order of aircraft—six more B747-300s plus six A310s and four B757s. Technologically obsolete and fuel inefficient aircraft were meanwhile retired. (See Table 2 for Summary of the Aircraft Deliveries and New Orders.)

By April 1988 SIA's fleet will consist of the following:

9	B747-200B
14	B747-300SUD
6	A310
4	B757

What was the justification for all these purchases? Firstly, SIA was able to exploit its traffic rights through skillful marketing. This, in turn, helped to stimulate traffic enabling the airline to expand at a rate of about 25 per cent a year in the 1970s.

Secondly, to support SIA's high service standards the airline decided to invest in the latest technology. It has since been part of SIA's strategy to maintain a youthful fleet with the lowest operating costs. The two fuel crises in 1973 and 1979 vindicated these 'bold' decisions, since the new aircraft proved to be an excellent hedge against fly-away inflation.

Thirdly, the major purchases were made at the bottom of the business cycle; best deals were therefore struck. With the carefully phased-out delivery of these aircraft, SIA could take advantage of any upturn in the economic cycle when demand for additional capacity was strong.

Service

From the start SIA understood that superior service, especially the standard of inflight service was paramount in order to establish itself. To provide a service 'that even other airlines talk about' became the unofficial motto for SIA's employees beginning with its cabin staff. According to Fortune magazine 'the combination of gentleness and efficiency helps the airlines lure customers from competitors on routes that now span half the globe'. The unceasing pursuit of excellence continues in the air as well as on the ground.

SIA's passenger load factors have been consistently above 70 per cent for the greater part of the past 10 years (see Table 1). Accolades from the trade and customers too have borne out SIA's belief that a superior quality of service is paramount under conditions of open competition where carrier's network, frequency and capacity are generally equal.

Table 1. Load factors by year (%)

	Passenger load factor	Overall load factor
1973/1974	71	63
1974/1975	67	60
1975/1976	68	64
1976/1977	71	66
1977/1978	74	68
1978/1979	73	70
1979/1980	74	71
1980/1981	72	69
1981/1982	75	72
1982/1983	73	69

While the inflight service has been highly visible, the airline has also spared no expense to raise its standards on the ground. Ground services are reviewed continually to match the standard of service provided in the air. With the passenger foremost in mind, SIA has invested millions of dollars in computers to link its reservations network worldwide to provide instant access on schedules and seat availability.

Owing to its high inflight standards and charming cabin crew SIA has managed to capture the mystic of the Orient in its 'Singapore Girl' advertising theme. The 'aura' created by the Balmain-clad girls has made the stylized yellow bird logo of SIA instantly recognizeable everywhere. Advertising recall of SIA advertisements is generally one of the highest wherever polled. This evergreen theme has also won some of the most prestigious awards in the advertising industry including the 1983 Clio award for the best International Television and Cinema category. SIA has also won Clio awards for the best television commercial (1975) and best overall print campaign (in 1976 and 1977).

Human Resources

Because Singapore lacked natural resources it has had to rely on its human resources to upgrade itself. Recognizing this, investment in human resources has been one of the cardinal facets of SIA's game plan.

Recruitment

During the recruitment phase, the best available personnel are sought. The new recruits are exposed to various departments and on-the-job training. High priority is given to staff training and

development in diverse forms, both in-house and out-house, locally and overseas. Total expenditure in this area of staff development and training ranges between U.S.$15m and U.S.$20m annually.

This huge investment has been well spent. For example, its engineering staff can do almost all the maintenance on the latest generation of aircraft and engines. Hitherto, a greater part of the maintenance was contracted out-house at higher cost.

As mentioned earlier innovation and creative ideas are highly regarded and rewarded. Staff are continuously encouraged to send in ideas which save costs, increase revenue or productivity or upgrade service. Numerous ideas have been recognized, rewarded and implemented. Not long ago S$50,000 was awarded for an idea which saves the company about S$1·5m a year on fuel. It is through such schemes that employees are encouraged to give of their best.

Innovations

The innovative spirit also gave the travelling public the first slumberettes on B747 upper decks, jackpot machines to relieve boredom and Round-the-World fares. SIA also became the first airline, apart from British Airways and Air France, to operate the Concorde which cut travelling time, between London and Singapore, to $9\frac{1}{2}$ hours. This not only fulfilled SIA's goal to provide total service to the public but also enhanced SIA's reputation and image in the industry.

Behind the service standards lies the corporate philosophy supporting it. Among the attributes ingrained into employees are teamwork and the pursuit of excellence. The smallest possible units are created to carry out required tasks. Authority is delegated down to the lowest level consistent with accountability and efficiency. Decentralized decision-making enables fast reaction from the man-on-the-spot and especially the sales staff in the field. Executives are encouraged to progress to 'problem-solving' and on to opportunity-finding. Training and retraining remains the unwavering object of the company.

Productivity

Productivity is SIA's catchword in its drive for excellence. Staff recognize that survival in today's harsh competitive environment rests on raising their own productivity. With assurances from management that retrenchment is not the objective in seeking productivity gains, employees have been forthcoming with suggestions with improvements. SIA's employee productivity measured against the number of CTKs produced, ranks amongst the highest in the airline league (see Table 2).

Table 2. CTKs/employee

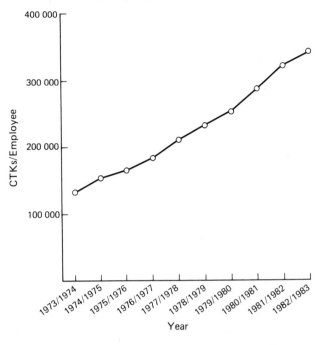

Note : Lufthansa (1982)   209,075 CTKs/Employee
        Swissair (1982)   170,221 CTKs/Employee
        KLM   (1982/83)   256,120 CTKs/Employee
        SIA   (1982/83)   339,232 CTKs/Employee

SIA intrinsically believes in being slim and trim. Staff recruitment is tightly controlled and is closely related to capacity growth rates. Staff made surplus through technology are either retrained or redeployed or induced to leave through generous redundancy schemes.

Industrial Relations

Because of the huge investment in human resources it is not surprising that Management and Unions try to co-exist for the good of the airline. Most industrial relations problems are solved amicably.

The cordial Management–Union atmosphere enables Management to concentrate on its task of running the airline instead of being preoccupied with 'public relations battles against criticisms and fighting for support of government and unions'.

Quality of Management

Of all the major and well-established airlines in the world, SIA has one of the youngest management teams. The average manager is in his late 30s with executive directors only 3–4 years older.

The young and dynamic team has been able to react quickly and decisively in decision-making. Luckily

for SIA the government does not interfere in day-to-day affairs and quick decisions can be made and actions taken.

Financial Conservatism

Management also believes in prudent financial management. New aircraft, for example, are depreciated over 10 years. This policy of accelerated depreciation reflects the rapid and continuing increase in the cost of new aircraft. Start up costs of aircraft are also written off fairly quickly. This has enabled SIA to finance a huge portion of its aircraft and other capital expenditure from self-generated funds. Because of SIA's credit standing, it has been able to tap the market for funds at the finest rates.

The Role of Corporate Planning

When SIA was expanding at double digit growth rates the Company Planning Department was preoccupied mainly with fleet planning. Over the last 2 years, with both capacity and traffic growth showing modest growth, the Company Planning Department became actively involved in identifying and establishing Corporate Objectives and Corporate Goals. To support the accomplishment of Corporate Goals, the Company Planning Department acted as a facilitator and catalyst and got the Divisions to establish their respective Divisional Goals. Consequently the smallest department in the Company was functionally linked in one way or another to the broader Corporate Objectives and Corporate Goals. In this way staff at various levels were motivated to do their best since the goals were well defined and measureable. The Company Planning Department monitored the progress of the goals, monthly, on behalf of management.

More importantly, in the realm of strategy formulation, the Company Planning Department consolidated the 'Environmental and Resource Analysis' inputs from all the departments and prepared an 'Issue Analysis'. Essentially this 'Issue Analysis' provided the kernel for management response and strategic thought and eventual functional strategy development. Implementation was, of course, decentralized.

Strategic Issues for the Future

The Company, historically, experienced capacity growth rates close to 20 per cent per annum. This was possible thanks to the systematic exercise of attractive traffic rights. Most of the relatively attractive traffic rights have now been used up. Meanwhile the global economic recession has served to heighten protectionist sentiments in several airline quarters. The prognosis is that we have to live with modest to low capacity growth rates in the future.

Strategically, we are now preoccupied with issues such as how to maintain profitability in the face of slow growth and rising costs. Also, in a low growth regime, how do you keep improving productivity continuously? There are other issues; and these feature prominently in the search for suitable strategies.

Conclusion

Through sheer hard work, innovation, bold and pragmatic decisions and huge investment in the staff SIA has grown from its humble origins to serve 36 cities in 27 countries. Its strategy is quite simple. It believes in giving the customer a quality service at a competitive price while earning a small return. This has been made possible by the high investment in the most up-to-date equipment and facilities and in staff training and development.

In short, SIA's success is founded on the prudent practice of sound and well-tried business fundamentals rather than any earth-shattering or new corporate strategies.

Integrating Information Systems for Competitive Advantage at Merrill Lynch

Elaine M. Koerner

Innovative technology has taken a back seat at Merrill Lynch, at least temporarily. Bringing costs down and keeping them down is much more the focus of attention these days, both within the operations and systems part of the business and right across the firm. With competitive pressure mounting both at home from commercial banks and abroad from the European Community and the Japanese, the rationale for deploying technology largely is a process of pragmatic justification rather than a pitch for creative experimentation.

Gerald H. Ely

'There is a difference between being technology-driven and being innovative. There is a difference between deploying technology to achieve clearly-defined goals and looking for opportunities to try out new technologies. Over the past 3 years, we have been driven by one overriding aim: to get our costs down.'

The person speaking is Gerald H. Ely, first vice president and director of the information systems division at Merrill Lynch. Ely is a versatile man. From 1981 to 1984, he was director of technology planning at the company, a position in which his charge was to invest in innovative technology not only to enhance the operations of the firm but also to explore other more high-risk ventures away from core businesses. The result was projects such as Teleport, an initiative initially undertaken with the New York Port Authority to enhance the company's communications infrastructure that eventually evolved into a separate business of its own with operations in other U.S. cities.

Today, the technology planning unit at Merrill Lynch no longer exists. Innovative technology within the company also appears to be something of

the past, at least for the moment. Times are not so easy. As of mid 1989, the consumer markets sector of the business was having a good, steady year though not a banner year. Consumer markets offer brokerage and other financial services such as investment, insurance and trust products and services for individuals and small to mid-size firms primarily in the United States. The capital markets side which caters to large corporations, institutions, and governments on a global basis, was having mixed results, though second quarter results showed a continued number one ranking in the global and domestic underwriting of debt and equity securities. To home in on core businesses and generate additional capital, the company announced the sale of its entire residential real estate sales and relocation businesses to Prudential Insurance Co. of America for $300m.

Elaine Koerner is a freelance journalist living in Washington D.C.

Gerald Ely has moved on with the times, shifting his focus from technological innovation to technological integration. Productivity, which Ely says will be the password of the 1990s for the entire financial services business, already has become the password at Merrill Lynch. To make it a reality and to bring costs down, Ely has set up an applications productivity task force whose members consist of the directors of technology development responsible for each of the firm's major business sectors.

The task force has been given a 3-year deadline and an onerous task: to improve productivity by 100 per cent within the technology systems applications and development area of the business. The strategy they are pursuing to meet the challenge is based largely on integrating and simplifying a diverse collection of information systems (see Figure 1), a mammoth undertaking which will have a ripple effect throughout the organization.

Systems		Databases	
On line	90	Securities	63
Mixed	86	Trade History	52
Batch	157	Customer	60
Minis	34	Holdings	42
LANs	78	Accounting	58
Other	90	Activity	60
	535		335

Figure 1. Current systems survey

At present, Merrill Lynch spends approximately $165m per year on systems applications and development. It is this figure that the productivity task force must bring down. If corporate investment in technology goods and services plus indirect communications charges is brought into the equation, the total figure climbs to nearly $1·5bn a year.

The bulk of this billion-dollar-plus investment goes into the budget of the operations, systems and telecommunications sector, one of five major groups in the company and the sector within which Gerry Ely's information systems division is housed. In total, the sector has nearly 12,000 employees, 1500 of whom are technology developers whose unit heads are linked to business units in other parts of the organization. It is this same key group of individuals who have been commandeered to serve on the productivity task force and bring down the costs within their departments.

Technology clearly continues to be closely scrutinized, though the impetus behind it has changed. The head of operations, systems and telecommunications, executive vice president DuWayne J. Peterson, reports directly to president and chief operating officer Daniel P. Tully (see Figure 2). So do the heads of the company's two major business sectors, consumer markets and capital markets, as well as the other major business unit directors. The operations, systems and telecommunications sector has been assigned a three-pronged mission: to deliver the highest-quality service to Merrill Lynch clients; to be the low-cost producer and distributor of these services; and to upgrade the firm's technology, whenever required, to pursue new business opportunities.

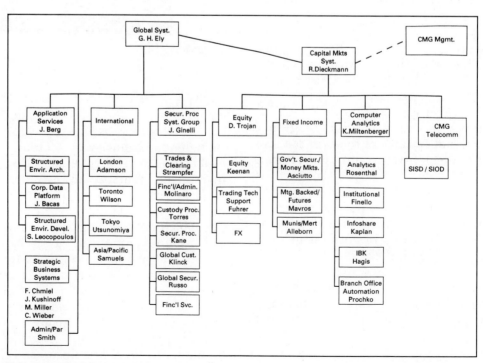

Figure 2. Organization chart

The Productivity Project

Attaining the status of low-cost producer and distributor is on the mind of Ely and his colleagues at the moment. This goal and the mission of the productivity task force neatly dovetail.

The planning framework for the productivity initiative consists of six areas, each of which requires co-ordinated strategic actions in order to increase productivity and cut systems costs: architecture, compensation and reward, measurement, product-ivity tools, staff development, and end user comput-ing (see Figure 3). The primary goal is to cut costs, thereby gaining competitive advantage through faster systems that are more flexible and easier to use (see Figure 4). To reach one of the initiative's primary goals, that of restructuring the develop-

ment environment through integrating the systems architecture, several key platforms will be built.

'The first and most crucial platform we are looking at is a data platform,' says Ely. 'At present, we may have 50 or 60 files that have the same information in them. Our aim is to build a data platform with common access to all of our major databases—and we have identified eight of these—so a person only goes to one place consistently across all of our systems for things like customer data, trade data, or product data.'

The total number of platforms to be built has not been determined, but Ely hazards a guess at perhaps three or four: the one for the retail infrastructure, the one for the global trading world, a third for banking and trust businesses that are not strictly

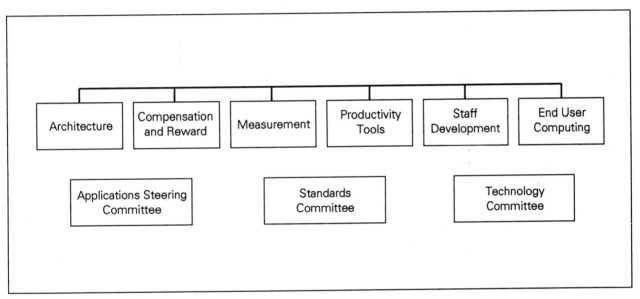

Figure 3. The applications productivity initiative

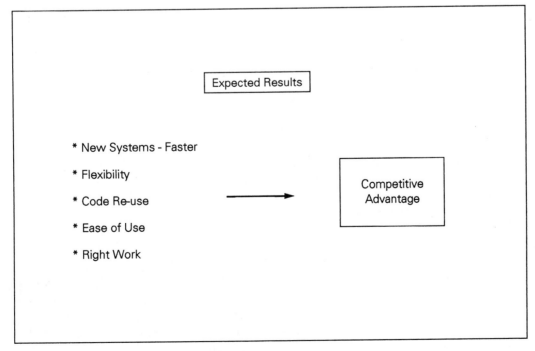

Figure 4. Competitive advantage through systems

retail, and perhaps a fourth for other types of financial services. Platforms will be assembled by picking and choosing pieces from vendors and using them to integrate existing systems and construct what will become a Merrill Lynch platform.

The thinking behind the initiative is that an integrated systems architecture, combined with effective design, development, and maintenance tools, should yield the payoff of better end user computing. By giving the end user an easier and more effective product to work with, costs should be reduced and productivity should go up, so the reasoning goes.

Training end users to work within the new systems architecture using the new tools will present challenges of its own. Overall across the firm, Merrill Lynch spends in the range of $15m on technology training. This figure is expected to remain constant. The rationale is that though fewer people may be involved as the human resource side is scaled down, the technological scale-up embodied in information engineering tools currently being tested requires a relatively high degree of under-standing and therefore more intensive training.

'When it becomes fully understood, the platform initiative will be seen as a corporate initiative pitched at the level of going out and acquiring a new business,' Ely claims. 'There are some big chunks that have to the chewed into building platforms. For instance, so far as the building of the workstation platforms for capital markets on the trading systems side goes, I can absorb that into the work I'm doing. But I can't incorporate databases converted into a standard format with access across all applications unless we have a major initiative that brings together everything and it gets funded that way. Many tens of millions of dollars may be invested. You have to spend money to get productive.'

Ely's view is that successful firms stand apart because they limit the technological choices, educate and train people in the right skills, and motivate them to work in this environment. Merrill Lynch aims to do the same, he says, but the company is big and so that challenge is big. Ely says the real economies are likely to be in capital markets; more economies will emerge at the end user part of the business. The initiative will also increase efficiency in consumer market development. With astute management, he says, increased productivity in the short term will enable some of the money saved to fund some of the longer-term developments.

A cost-cutting yardstick also played a large part in the company's decision to implement another technology project. Under a $50m contract the firm announced in September of 1989, it will become the first customer of network management services jointly provided by IBM and MCI Communi-cations Corporation.

In relating this project to the technology initiative, DuWayne Peterson explains, 'We want to have the best technology available for rolling out the systems architecture strategy.' But savings as well as quality undoubtedly influenced the decision to give the project the green light. For no more money than the firm would have paid to operate its existing system over the next 5 years, it has entrusted a major upgrade of its corporate network to IBM and MCI during their early days as joint providers of this service to other companies. The contract calls for the two companies to convert Merrill Lynch's current network management system to an intelligent, integrated multivendor system. The agreement represents the next phase of a project begun in 1988 to re-evaluate Merrill Lynch's telecommunications network. Under a $150m contract, MCI will become the sole provider of the company's telecom-munications services with the aim of reducing costs by more than $100m over a 5-year period.

From Instigation to Implementation

Bruce A. Turkstra, senior vice president of global information services and Ely's counterpart in the services side of the business, describes technology management at Merrill Lynch as 'very much a hybrid organizational approach'. Sometimes there is a mainstream strategy and sometimes there is a 'pocket' strategy that inspires it. But the day-to-day management generally is carried out by individual technology development units that are addressing sets of internal client needs, the clients being the business units.

'This tends to be a very technology-intensive business from a user perspective,' Turkstra points out. 'We are dealing with very knowledgeable internal clients. Often, a set of solutions will be driven by the client into the holding company.'

Bruce A. Turkstra

The recent decision to move into image processing technology for processing new account applications is a good example of a client-driven technology solution being brought to fruition. Under a contract awarded to Integrated Automation, a Litton subsidiary, the firm is overhauling its account opening system to make the process more efficient and cost-effective. The idea was generated out of a combination of the operations area's view of what they had to improve from a cost perspective, and the systems development group coming up with a technical solution that fits their needs. The operations people who manage the service centres and the development group came to Turkstra's people and helped them to choose an appropriate systems vendor. This instigation by the internal client community is fairly typical.

'Resource allocation decisions at Merrill Lynch tend to be pushed down into the organization,' Turkstra explains. 'This tends to be a very agile business. It is very difficult given the complexity of technology today to ask central functions to become experts and pass judgements on the merits of particular types of technology. The approval process must not be too centralized if you are going to be able to react to the changing market.'

Funding and approval of small projects is a straightforward process in which the systems development people ask their internal client for approval and the work is funded from the business unit budget. However, if the project represents an investment in capital of over $2m, a capital commitment process is set in motion. Corporate approval entails gaining agreement from the executive committee. Alternatives have to be weighed and everyone outside the central function has to sign the proposal. Once it gains corporate approval, it is funded by the firm.

Merrill Lynch's decision to move into the foreign exchange business is a case of a large project using innovative technology whose approval required the blessing of the executive committee. The cost, revenue, and profit projections for the first 5 years were submitted with the proposal. The impetus for building a global system to support the new business came from those responsible for foreign exchange within the capital markets sector. The business unit people called in the systems and operations people and once corporate approval was obtained, the process of building the system began. An outside vendor from California is supplying most of the basic software for the workstations. This software is being combined with existing software and new internally developed software, all of which are being run on IBM and SUN workstations. The first part of the system has been implemented around the world and the second phase is now being developed.

Besides being used to enhance revenue generation, technology continues to be applied to cut costs. For instance, image processing is being harnessed as a major cost reduction and efficiency tool within the company's security processing areas. Workstation technology is being developed both in the capital markets sector at the trader desk and in the retail side of the business. In the retail business, Automatic Data Processing (ADP) has taken over a project that was initiated in the early 1980s as a joint venture with IBM. Though the original project was abandoned, ADP and the company are working from some of the original concepts to design and implement the information delivery system. Named PRISM, the software for the workstation system runs on IBM PS/2 computers and is aimed at enabling the firm's 500 domestic retail offices, which are the homebase for its 11,000 financial consultants, to access quickly account information, market quotes, news stories, and other data. It is envisaged that the workstation also will enhance the efficiency of processing orders.

To accompany the changeover to the PRISM system, a carefully orchestrated training program is being carried out. Training begins roughly 6 weeks before the conversion and includes the installation of a 'live' workstation. Each financial consultant takes a 1-hour hands-on training session prior to the conversion. The conversion takes place over a weekend, with branch personnel reporting to the office for a few hours on Sunday for training and practice in preparation for the beginning of the next workweek. An internal group called the Advanced Office Systems Group is responsible for the process.

More general technology training also is in evidence throughout the company. Corporate headquarters at the World Financial Center in lower Manhattan has its own technology training centre. Here, Merrill Lynch capital markets clients and producers come to receive training in trading analysis. The centre also serves as a resource for PC-based training for any department within the firm. It was developed by a group called the Capital Markets Professional Group and is supported by the professional development group within the operations, systems and telecommunications sector.

Management Scientists, Not Watchdogs

Upstream from technology trainers are those whose responsibility it is to identify which technology is appropriate in the first place, and where and what sort of technology changes are needed in the organization. Bruce Turkstra says that the ability to recognize such circumstances is important, but he has a basic problem with setting up such watchdog functions when technology is changing so fast.

In place of an internal watchdog group, the firm relies on a small cluster of 10 professionals with mathematical modelling expertise called the Management Science Group. This group acts as an internal resource for ideas about how to put information systems to work and for assistance in implementing solutions. Hired from RCA in 1986 by DuWayne Peterson less than 6 months after he joined the firm, the group is part of the operations, systems and telecommunications sector and is consulted internally on a variety of corporate projects.

The aim of recruiting this group into Merrill Lynch was to bring the scientific community into the corporate world but keep one foot in each camp. Mathematical and statistical expertise are applied to corporate projects, using new scientific developments and procedures where they are relevant. One of the group's recent undertakings was to review the cost-efficiency of the company's data centres. As a result of its findings, the firm is now reducing the number of data centres from seven to two.

The Management Science Group has also developed an expert system that is being used at headquarters by analysts in the credit administration department. Its proponents say the system has improved turn-around time in responding to requests to raise credit authorizations, has standardized credit decisions, and has increased the confidence of each analyst acting independently in the assessment of risk. It is also being used as a training tool.

Several other groups within the firm keep their eyes on technology changes. One of them, the Technology Committee, cuts across the entire company and is made up of technology leaders from different departments within the firm. The committee tends to act as an information-sharing forum rather than a decisionmaking body.

Measuring Up to the Task

Clearly, an intensive campaign is underway at Merrill Lynch to cut costs right across the firm. Savings gained through efficient information systems, are playing a big part in the process. And, according to Gerry Ely, considerable progress is being made. The cost of information technology across the company has been down a percentage point or two over the past few years, a big improvement over the 20 per cent a year compounded rise that occurred during the mid 1980s. But the firm still has some way to go. Maintaining the pressure to get technology costs down could become crucial given the competitive challenges looming both at home and abroad.

First, large U.S. commercial banks may have the opportunity to make strong inroads into domestic financial services such as the securities business as provisions under the Banking Act of 1933 (known as Glass-Steagall) get chipped away and a less tightly regulated industry emerges. These banks may also become formidable competitors in global capital markets.

Besides this domestic challenge, Merrill Lynch faces several global tests of its competitive strength. European banks and security houses are expanding their transcontinental presence in preparation for the European single market. Also, Japanese securities firms, which already dominate the Eurobond market and dwarf U.S.-based and European firms in terms of market capitalization, are rapidly building their capital markets businesses domestically and abroad.

So far as the 1992 challenge goes, Merrill Lynch already has a presence in France, Germany, Italy, Spain, Portugal, and a large presence in the United Kingdom. According to Bruce Turkstra, the company is in the process of trying to re-position its products so that they can be efficiently delivered under a number of scenarios that may emerge.

The Japanese challenge may be a matter of graver concern. Size is a matter over which Merrill Lynch and other financial services organizations have little control. The firm is moving ahead in several areas that have been identified as contributing to Japanese success. The first is the ability of Japanese corporate managers to plan and target resources effectively. The second is more difficult to copy: the ability of Japanese firms to have direct access to state-of-the-art electronic and communications technologies through other firms in their international trading groups.

Merrill Lynch management recognizes the importance of these advantages and is attempting to keep abreast of new technologies. But, as Gerry Ely puts it, 'Globalization presents complex and difficult issues that require more than just technological solutions. Management, cultural, and personnel issues are equally important. We still haven't proven that we can go into foreign lands and compete as well as we do on Wall Street. The network is a people and a business network, not just a telecommunications network.'

The Brains Behind the Business

The human network behind the technology at Merrill Lynch brings a collaborative spirit to new endeavours, in part because the internal clients are quite knowledgeable users. According to Bruce Turkstra, 'There is a definite shift in tone around here over the past 5 years. It used to be, "We are the people you come to for technical solutions." Now it's "let us help you understand this technology and explore whether it works, what will be its effect on your cost structure and whether there may be different approaches." '

'We are on a geometric curve relative to technology options. Now a manager has a broad array of technical options from which to choose. The optimum solution today may be suboptimal 3 years from now. We are trained to maintain a degree of flexibility and openness and not get wedded to historic solutions.'

His view is that technology experience is not as relevant in the current environment as it was in a more stable environment. Relevant experience does come into play, however, in having a sense of the business risks inherent in any choice. Turkstra advises that undercapitalized firms generally should be avoided when selecting a technology vendor. He suggests that these three questions be asked:

(1) Will the firm be likely to stay in business for a while?

(2) Is the technology something that can be built on?

(3) Can I understand the growth path?

The qualities Turkstra requires in a good technology manager include characteristics that are useful for the present but also those that could be useful in the future:

☆ a good mind,

☆ creative instincts,

☆ willingness to try new technologies,

☆ willingness to make an adroit leap of faith when required,

☆ flexibility, and

☆ openness.

The ultimate test is whether a manager can successfully apply technology. Effective operational skills should include:

☆ credibility in the client community,

☆ ability to analyse and assess technology,

☆ ability to work with people and sell solutions,

☆ ability to implement technology within an infrastructure where it might not perfectly fit.

The View from the Top

Top management's thinking about technology is conservative. The company is not timid about deploying technology, but the approach is incremental rather than discontinuous. Turkstra believes that technology applications are concentrated these days on the trading floor, smoothing the flow of operations, and reducing head count, areas which generally involve incremental changes rather than basic departures from the past.

Gerry Ely, too, points out that the company's past investments have allowed it to cut costs but not always to gain a strategic advantage. He says the time that is put into being a pioneer often makes it easier for competitors to catch up. In his words, *Strategic investments help to create a level playing field as often as they provide a technological or strategic advantage.* The present technological goals will become even more important in the future. These are:

☆ cost control,

☆ globalization,

☆ risk management,

☆ analysis,

☆ information distribution, and

☆ end-user computing.

However, end-user computing, which is today's problem, will require some of tomorrow's solutions. Ely recognizes that innovation can never be put too far back on the shelf.

DuWayne Peterson also suggests that there is a fine line between keeping up with the times and falling behind.

He says: 'We are not ignorant, nor are we risk-averse to the point where we won't try out new technology. We have our eye on what is going on out there. But we don't want to go down a blind alley. I don't want to give the impression that we are spending millions of dollars on a technological whim. These are cost-cutting times.'

He suggests that innovation is not being automatically ruled out in strategic planning even in these relatively austere times. He says, 'I do not want the word to get out that we are so buttoned down that we won't talk to anybody. I'll talk to anybody once. Sometimes it's a 2-minute conversation and sometimes it leads into a prototype.'

His advice to technology managers is:

☆ avoid 'the bleeding edge'; don't make your mission to be first with everything that comes down the road;

☆ maintain a continuous dialogue with vendors and universities;

☆ maintain a network with those you trust, those who have a good track record; and

☆ remain open and continue to review what is going on.

Conclusion

The use of technology to promote financial services at Merrill Lynch takes its lead from the overall operating climate. The securities market today is highly competitive. The company whose goal in the early days was 'to bring Wall Street to Main Street' now must not only maintain its prominent position on Main Street but also establish a powerful global presence.

Management at Merrill Lynch is using new technology to reduce costs and thereby build a strong market position. State-of-the-art technology is being sought. Innovation is applied very selectively. Initiatives are under way both in specific business sectors and within administrative functions to move the company step by step to the next generation of delivery systems, workstations, and end-user computing.

J. A. Byrne, Is your company too big?, *Business Week,* 84–94, 27 March (1989).

B. D. Fromson, Merrill Lynch the stumbling herd, *Fortune,* 44–50, 20 June (1988).

S. Swartz, Merrill Lynch, facing growing competition, reaches a crossroads, *Wall Street Journal,* 12 August (1986).

G. H. Ely, Staying innovative in a down market, *Institutional Investor,* 12–17, June (1988).

Bibliography

A. I. Marcus and H. P. Segal, *Technology in America—a Brief History,* Harcourt Brace Jovanovich, New York (1989).

B. R. Guile and J. B. Quinn, editors, *Technology in Services: Policies for Growth, Trade, and Employment,* National Academy Press, Washington, D.C. (1988).

Related references

W. Adriaans, Planning an information system at Netherlands gas, *Long Range Planning,* June (1989).

R. I. Benjamin *et al.,* Electronic data interchange: How much competitive advantage? *Long Range Planning,* February (1990).

C. Jackson, Building competitive advantage through information technology, *Long Range Planning,* August (1989).

C. Palmer, Using IT for competitive advantage at Thomson Holiday, *Long Range Planning,* December (1988).

PART TWO

Accelerating Successful Implementation

Building a Customer-orientated Organization at Citibank

Frank Cornish

In this article a Vice-President of Citibank NA describes some of the steps they have taken to ensure that service quality remains a key objective of the organization; and service quality does not apply only to the customer base. The same principles apply internally within the organization.

In a service industry, particularly, the key long-term competitive advantage between suppliers is service quality. Whilst price is an important element in the sales equation, it is not the sole determinate, and although technology and productivity provide a company with advantages, sooner or later competitors catch up. Therefore, to remain in a leadership position we must maintain service quality as the pre-eminent objective. Figure 1 shows how this philosophy has helped us to increase Citibank U.K.'s business with other financial institutions.

In this article, I would like to describe some of the steps Citibank has taken to ensure that service quality remains a key objective of our organization.

(1) *Explode the Myth That Quality Costs Money*
Service quality means getting it right first time, but this need not be a costly objective. In fact, by getting it right the first time, you avoid the cost of error correction and customer dissatisfaction. Probably a considerable percentage of your expense base is related to:

(a) making the error in the first place, and
(b) the cost of correcting it.

It is of course true that a selling opportunity occurs at the time you correct errors to the customer's satisfaction, but too many errors will eventually lose the customer.

Frank Cornish is a Vice-President of Citibank NA Financial Institutions Group U.K.

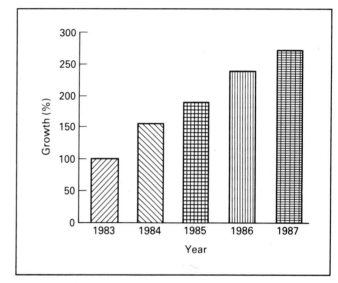

Figure 1. Citibank Financial Institutions Group U.K. earnings growth index (1983 = 100%)

(2) *Encourage Staff to Communicate With Customers by Freeing Them From Routine Tasks*
We isolate routine tasks by means of production analysis techniques, and then introduce temporary staff and part-timers to handle these time consuming jobs. This enables us to place core personnel in positions of responsibility and customer contact, and we encourage our people to talk to the customer.

When processing personnel talk to their customer counterparts it builds the relationship, and when the financial director or the chief executive officer wishes to change an existing relationship it is surprising how much input the processing people have in the decision.

Occasionally somebody say 'Mrs Smith spends so much time worrying about ABC Ltd she should go and work for them'. In Mrs Smith we have identified the kind of person who will make our business more successful.

(3) Build Service Quality Into the Goals of Every Staff Member

At Citibank we set annual targets of performance for our staff. Amongst these we build in service quality goals such as customer calling or transactional error rates. However, caution is called for when setting goals for performance standards. We have developed a method based upon reasonable expectancies, i.e. the number of transactions an individual can perform per hour, etc. but we also work closely with first level supervisors, who monitor and adjust the standards before final agreement. By doing this, progress is checked against their own agreed numbers and not Citibank's. We have a process of goal-setting and appraisal to indicate to our staff what is expected of them and how we can help them meet their objectives.

(4) Reward High/Top Performers

Our compensation policies are designed to ensure that we differentiate between good, average and poor performers. Top performers are rewarded more than staff who just meet the standard. Bonus schemes are another method of rewarding high performance.

(5) Introduce Service Excellence Awards, Productivity Schemes and Perfect Attendance Awards

Where our personnel have earned praise from our customers, or if they become more productive, we reward them in a tangible and open manner. We award them plaques, certificates or desk-top displays that clearly demonstrate they are examples for everyone to follow. Award ceremonies are conducted at staff meetings, hosted by the most senior company manager available at the time, and congratulatory letters are always signed by the Chairman or President. Appreciation of these award schemes is evident in that staff choose to display their awards.

(6) Conduct Breakfast and Lunch Sessions With All Staff

Structured, but informal meetings directed towards understanding the attitudes and problems of the staff member, are held regularly. These are hosted by the senior manager of the area, without the immediate supervisors attending. This encourages an open and free dialogue between participants.

The success of the process however, depends on the problems and opportunities identified being followed up, and participants being kept informed. This course of action should only be started if it is intended to maintain it as an ongoing activity.

(7) Customer Feedback

We need to measure how well we are performing to find the strong and weak points in the organization and there are several methods of gauging the customer's level of satisfaction.

Customer Roundtable. One way is the 'Customer Roundtable'. We invite a handful of customers, from the same business sector, to lunch at Citibank. Then, using a trained group leader, we ask them carefully chosen questions which invite customer comment. We find that customers with problems are balanced by those who are pleased with our service, and customers often tell each other how best to work with us.

Customers like to give their comments. They see that we value their opinions and they feel valued.

Then, we follow-up the 'Roundtable'. We try to build on what we are good at, fix what needs to be fixed and be honest and open about things which we cannot do. Follow-up action is crucial as it gets the message around the market-place that Citibank is a responsive organization.

Market research. Another key method of obtaining customer feedback is the market survey. This process ensures that we understand how our customers feel about us.

Product development. We also involve the customer actively when developing, or changing our technology. Customers are surprisingly enthusiastic when consulted about changes we wish to make to our service. It also helps us to avoid making mistakes.

Customer enquiries. Another way of gathering customer information is to monitor enquiry levels. Some of our work is devoted to answering customer requests for information. Our approach to this is to have customer service units staffed by skilled personnel who can follow-up customer enquires quickly and accurately. We monitor those enquiries on minicomputers so that the account officer, when making a customer call, immediately has available a history of the operational relationship. We acknowledge all enquiries with a unique reference number and always keep the customer updated as to the status of the enquiry, on a regular basis. The responsibility for resolution always remains with the same staff member.

Training and Personal Development

We realized, within Citibank, that we could achieve a great deal more by the correct level and proper focus of training. With the aid of our Training Department, we have developed programmes of continuous training for all levels of staff, to help them develop techniques which will enable them to perform more effectively and to judge how they are performing.

We also offer, in-house, the 'New Age Thinking' Programme, developed by Louis Tice, founder and chairman of the Pacific Institute. This programme is designed to assist staff to develop their latent potential in all spheres of their lives, and promote greater productivity and job satisfaction by helping participants gain:

☆ Insight into why they think, feel and act the way they do.

☆ Ideas they can use to increase their creativity.

☆ Principles of decision-making.

☆ Ways of improving their confidence in their own ability.

☆ Methods of handling stress and the pressures of everyday living.

☆ A system of goal-setting linked to these objectives.

☆ We believe that this training programme, by improving the individual's performance, improves the organization, and it is now offered to all members of the Financial Institutions Group, and in other parts of Citicorp.

These are some of the major initiatives we are using to reinforce the message to staff that service quality is the single most important factor which differentiates Citibank in the market-place.

Service quality applies not only to our customers. It is just as important to follow these principles internally. We are all 'givers' and 'receivers'. We need to specify clearly and get agreement to what we expect to receive, and what we intend to produce. By 'contracts' such as these, costly aggravations can be eliminated.

Bridging the Awful Gap Between Strategy and Action

Roy Wernham, British Telecom, London, U.K.

This article describes the lessons learned from a study carried out within British Telecommunications as part of the author's doctoral research programme. It was found that strategy was formulated and implemented, with direct action taken and resources committed, by Divisional managers at all three organizational levels in BT so that implementation did not always follow the lines intended by the HQ strategic planners. Implementation was found to be an interactive rather than a rational/sequential process. Marked variations in practice were observed and explanations for these are offered. The relative success of the strategies differed widely, both overall and within the divisional field units. The manner of implementation and factors managers perceived to help and hinder it were studied. Success or failure was felt to hinge on getting a few basics right: resources, organizational 'fit', historical performance and the expectations it generated (track record), information and support, market acceptance, technical competence, consistent goals and top management support.

Introduction

There has been much recent interest in the problems of implementing strategy in academic circles as well as among practising managers.[1] The essential reason for this interest is the widely shared experience that all too often plans don't work as their authors intended. This article describes a programme of research by the author into the problems of implementation in a (then) large Nationalized Industry, British Telecommunications (BT).[2]

Planning in BT

BT was formed from the telecommunications part of the former Post Office (PO) Corporation in 1981. The PO began corporate planning in 1971; an early PO Board paper on the subject indicated that its purpose was 'to provide a stable and coherent basis for planning throughout the Business'. This was seen to be particularly desirable in telecommunications, a capital intensive industry with long lead times. Business Plans have been made annually almost every year since. The planning team suspected that often past Plans might not have proved to be the blueprints for action that their authors had intended; a backward look comparison of the 10 and 5-year forecasts, and strategic outlines in the 1971 and 1975 Plans, with what had happened confirmed the doubts. Had external events intervened or were the plans themselves deficient? What happens during implementation? Questions like these led to the research. It was quickly apparent that the PO experience was not unusual.[3,4] Taylor's note[3] that 'No plan survives contact with reality' was particularly arresting. The research aimed to explore the nature of this 'reality' and how it affects implementation.

Planning in the Nationalized Industries was greatly encouraged by successive Governments throughout the 1970s, partly as an aid to Government understanding of their investment plans in the context of longer term strategies.[5] Moreover, such plans provided Government with an additional mechanism to influence or control development of the Industries.[6] While there has been some study of the economic and legislative aspects of Nationalized Enterprises, little is known about the way in which they are managed.[7-9] There are grounds for suspecting that their special relationship with the political scene brings with it some unique problems.[10,11] While there have been some empirical studies of strategy formulation, little field research has so far been undertaken on implementation.[12-14]

Traditional Model of Strategy and its Implementation

The term strategy comes from the Greek 'strategos' meaning the art of the general. There is no clear

Dr. Wernham is Deputy Corporate Planner for British Telecommunications plc, 2–12 Gresham Street, London EC2V 7AG.

consensus in the academic literature on how it should be defined. What is perhaps the dominant school of thought has been followed here in regarding it broadly as the allocation of resources to achieve certain aims or objectives.

The usual textbook view of strategic management is of a highly rational, analytical process with broad policies being laid down at top levels and translated into progressively more detailed sub-plans as they descend in straight line fashion through a homogeneous and subservient organization. Strategy formulation and implementation is generally shown as a rational/sequential process (Figure 1). An analysis of the environment and of the organization's current position, a WOTS UP (Weaknesses, Opportunity, Threats and Strengths Underlying Planning) analysis,[15] leads to clear, preferably quantified goals. Alternative ways of reaching these goals are considered and the most promising selected. It is then implemented and progress is measured and controlled.

This tidy and straightforward view of the process rests on a number of important assumptions including:

☆ The process is indeed a chain reaction of the kind just outlined.

☆ The organization's environment is stable or if it is changing, docs so in discrete, tidy steps.

☆ The organization is homogeneous, a unity rather than a coalition.

☆ Top management's goals and values are shared or at least accepted throughout the organization and they have the power to impose their will if need be.

☆ The chosen alternative is capable of being implemented.

☆ Sufficient resources will be allocated to enable the plan to be carried forward as defined.

The Traditional View revisited

In recent times, a number of these assumptions have been challenged by both theory and research which suggests that:

☆ Many organizations must cope with turbulent environments where change is fast; the problems are novel and hard to deal with.[16]

☆ In these circumstances, it may not be appropriate to have closely specified, quantified goals which may not remain stable long enough to be achieved, something broader and fuzzier may be better.[17]

☆ The organization may not be homogeneous but a coalition of subdivisions, all to a degree doing their own thing—particularly true of Divisional firms as compared with the Functional organizations in which the traditional model took root.[18]

☆ The process may be interactive rather than a chain as Figure 2 seeks to show.

There are, then doubts about how far the traditional model represents the way in which the real world works, and whether it is oversimplified for presentational or teaching purposes to the extent that it seriously distorts the reality. What does happen then managers try to put plans into action? What problems tend to occur and what helps them achieve their goals? The author set out on a programme of research to try and address these

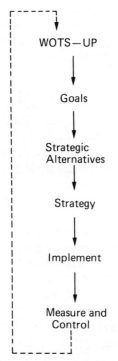

Figure 1. The traditional model of strategic managment

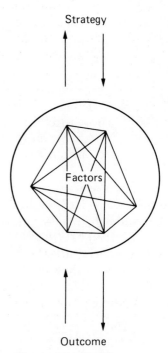

Figure 2. An alternative view

questions. The methods used and findings will now be discussed.

Aims and Method, of the Research

The overall aim was to identify the factors influencing the implementation of strategy within BT and assess their relative importance. Attention focused on three representative topics which were used as 'tracers' and were followed through the BT organization much as a geologist might 'label' a subterranean water course with fluorescein to trace its path.

The three tracers were:

☆ MAC (Measurement and Analysis Centres)—a system to generate and trace the progress of tests calls placed through the telephone network to measure the quality of service being provided and identify faults.

☆ Radiopaging—a service whereby a person who is out of the office but is carrying a pocket 'bleeper' can be alerted through a radio signal that he is required.

☆ SRT (Special Range Telephone)—a new range of decorative or fashionable telephones for customers who wish to have a telephone that has a distinctive appearance.

National HQ Managers, Regional Chairmen/ Directors (RDs) and Area General Managers (GMs) from England and Wales, were interviewed; they are referred to collectively as Unit Managers (UMs). During the study, tape-recorded interviews were obtained with some 64 UMs and analysed exhaustively. The interviews covered general material as well as the three selected tracers, each of which represented one aspect of BT's overall customer service strategy, being followed through the organization to see what happened to it. The fieldwork took place during the passage through Parliament of the Telecommunications' Act 1981 which established BT as a separate Corporation from the Post Office and opened the way to competition in areas where BT had previously enjoyed a monopoly.

Discussion of Results

Strategic Management Process
This study questions much of the traditional model of strategic management finding rather a process of interactions between coalitions of semi-autonomous units, with common cultural ties and identity. Each level of the organization, including HQ, tried to put its own stamp on events. Areas and Regions frequently did not accept HQ initiatives passively but would try to adapt or even reject them.

Political manoeuvring was readily apparent with different players manipulating the power bases they had, often to obtain extra resources. The attempts could take a number of forms. There could be a straight request with no duress. Junior managers in the higher level Unit, might be lobbied so as to seek their help in pressing a case. Favours might be offered or the target manager(s) invited to lunch. Some UMs attempted to use their own co-operation as a bargaining counter in a way that could embarrass the higher level Unit unless their wishes were met. Sometimes a number of lower level UMs would co-ordinate their actions or approaches to the higher level Unit where it was a matter of common concern. A delicate balancing act could be observed between UMs who were at some times dependent upon one another, and at other times rivals for available resources. As some of those interviewed put it:

> 'I have used every method in the book, or out of the book, dirty or otherwise, in order to get more than my share because I think the (unit) needs it . . . I have gone as far as cultivating (X) because I think he's got the ear of (Y) so you get at the power base . . . I've invited X (here), I've listened to him . . . that sort of thing brings dividends.'

> 'We fetched the (junior managers) over from (HQ) to get them on our side who would then persuade (their boss).'

> 'At a meeting (with a senior HQ manager) I made absolutely clear that unless we had (more resources) . . . we would (not co-operate). It was sheer blackmail by me.'

HQ managers appeared to try and restrict the options open to the field Units, to define the strategy to be adopted quite narrowly and themselves take on parts of the work. These efforts often failed:

> 'I said to (my junior managers), I don't care how you get hold of them, just get some and they did. I'm not sure how they did it—I never asked— . . . There were very strict controls put on (these items) so our more enterprising managers broke the rules and quite rightly so.'

Paradoxically, most field UMs perceived themselves to have a good deal of room for manoeuvre in general.

> 'You meet these people from (HQ). They waffle and then they go home and to hell with it. They don't really control what goes on here. They might think they do but they don't really.'

The basic message here is that the view found in many management texts of a powerful HQ able to impose its will on compliant field units exaggerates both the power of the HQ and the compliance of the field. Both have their own resources of power, eg to give or withhold money or co-operation, and mobilize these resources to achieve particular ends. The astute planner will use this process by appreciating what are the goals of the parties and the bargaining resources they possess (including himself) and ensuring that he is able to offer others something they want.

A related feature that emerged was:

Contacts between UMs. Frequency of reported contacts between UMs varied enormously and showed a strong inverse relationship with distance. UMs of Units located in the large conurbations had very frequent contacts, apparently because the BT administrative boundaries did not correspond with the natural boundaries of the communities being served. Action by one Unit could have market or personnel implications for adjacent Units or for others even further afield due to what was described shared community of interest.

As one local UM described the relationship with his colleagues in a large conurbation:

> 'We telephone one another pretty frequently. We meet both formally and informally. I guess there is not much of import that goes on within (this city) that we don't all know . . . and warn others before it hits them . . . Very tight. You can't run it any other way . . . It is very tight knit . . . We meet, even if its a social thing—but work gets done even at a social thing—once a fortnight. Physically we are in the same room.'

This had important repercussions at the next higher level (Region). Where a strong community of interest existed—mainly in the largest conurbations—there were frequent contacts between local UMs and with Regions undertaking some of the functions exercises elsewhere at the lower level, for example, promotional activities.

> 'I can't do anything on my own. We represent only a part of (conurbation). Any approach has to be co-ordinated and done through the Regional office.'

The Regional role was not always welcome:

> 'You need to be watchful. It isn't them and us but you do need to watch the fortunes of the Area *vis-a-vis* the Region.'

Where there was less community of interest, UMs contacted one another much less frequently and perceived much greater autonomy, but usually contacted UMs in their own Region more than those in other Regions.

> 'We are independent operators . . . I like to think we are a little like feudal barons . . . There is no question that every day or so we ring other Unit managers up, we don't.'

> 'I don't find it necessary to talk to other Unit managers though I'm not too proud to seek advice if I need it.'

In some exceptional cases, contacts between neighbouring UMs in different Regions were frequent; in each case, a strong community of interest existed across the Regional boundary. Thus the local Units (geographical Divisions) were far from being homogeneous, those in the largest conurbations having substantially different characteristics from those elsewhere.

Interview Findings for Individual Tracers

Findings on the individual tracers may be summarized thus:

MAC was widely welcomed by UMs and seen as important because it would provide a much needed facility to give a better measure of the standard of service being provided and thereby enable service to be improved. It was given high priority. It was put into the larger centres first to maximize the short-term benefits from it. Detailed implementing action was undertaken at all levels, with HQ in particular providing advice and technical services and having a major say in how the programme was constructed, i.e. the order in which field Units received their equipment.

Radiopaging was put into eight major centres first and had been heavily delayed, in part by development of the integrated national system, chosen in preference to the discrete local services with which a competitor had achieved modest success. BT Radiopaging was perceived as a technically valid response to the market need and fitted in well with the existing organization; few wholly new or different procedures were required. However delays had been experienced and were said to have been inadequately communicated to field Units. As a new and potentially useful service for business customers, it was well regarded but was accorded a lower priority than MAC by most, but not all, UMs. Much promotional material was produced centrally and some specific action, e.g., advertising, was undertaken at all three levels.

SRT was regarded as a residential service and was seen by some UMs as a rapid response to the challenge of competition from private retailers of decorator or fashion phones—although its origins lay well before that. It was felt to have public relations value in demonstrating to both staff and customers alike that BT intended to compete effectively in the residential telephone terminal market. Past shortages of materials of SRTs and other products had produced a mistrust, a lack of confidence among field UMs and their staff. The Range, was, with a few exceptions seen as a valid response to the requirements of the market. The administrative arrangements placed unusual demands on those in the field trying to sell SRTs; they were only partially successful, being disregarded by many UMs. The HQ Unit took direct action by selling SRTs at exhibitions and by placing national press advertisements with responses to be made to HQ rather than to local Units.

Tracer Strategy Adaptations
While the *aims* declared by the various Units for each of the tracers showed little variation, their *strategies* varied somewhat from each other and

from those put forward by the HQ UMs. For MAC, little variance from the HQ strategy was observed and there were no major inconsistencies between it and what the field Units were doing. For Radiopaging and SRT however, there was much less agreement and several inconsistencies in approach.

HQ/Regional/Area Differences. Answers by HQ, Regional and Area UMs were compared for each of the major dimensions on which data was collected. UMs were generally agreed on aims and the factors that had helped implementation. There was wide agreement among field UMs about the problems there had been but striking disagreement between them and the HQ UMs. There was also much disagreement on the strategy being followed and how well implementation had gone overall— suggesting that each level formed its own partisan view of such matters. HQ UMs were about as likely to *agree* with the field UMs as were field UMs to agree with each other. They were far more likely to *disagree* with field UMs than were field UMs to disagree with one another. It appeared then that feedback of information to HQ was defective at least in respect of the bad news, points of disagreement between the field and HQ (Figure 3).

Problems of Implementation

A number of general problems emerged from the research which were observed to a greater or lesser extent in respect of all three tracers. These are listed in Figure 4 and are presented broadly in order of the frequency with which they were mentioned by respondents.

Resources. The resources either of men, money or materials were often not available where and when they were required. There were two aspects to this:

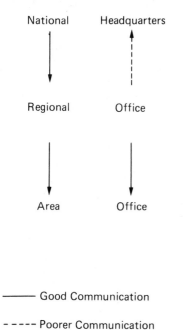

——— Good Communication

- - - - - Poorer Communication

Figure 3. Transfers of information between levels

Problems

Resources—Money, Men, Materials

Other Priorities

Organizational Validity

History, Confidence

Delay

Lack of Information/Timing Ads

Market Validity

Technical Validity

Conflicting Goals

Figure 4. Problems of implementation

the absolute volume of resources might be inadequate for all that was expected to be achieved; the relative volume of resources was inadequate owing to other competing uses being given higher priority.

> 'It's been made very clear to me that you can do whatever you like so long as you don't ask for any money.'

> 'It's more a question of priorities than actual staff shortages. At the end of the day manpower problems are a matter of priorities. We always have resource problems.'

Certain aims were widely perceived by UMs as much more important than others and plans which were felt to contribute to their achievement were given higher priority—and hence resources—than were others.

Organizational Validity. Organizational validity[12] is an indicator of how well a plan 'fits into' the existing organization and procedures. To the extent that people were required to adapt widely their existing patterns of behaviour, problems were likely to occur. Following an existing procedure or a slight adaptation to it is much easier to absorb and creates less resistance than wholesale change.

> 'The rules for stocking them are too involved. My simple mind says beat the system. So we have a few hidden away.'

> 'There were a series of silly rules governing product B which seemed to hamstring the whole thing.'

History. A word that frequently came up in the interviews was 'confidence'. Confidence that others would deliver what they promised. Confidence was based on the track record of present plans or other plans that the implementers felt were related. Just as nothing 'succeeds like success', it seems that nothing 'fails like failure'. Reputation is a very hard parameter to measure but is important for all that.

> 'You have a human problem. When supply has been bad, they are a little careful before they flog it too

wholeheartedly in case they personally look silly to their customer. That is a hurdle that has to be got over. Well it has been got over with product A, the arithmetic seems to have been done correctly at the moment. You see, I'm doing it too, saying 'at the moment'. Next year I might be telling you a different story.'

Delay. This is effectively a subset of the last point. Overoptimism, especially in estimates of timing, had been a hallmark of all three tracers in the research. It had moreover, contributed to a loss of confidence among the field staff who, having seen one schedule fail, were less inclined to believe the next.

> 'One thing you do need to realize is the time it takes to introduce an idea and make it effective, it depends on what it is but it's a lot longer than people think . . . it's 2 years before it's really moving in my experience.'

> 'The thing goes back. It was going to be December, then May, now June. It drives me crackers.'

Lack of Information/Support. Back up materials whether publicity information, software or just plain know-how were important elements in acting upon plans. Lack of adequate support quickly eroded confidence and led to available effort being transferred elsewhere as confidence flagged.

> 'Information doesn't come down the line freely. Business men ask me what products we have coming along. I haven't a clue.'

> 'We have no means of finding out when out of stock items will be available again, which is awkward because that is always the next question, the customer asks . . . and you are made to look stupid when you say you don't know.'

Market Validity. This concept refers to the extent to which the product or service is viewed by those at the front line of the organization as meeting the market need as they see it. Did it do what they felt that customers wanted to do? Where it did, the chances of successful implementation were greater, perhaps because the market reacted more favourably or perhaps those implementing it scented success and put more effort into it. These trends are likely anyway to be mutually reinforcing.

> 'I tried to sell product *C* to a builder but it developed that the initial area of coverage was not wide enough for him.'

> 'Strangely enough, range *A* don't sell all that well here . . . While (we) are doing well in general terms, range *A* no.'

Technical Validity. Technical validity indicates how far the product or service matches up to its specification and the hardware performs the functions claimed for it. Once again this is in essence a test of credibility and a matter which will either add to, or subtract from, the confidence of the staff concerned with its introduction and their motivation to achieve.

> 'I get the feeling they are cheap and nasty.'

> 'People can't have model *A* and model *B* on the same installation. They can (here). It's a popular combination. We modify the wiring.'

Conflicting Goals. Internal inconsistencies within the goals of the strategy being pursued were found to have a demotivating effect and to cause confusion among those concerned with implementation. There may well be intrinsic conflicts to be resolved, e.g. between secure storage and handling of stocks and giving customers maximum exposure to the product to achieve higher sales.

Where there are, it is as well that they should be made explicit and the means for their resolution clearly defined if confusion at grass roots level is to be avoided.

> 'Monitoring existing services versus provision of new is a long standing problem. The facile way out is to say they are equally important but it is not always possible.'

> 'There is a conflict between our tradition of providing a uniform service, anywhere in the country, at a standard price, regardless of cost, moving away from that to meeting competition where you have got to balance your tariffs in relation to the cost of providing the service.'

Factors Making Implementation More Effective

In an attempt to look at the reverse side of the 'problems' coin, the research pinpointed certain factors that were found to be helpful in making implementation more effective, things that were felt to have gone well. There were positive features to be applied as well as traps to be avoided (Figure 5).

Some of the main factors assisting implementation that emerged were:

Superordinate Goal. The existence of a superordinate or higher organizational goal, with which the strategy could be clearly identified and which it was seen to be contributing directly towards, was found to be of great value. It was then much more apparent to implementing staff that the strategy was

Superordinate Goal

Resources

Technical Validity

Market Validity

Information and Support

Staff Enthusiasm/Confidence

Top Management Backing

Figure 5. Factors assisting implementation

making a real and direct contribution to the overall effectiveness of the organization rather than appearing simply as an end in itself or as a largely optional extra having dubious value for the enterprise.

'We are not satisfied with the performance of the network and saw this as a way of improving it.'

Resources. The assumption that resources are available, resources in the widest sense presents problems that are not trivial. It was found that people were often asked to do tasks and then denied the money, manpower, expertise or consumable materials which they felt they would need to accomplish it. The provision of adequate resources (though not transferable to other projects) was a powerful aid to success.

'It is one of those things we did when we said we would . . . The bits all came and reasonably on time. I might not like the priorities but they are more difficult to dodge if I've got the bits.'

Technical Validity. It seems that nothing succeeds like success. Producing a product or service that lives up to the claims made for it in the sense of the technical performance of the hardware seemed to breed a confidence in those who implemented it that inspired a genuine enthusiasm and laid the groundwork for further success. Difficulties that were perceived as teething troubles were a different category; the existence of a sound concept, adequately engineered appeared to be the key.

'The main thing is (project X) is basically a good tool anyway. The concept is naturally right.'

'The most impressive thing about it is that it works.'

Market Validity. Production of a service or product that meets a genuine need is a powerful factor for success. The value of a product like the national Radiopaging service to customers was quickly evident through word of mouth recommendations and the ease with which sales were made. There was little doubt about customer acceptance or that the enthusiasms of staff and customers alike were genuine and perhaps mutually reinforcing.

'We have got several hundred customers lined up—spontaneous demand.'

'We are onto a winner with Radiopaging. We can't fail. Customers will be falling over themselves to have them.'

Information and Support. Really a part of the total resources question is provision of adequate and reliable information and supporting materials such as sales brochures and literature. Provision of reliable information e.g. on date of introduction helped to breed confidence in the product and in the competence of the team producing it—just as failure in this direction eroded confidence. It appears that the team that is seen to do its homework and does not hide potential problems is more credible than that which gets things wrong or paints a falsely optimistic picture.

'There has been a lot of assistance from Regional and national HQs to draw it together.'

'Headquarters have spent quite a bit of effort in time and money on that sort of promotion which gives the awareness that we capitalize on.'

Staff Enthusiasm/Confidence. A powerful factor was the confidence and enthusiasm of the implementing staff stemming from such things as their faith in the product and service being produced and their perception of the competence of the team producing it. All the other factors mentioned had a bearing on this. With it, implementation has every prospect of success, without it, an uphill struggle is certain.

'The (Unit) now loves (X) and has taken it in as part of its own business and that is a very good sign.'

'The local supervisor is very, very keen on it. They guard it you know. Even I am not allowed to go into the wrong room in case I press the wrong knob and undo all the hard work they have put in.'

Top Management Backing. According to the textbook view, see Steiner[15] for example, top management backing is essential for success. While it was mentioned by respondents as a factor that had contributed to successful implementation in this research, it did not emerge as being so important as the other factors listed above. It helps but it probably will not pull a bad scheme from the fire.

'Y was very keen on this, has been all through, so I don't think there has been any lack of urgency there.'

Conclusions

The traditional textbook strategic management view, that a strategy is successively defined in greater detail as it progresses in a logical 'cascade' from higher to lower levels within a homogeneous organization needs to be qualified. Each organizational level appears to take action to put its own stamp on the strategy, so that strategy formulation and implementation are part of a continuous interactive process, rather than successive steps in a linear sequence and are therefore much less 'top down' than many texts would have us believe. Unit Managers at all levels perceived considerable scope to formulate their own strategies.

The view of the world as seen by managers in different parts of the organization looks very different—much as the view from the penthouse suite of a tall building differs from that at ground level overlooking the dustbins—despite the existence of shared patterns of judgment. For example, HQ UMs' views of how successful implementation had been did not square well with those of field UMs. (Success of implementation was measured by objective criteria where measures existed, e.g. number of units sold, or by subjective criteria where they do not, e.g. reputation among users).

A number of factors were found which consistently caused problems in implementation and contributed to delay. The principal factors were:

☆ Lack of resources in the widest sense. This included money, materials and men but extended beyond simple numbers to include the existence of adequate knowledge, men with the right skills and support functions.

☆ Historical performance of current and past plans ('track record') and the expectations of success or failure that have been created.

☆ Lack of fit between: the actual hardware performance and specification; market performance and need; organizational demands imposed by both new and existing practices.

☆ Deficiencies in the transfer of information between Units at different levels.

☆ Requirements to achieve conflicting goals.

Certain factors were found to assist implementation. The main ones were:

☆ Adequate provision of resources.

☆ Matching: hardware performance to expectation; market performance to need; organizational procedures to current practices.

☆ Senior management support: success was associated with enthusiasm on the part of senior managers though the connection was less strong than might have been expected.

☆ Direct contribution to a major and widely acknowledged organizational aim.

☆ Staff confidence in the strategy being pursued which was in turn a function of information, training and historical experience.

A fact that stood out very clearly, and came as something of a surprise in view of the literature on resistance to change, was that change was by no means always resisted. Indeed it was often warmly welcomed by organizational members who saw real benefits flowing from it. As one manager put it:

'X has met 100% acceptance in the field and really has been the answer to the maiden's prayer there.'

Application

Perhaps the most obvious conclusion, but one that all too often goes unrecognized, is that strategy cannot be formulated on a blank sheet of paper as if no constraints exist or there is no past to come to terms with. The real world is complex and the manager who ignores its complexity will suffer from problems of implementation. Important components of this complex reality, many of them 'obvious' yet frequently neglected, include:

☆ *Resources* in the broadest sense. It is a necessary but not sufficient condition that these must be adequate. This means ensuring that the necessary manpower is available, with the mix of skills and knowledge needed to do the job, that they have the tools and materials and organizational support to do the job and the necessary funds are there (and cannot be siphoned off for use on something else!).

☆ Organizations find it easier to go on doing the kind of things they have done before, the better a new strategy *fits* the old, with differences minimized rather than exaggerated, the better its chances of success. Old habits and procedures that are ingrained die hard and change slowly and with difficulty. Often much can be done by adapting an existing framework thereby achieving a smoother, faster, transition with less disruption and fewer hiccups than the ostrich-like policy of attempting to start from a clean sheet and pretending that the past does not exist to colour attitudes and work habits.

☆ Faced with *conflicting goals*, managers select those which best suit their circumstances of the moment at the expense of the others. A requirement to achieve several conflicting goals presents a reluctant manager with an ideal opportunity to choose the things he wants to do and duck what he does not want to do. A coherent set of goals, even if they cannot all be specified in detail, give greater consistency.

☆ The attitudes of senior staff are important, but so too are those at lower levels. *Resistance to change is not inevitable*, attitudes depend on how people perceive changes affecting them in their job. There is evidence that change is welcomed and not resisted if it is perceived to be for the 'better'. The textbooks stress the need for top management support. This piece of research suggests that it is indeed helpful but will not compensate for a bad plan. Where staff felt that a change was 'good', it was widely welcomed. Only 'bad' change was resisted. The attitude of top management was largely irrelevant. The moral here is to seek out and stress the advantages of a proposed change so that it is perceived as beneficial and welcomed rather than try to rely on force majeure which can be resisted successfully on occasion by those lower down in the organization.

☆ *Confidence* is elusive and hard to define but a vitally important factor. Past experience conditions attitudes to future developments and people's expectations. Whether as individuals or organizations, we are all prisoners of our past. Today's overpromise is tomorrow's albatross. The need to develop a reputation for competence and being able to deliver what is promised is essential.

☆ The *technology* and the *marketing* arrangements must be fit for the purpose to which they are applied (and strategic planners are both producers and marketeers). This is related to the previous point. A product that does reliably what it is supposed to do or marketing arrangements that meet the real needs of customers give all concerned a confidence that shows. No amount of window dressing can compensate for a faulty product. The right product is the starting point—and that goes for planners too.

Acknowledgement—This paper is based on part of the author's Ph.D. thesis at City University Business School. The views expressed are those of the author and do not necessarily represent those of British Telecommunications, British Telecommunications plc, or the City University. The author gratefully acknowledges the assistance of British Telecommunications who funded the research, and also of Mr. A. J. B. Scholefield and the referees for helpful suggestions.

References

(1) SSRC, *Central–Local Government Relationships,* Social Science Research Council, London (1979).

(2) R. Wernham, *A Study of Strategy Implementation in a Major UK Nationalised Industry,* unpublished PhD thesis, City University Business School (1982).

(3) B. Taylor, New dimensions in corporate planning, *Long Range Planning,* 9 (6), 80–106 (1976).

(4) J. M. Hobbs and D. F. Heany, Coupling strategy to operating plans, *Harvard Business Review,* pp. 119–127, May–June (1977).

(5) Cmnd 7131, *The Nationalised Industries,* (HMSO, London) (1978).

(6) D. J. Harris and B. C. L. Davies, Corporate planning as a control system in UK nationalised industries, *Long Range Planning,* 14 (1), 15–22 (1981).

(7) Y. Aharoni, Performance evaluation of state owned enterprises, *Management Science,* 27 (11), 1340–1347 (1981).

(8) A. Y. Lewin, Research on state-owned enterprises introduction, *Management Science,* 27 (11), 1324–1325 (1981).

(9) J. Zif, Managerial strategic behaviour in state-owned enterprises—Business and political orientations, *Management Science,* 27 (11), 1326–1339 (1981).

(10) J. G. Smith, Strategy—The key to planning in the public corporation, *Long Range Planning,* 14 (6), 24–31 (1981).

(11) J. L. Bower, Effective public management, *Harvard Business Review,* pp. 131–140, March–April (1977).

(12) R. L. Schultz and D. P. Slevin, Implementing operations research/management science, American Elsevier, New York (1975).

(13) C. W. Hofer, Research on strategic planning, *Journal of Economics and Business,* pp. 261–285, Spring–Summer (1976).

(14) E. Bardach, *The Implementation Game,* MIT Press, Cambridge, Mass. (1977).

(15) G. A. Steiner, *Top Management Planning,* Macmillan, New York (1969).

(16) H. I. Ansoff, *Strategic Management,* Macmillan, London (1979).

(17) J. B. Quinn, Strategic goals: process and politics, *The McKinsey Quarterly,* pp. 35–53, Winter (1979).

(18) R. M. Cyert and J. G. March, *A Behavioural Theory of the Firm,* Prentice-Hall, Englewood Cliffs, N.J. (1963).

Woolworth's Drive for Excellence

Don Rose

This article describes the turnaround of a giant retail store which by 1982 had acquired a bad public image for inferior quality goods, poor service and outmoded ideas. A new management team was installed which redefined the company philosophy and adopted a policy of staff and customer care. Personnel and management structures were reorganized, a system of intensive management training undertaken, and new approaches to recruitment and induction of staff introduced. A programme of excellence to motivate and reward staff and training in merchandise knowledge to produce a more sophisticated retail sales force, and the company have shown increased profits and greater customer satisfaction.

In November 1982, when the Paternoster consortium of City financiers acquired F. W. Woolworth from the American parent company, the retail giant was regarded as the 'sick man' of British retailing. It suffered from a poor image with the City, its suppliers and the British public.

The new management team identified key problems which were substantiated both by research and performance figures. Woolworths had:

☆ Become a 'store of last resort' with an unacceptably low average spend per shopping trip.

☆ An outmoded concept of retailing.

☆ Over 1000 stores, many either too small in growth centres or too large in declining centres.

☆ Some 8000 suppliers providing inferior quality merchandise.

☆ No recognition as a serious retailer with good management—neither by the business community nor the media.

☆ Over 30,000 demotivated staff who had become the benchmark for poor service.

The new management decided on a rescue mission which was launched in March 1986 under the banner 'Operation Focus'. It was to involve:

Don Rose is Personnel Director of Woolworths plc.

☆ The disposal of low-profit sites with the least potential.

☆ The identification and development of new, more appropriate sites and the rationalization of existing store sizes where appropriate.

☆ A multi-million pound refurbishment programme: by the end of 1987, 160 stores had been totally refurbished—some 2·3 million square feet of selling space—and the remainder re-merchandised.

☆ The creation of a new trading concept focusing on six areas of strength, in order to reposition the chain as a specialist in key areas.

☆ A reduction in the number of suppliers to just over 1000.

☆ A significant reorganization and culture change through a specially-designed, multi-million pound staff training and development programme.

The new management recognized that a highly efficient and motivated staff would play a key role in this rescue mission. Indeed, innovations in the battle for high street sales had reached a stage where quality of service was now very often the only advantage one retailer could offer over another. Accordingly, the change was towards customer service and satisfaction.

Attitudes of Staff and Store Management
The attitudes of staff are best summarized by the results of an attitude survey which achieved an 85 per cent response:

☆ Managers were not communicating with staff.

☆ Staff were frightened to express their views openly because they were afraid of the likely reaction.

☆ Sales staff were afraid of customers—they had been hired to man tills and fill shelves and had little confidence if asked to operate outside these parameters.

☆ Staff lacked pride.

☆ Managers regarded themselves as managers of systems, procedures, stock and property—people were there to be directed, manipulated and disciplined.

Overall, Woolworths' management style was authoritarian and driven by fear. Staff were told to get on with a job and not to ask questions.

As a result, sales staff became cynical. They believed their jobs were dull and humdrum. This was, not surprisingly, increasingly apparent to customers.

Attitudes of Line and Personnel Management
A similar study was carried out among Line and Personnel Managers to determine what they perceived as the major contribution the personnel function could make to organizational effectiveness.

Line Managers identified three areas where the personnel function could better satisfy their needs. These were:

(i) Recruitment and selection
(ii) Training and development
(iii) General support and guidance

Line Managers saw customer care and positive company results as the basis of personnel management excellence. Attitudes had to be changed within the personnel department if it was to better serve the needs of the business.

Recruitment and Training Policies
Traditionally, Woolworths recruited via Job Centres. Recruitment interviews lasted about 10 minutes. Induction took 20 minutes. Training consisted of on-the-job learning.

The Personnel Structure
Until 1980 there had been no board-level responsibility for personnel at Woolworths. The Personnel Controller reported to the Store Operations Director. Regional Personnel Managers (RPMs) reported to, and were paid by, Regional Managers—resulting in the RPM taking on the role of 'bag carrier' for the Regional Manager. Area Personnel Officers reported to District Managers at the next level down.

The problems which existed can be summarized as follows:

☆ The personnel function was shackled to line management, and therefore unable to set and maintain its own standards

☆ Recruitment and training procedures were inadequate

☆ Serious attitude problems existed at store management level

☆ Personnel management itself needed to be re-educated

Adopting a New Philosophy
As a result of surveys, Woolworths redefined the aims of its personnel strategy. 'People Serving People' was adopted as the phrase to summarize the company's new staff and customer care philosophy. This would be achieved by demonstrating the importance of:

(i) Concern for the customer: creating a friendly environment in stores which makes customers feel welcome so that they will continue to shop at Woolworths.
(ii) Concern for staff: recognizing the role of the sales assistant as the most important member of the team because this is the vital point of contact with customers.
(iii) Concern for the community: a commitment to prove that Woolworths has an important role to play in local communities.

Reorganizing the Personnel Structure
Following the appointment of a new Personnel Director in 1985, control of the personnel function was moved from the hands of Line Managers to the Regional Personnel Managers who now reported direct to the Personnel Director.

Area Personnel Officers reporting to Regional Personnel Managers were renamed Area Personnel and Training Officers (APTOs) with specific responsibility for personnel *standards*.

To improve the level of service to each store, additional APTOs were recruited and existing APTOs retrained. Each was made responsible for 12 stores and committed to visiting each store every 7 days.

It is indicative of Woolworths' commitment to APTOs and their new role that training of the 100 prospective APTOs, from initial planning to completion, took only 4 months.

Finally, the areas of responsibility for APTOs were succinctly and memorably defined by the mnemonic RITA—Recruitment, Induction, Training and Advice.

Reorganizing the Management Structure
With the implementation of Operation Focus, Woolworths needed to reorganize its management structure at store level.

Merchandise in the stores was rationalized and concentrated into six key departments or 'Focus Areas', and the basic unit of management was defined as the merchandise team—one per focus area and each headed by a Section Manager.

The existence of both Assistant Store Managers and Staff Managers mitigated against the Store Managers' ability to be truly responsible for the management of store staff. Woolworths phased out these two roles with the result that section managers now have a 'real' job—resulting in a more simplified structure and more clearly defined roles.

The new structure put more emphasis on personal responsibility, more scope for the development of teams and freer, more open, communication.

As each store is refurbished in line with Operation Focus, a team goes in to give special training in the new responsibilities and modes of behaviour. Staff are also issued with smart new uniforms to replace the old overalls.

The overall result has been a new understanding by each staff member of the importance of his or her role in the future success of the chain. Staff have a renewed sense of pride in their jobs and an evident confidence in dealing with customers.

Manager Training

Research identified the fact that managers were essentially bureaucrats—managing systems, stock and procedure. Therefore, if the new store structure was to work, and if Woolworths was to fulfil the primary aim of serving customers, it had to effect a fundamental shift in the attitudes and behaviour of managers.

Woolworths sent a clear signal across the company: management means doing things right, but leadership means doing the right things.

The physical manifestation of this is a 3-year tailormade management training programme at Henley Management College for all Woolworths' 1200 managers, including Store and Head Office Managers, emphasizing:

(i) Leadership and the Team
(ii) Leadership and the Customer
(iii) Leadership and the Business.

The course, which is residential, is business-driven and designed specifically to build managers' leadership skills.

Under the strategic banner, 'Working and Winning Together', Store and Section Managers are taught how to conduct team meetings and to encourage two-way communication. Consultation via elected representatives at each level is a key part of the process.

A New Approach to Recruitment and Induction

In response to research conducted with line managers, recruitment and induction of store staff are now given a high priority. Woolworths provides the appropriate facilities and trained interviewers to conduct all recruitment interviews, as well as using high-profile advertizing in the community to attract applicants.

Store and Section Managers are responsible for recruitment and, as 'licensed' interviewers, are trained in the art of interviewing and selection.

Successful candidates spend their first day away from the store, participating in the induction programme which involves:

(i) a welcome to Woolworths and explanation of the chain's trading philosophy and high street positioning, and
(ii) an explanation of the importance of good customer service, the sales assistant's role and the support which sales assistants will receive from other functions within the organization.

Woolworths has also produced its own induction magazine—'The Woolworths Scene'—which is given to all new recruits prior to joining. It is presented in a bright, readable format and outlines not only the 'dos and don'ts' of sales assistant work, but also gives tips on make-up, presentation, diet, how the company is organized, and what it is like to work in a store.

The Excellence Programme

This was introduced in July 1987, designed to motivate and reward—offering rewards to staff in recognition of their achievements and progress towards standards of personal and team 'excellence'.

The programme divides up as follows:

(i) *Section I—Skills and Behaviour*
E—Induction: welcomes new recruits to Woolworths and demonstrates that working for the company is both enjoyable and rewarding.

X—Feelings: designed to help staff feel good about themselves, behave positively to customers and colleagues, and hence improve the shopping environment.

C—Till Skills: covers the different ways in which a customer can pay for goods, how to operate the till, and how to order goods.

E—Secondary Selling: encourages staff to work towards additional sales through better, more thoughtful customer contact.

(ii) *Section II—Merchandise Knowledge*
This consists of training programmes designed to cover all merchandise areas—teaching staff how to handle individual ranges correctly and looking at the special types of display used for each merchandise area.

L—Entertainment
L—Gifts and Sweets
E—Kids
N—Looks
C—Kitchen
E—Home and Garden

As staff pass each test they are awarded letters. When they get to *EXCEL* they get a cash award. When staff finish Section II of the training programme they receive additional cash bonuses and complete the *EXCELLENCE* badge.

After 1 year, staff are re-tested to ensure continuity of the programme—failure in any area could result in the loss of a letter.

Results

The results of the Excellence Programme were:

Greater satisfaction with service amongst Woolworth's 9·5 million customers per week—as shown by in-depth research before and after the implementation of the training programme.

Reduced number of customer complaints, which are logged weekly: so far this year there has been a reduction of 21 per cent on the same period last year.

Pre- and post-opening research for the refurbished store in Leicester revealed that:

☆ staff were found to be readily available, friendly, polite, willing and helpful whenever requests were made of them

☆ consequently, customers felt that the level of service was superior to that which had been provided in the past

☆ staff uniforms were considered by customers as both modern and attractive.

Recognition outside the company of Woolworth's staff training developments: major organizations such as Laing Homes and Harrods have been so impressed that they have asked Woolworths for advice on tailoring similar schemes for themselves.

30,000 motivated staff who have all helped Woolworths achieve greater profits: since the introduction of Operation Focus, pre-tax profit for Woolworths has risen to £45m in 1987/1988 from a loss of £5m in 1984/1985.

Sales per square foot have increased by an average of 15 per cent.

Increased sales in stores where the training has been carried out; for example staff in the recently refurbished Southport store have the highest number of *EXCELLENCE* stars of any of the Woolworths stores and sales have risen by 16 per cent.

Controlling Overseas Insurance Subsidiaries

Giorgio Petroni

The development of the economy in the industrialized countries, together with the integration of markets this entails, has brought about a net growth in insurance services. Insurance companies operating at an international level are devoting particular attention to their planning and control systems. This article, which is the product of a survey dealing with the operations of the largest American and European insurance companies, describes three general modes of approach to the problem.

Introduction

The phenomenon of 'market globalization', which has been accelerating markedly, starting from the mid 1970s, continues to involve the international market sector to an ever-increasing extent. Indeed, over the last 10 years, the latter has reported a considerable growth in overall demand, on the one hand, and a noticeable evolution in the structure of the supply, in the other. The largest American and European companies have actually widened their sphere of activity, for various reasons, in order to bypass the limitations of their country of origin and consolidate their presence in the international markets.

Basically, the reasons for this evolution are:

☆ Economic activity has become increasingly vulnerable. This increase stems from developments in production and from market integration. In other words, the highly industrialized countries are facing a progressive expansion in the area of risk so that a company which, for example, makes heavy use of computer science and telecommunications in its production processes, business activities and administration is now more vulnerable than an organization which is characterized by the traditional pattern of work distribution and execution. The computer, in fact, represents a nerve centre from the vulnerability viewpoint. Moreover, the possibility of interrupted production when goods are to be sent abroad will have far more serious consequences economically-speaking than if the organization operated solely in the home market.[1]

☆ The modern industrial company is, moreover, subject to risks which, just a few decades ago, were practically unknown, i.e. pollution problems, or product liability.

☆ The ever-expanding presence of the industrial company in the international markets implies a need for a greater range of services (e.g. financial and insurance services).[2] Indeed, these tend increasingly to become a means of competing, so that their quality and cost assume a determinating value. Many multinational industrial organizations have, over the last few years, set up or acquired insurance companies (captive companies) to obtain a better service at a lower cost, as well as to have an additional profit-making centre in their diversification strategy.

☆ Developments in information science and 'deregulation' policies in the more industrialized countries have greatly contributed to the advent of a 'capital market' within which banks, insurance companies and organizations of financial intermediaries compete, for profit incentives. Within this competitive universe, various forms of horizontal and vertical integration are taking place (collaboration agreements, acquisitions and mergers) due to the great significance in this market of the so-called 'goal-oriented' economies. Being able to have an insurance company at one's disposal may therefore amount to having a head-start in the capital market.

☆ Finally, another reason for international-scale, industrial operation to seek to complement its structure lies in the relative availability of financial means. American and European insurance companies (which have been in operation for several decades and are therefore very likely

Professor Giorgio Petroni is President of the National Institute for Professional Insurance, Milan.

to have built up a substantial body of assets) can offer an industrial partner convenient cash availability for investment at a relatively low cost.

Thus the change in behaviour patterns which has been underway in the international markets for some time now prompted this survey, which was carried out, between February and September 1987, on the strategies employed by the main American and European insurance companies to get into the international markets. The survey proposed to identify the systems used for guidance and control of the foreign concerns adopted.

How the Material was Analysed

Three different models are presented for guidance and control of the foreign businesses adopted by insurance companies. These models are connected with the range of possible strategic orientations available and the approaches identified, when analytically described, form a classification of the behaviour of the following American companies:

Aetna
Allstate
American Reinsurance
Chubb & Son
Cigna
Hartford Group
Metropolitan Life
Nationwide
Prudential

In Europe, the approaches examined during the survey were drawn from:

Commercial Union
General Accident
Legal and General
National Netherland
Riunione Adriatica di Sicurtà (R.A.S.)
Skandia
Union des Assurances de Paris
Zurich Group
Winterthur

The information used to draw up the models described was collected during visits made to each individual organization, and emerged during discussions and interviews with whoever was responsible for foreign activities in the firms in question. The classification was created by taking a bird's eye view of the data emerging from the various meetings, while simultaneously comparing each series of facts with the others. The basic hypothesis which guided firstly the process of analysis and later that of model construction (classification) consisted in the conviction that guidance and control systems for foreign activities are organized and structured differently according to the way in which the companies are strategically oriented on the inter-national market; it naturally follows that these systems vary according to the motivations and underlying objectives which induce the companies to develop their activities beyond the limits of the home market.

Some Peculiarities of the Insurance Business

At this point, we might remind ourselves of several features which are peculiar to the insurance business, so that the inherent patterns lying within the various phases of the planning and control systems can be correctly identified:

In the first place, it should be pointed out that two co-existing and strictly complementary 'life cycles' are to be found in an insurance company's physiology: the technical–economic cycle and the financial cycle. In the first, earnings (that is, premiums) are set against costs (relating to claims, commissions payable to intermediaries and to the running of the business). Actuarial techniques permit calculation of the level of premium necessary to cover the costs of the claims (pure premium); to this (keeping to the rules of correct insurance management) must be added other portions of premium to form a whole which, when the rules of full-costing are applied, will allow the expenses involved in intermediation and in the running of the company to be covered with a reasonable profit margin. It is thus self-evident that, if the insurance entrepreneur abides scrupulously by the actuarial rules and correctly applies the full-costing method, there will be no risk of his making a loss. The financial circuit is built on the fact that an insurance company collects money (from premiums) before paying it out to those insured, generally following claims. Cash availability is thus created—cash which, when invested, yields a financial return.

It is a well-known fact that, nowadays, all over the world, with a few rare exceptions, an insurance company's income essentially derives from the financial and not the technical–economic cycle. The trend towards 'lowering one's guard' on the technical–economic side was triggered by the high inflation situation which impinged upon all the main industrialized countries from the mid 1970s onwards. The prospect of obtaining high financial returns from cash investments actually prompted firms to collect premiums with little regard for strict technical–actuarial procedures. In time, this trend turned out to be disastrous because when inflation dropped it became extremely difficult to earn anything—no matter whether one concentrated on the financial cycle or the technical–actuarial one. One illustration of this can be provided by the particularly negative trend of the combined claims/premiums ratio in the American market from the end of the seventies up to today (see Figure 1).

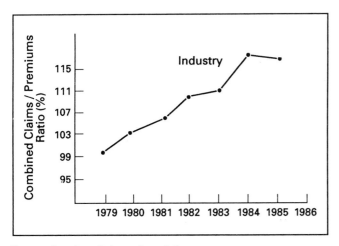

Source: American Science Foundation.

Figure 1. The increase in the U.S. insurance market

The reinsurance business is another exclusive feature of the insurance company. It is a mechanism whereby the entrepreneurial insurer tendentially shares out the 'specific weight' of each individual risk amongst a multiplicity of (assured) subjects which are typically international operators. The main insurance groups often own companies which provide reinsurance services. This practice automatically becomes a means of analysing and verifying the economic viability of the company to be reinsured (see Figure 2).[3]

It is part of the job of an insurer to carry out a statistical analysis of damages reported in the past for homogeneous families of risks (branches). The probability of damages occurring will subsequently be calculated using actuarial techniques, thus enabling the insurer (as seen below) to determine exactly how much should ideally be charged for a premium to cover the cost of such an eventuality (claim). The branches, which therefore constitute the essential reference unit for risk analysis and the taking on of risks, chiefly obey the logic of supply and not that of demand. The consumer units for insurance (individuals, families and firms) do in fact express a typology of needs which can only be satisfied by extracting guarantees from various different branches. A firm's risks can, for example, be covered by extracting guarantees (and combin-

ing them under a single policy) from the fire branch, the cargo branch, the machinery breakdown branch, the civil liability branch, the electronic risk branch and so on. 'Branch' is therefore not a conceptual equivalent of 'product', the latter being understood as a bundle of elements (perhaps intangible) that perfectly satisfies a specific need. When an insurance company starts functioning in this particular way, the impact on its planning and control systems will, of necessity, be severe. It can be clearly seen that, when guiding the development of an insurance company, the logic of the branches needs to be made compatible with that of insurance consumer units. More specifically, one comes up against the problem of deciding which unit of reference will be most effective for starting up the planning process, seeing that this same reference unit must enable those concerned to monitor both the development of the market (i.e. the demand) and also the technical—actuarial trends in all branches.

Lastly, the insurance company, in contrast with other industrial and service companies, has a 'long breathing space'. This implies that a satisfactory return on the investment made can sometimes only be obtained after a considerable time lapse (not less than 10 years, for example, in the life insurance business). At the same time, an insurance company with a rather precarious economic existence will 'expire' only after an extremely long illness—which may at times last for over 20 years. Generally speaking then, the 'pulse rate' of an insurance company is uncommonly slow when set in the context of the present industrial environment (see Figure 3).

This, in turn, implies that the presence of an insurance company in the sphere of an industrial group, besides providing an efficient diversification device, also plays an inherently anti-cyclic—and hence particularly important—role in the processes of creation and adoption of developmental strategies by complex organizations.[4] For a multinational industrial group, starting up an insurance company may yield the following benefits:

☆ Convenient cash reserves.

☆ Availability of a competent insurance service at a

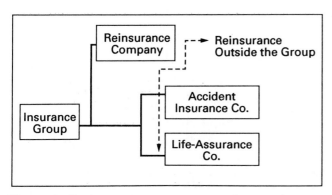

Figure 2. Reinsurance as a means of control

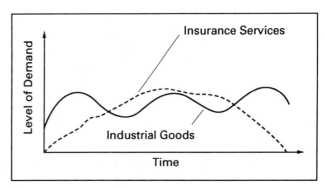

Figure 3. The trade cycle in insurance and industry

cost which may well be lower than current market prices.

☆ A significant opportunity to diversify.

☆ A convenient trading currency for making the acquisitions which best fit in with the strategic lines of development chosen.

☆ The use of a kind of 'flywheel' which, by its anti-cyclic action, can help to stabilize the expected inflow of revenue.

Why Expand Abroad?

The first objective of the survey as regards the model construction for the operations concerned, was to provide an answer to the (hardly trivial) question of the underlying motives which result in the development of insurance businesses abroad.[5] If we leave aside, for a moment, the factors illustrated in the previous section, which chiefly apply to insurance companies belonging to multinational industrial groups, the typology that emerged from our analysis was as follows:

In some cases, motivations of a political or economic–industrial kind are at the root of expansion abroad; Commercial Union, for example, developed largely in the Commonwealth countries (where, even today, it has a huge share of the market) obviously as a consequence of the expansion of British political and economic influence. Similarly, the hefty share of the market held by the Riunione Adriatica di Sicurtà (R.A.S.) in Austria and Germany (and also in some eastern European countries until the outbreak of the Second World War) should be viewed in its context. At the beginning of the last century, R.A.S. sprang up in Trieste, which was then the principal port of the Hapsburg empire, and started to expand outwards. Operations subsequently thrived in central and south America, primarily because of Italian cultural influence there, and due to the industrial settlements which had been founded in these countries by Italian immigrants from the beginning of the century onwards. Likewise, Winterthur began to develop so vigourously abroad, due to the fact that it is, by tradition, the insurer of SOC Schultzer, a large Swiss machinery-producing firm, whose expansion into the international market it promptly followed.

In other cases, expansion abroad is forced by limitation or saturation of home markets. This is almost certainly so in the case of the large Swiss multinationals, such as the Zurich Group and Winterthur; similarly, National Netherlands was spurred into looking for business opportunities abroad because of the limitations the home market presented. To a certain extent, even large English companies, such as Commercial Union and General Accident, see the overseas market as an essential part of their development, since the growth rate of the English market (apart from the so-called London market, which features predominantly international business) has been rather meagre for many years now. The conclusions drawn above are supported by the fact that, in 1986, the Zurich Group collected 75 per cent of its total premiums abroad, while Commercial Union and General Netherlands, which are in the same business, collected premiums abroad amounting to 60 per cent of the total.

Finally, in yet other cases, the reason for wanting to be decently ensconced in the overseas market derives from the possibilities this gives of obtaining a higher revenue, by seizing the opportunities—which occasionally present themselves—of obtaining attractive returns on investment.[6] It is definitely this last reason which prompted the recent expansion abroad of Legal and General, especially in the life insurance and personal line areas. The big American companies, such as Alstate, Metropolitan Life and the Prudential, which are paying great attention to certain Far East countries (e.g. Japan and Korea) are basically motivated by the same sort of incentives. Similarly, the entry of Chubb & Son and Loyal & Gimbal into the Italian market is obviously connected with the favourable prospects offered by this market, particularly in the field of life insurance and supplementary benefits, as a consequence of the serious state of crisis in the public social security system.

Guidance and Control

The strategic options which characterize development processes in other industrial and service companies are obviously valid for insurance companies too. Indeed, to further its overall aim of expanding abroad, an insurance company can choose either the path of 'make' or that of 'buy'. In the case of 'make', one question which typically presents itself is whether to set up a business abroad in collaboration with a company already operating in the chosen country or whether to go it alone. In the latter case, one usually starts with a liaison office and subsequently opens an agency, and then gradually set up a company as the business gets under way. If growth strategies for acquisitions have to be decided upon, the classic question arises—for insurance companies too—of whether to assume absolute control of the business concerns acquired and direct their operations, or whether to choose the more convenient solution of leaving management under the former owner, who will then, however, retain a share of the capital too.[7] Other no less important strategic decisions may consist in, or involve, defining the company's intended market profile (which type of service to offer to which type of clientele) which will naturally entail defining one's specialist role as regards supply and distribution channels.

These and other strategic orientations may be implemented by employing a variety of initiatives and means groupable under the following six headings.

Reinsurance Activities

It has already been pointed out that insuring the risks of a company automatically implies evaluating its economic viability; moreover, in the strategies of multi-business organizations, the procedure of reinsuring may allow the international transfer of funds to cover, for example, cash drains or to diversify investments, thus maximizing profitability. Reinsurance also constitutes an efficient means of implementing fiscal policies at an international level.

Economic Control of Insurance Operations

The usual problems to be tackled in this area are:

☆ Whether and how to draw up a consolidated balance sheet for foreign operations.

☆ What information to ask for from the foreign partners as regards the economic aspects of marketing intelligence.

☆ How to obtain an effective mix in the marketing intelligence between the technical–actuarial type of information and the strictly economic type.

☆ What information should be reported by the marketing intelligence system, apart from the technical–actuarial and the economic variety (e.g. information on trends in demand, on competitors' behaviour, on the opportunities and dangers inherent in certain market trends, etc.)

The behaviour of the organizations examined spotlights the general tendency to make use of a quarterly reporting system, providing essential information both about the general situation and evolution of the market and also on the economic conditions prevailing, besides news concerning technical–actuarial developments. Moreover, in most firms, the annual budget represents the appendix to a medium-term plan, which is normally designed to be implemented over a 3-year period. This business plan constitutes, in its turn, the operational version of a strategic plan which, in American corporations, appears to be given a far greater formal weight than occurs for the corresponding plans of their European counterparts.

Investment

One constant of the management teams which led the foreign companies (as far as the operations examined are concerned) consists in the issuing of guidelines and regulations pertaining to the areas in which cash deriving from premium collection is to be invested.[8]

Company and Equity Structure

Normally, the equity structure faithfully reflects the strategic orientation of a company. Indeed, the absolute control of equity generally indicates the will to control not only the revenue of a firm, but also its foreseeable development in the market. This motivation is usually combined with the strategic decision not to overstep the boundaries of the insurance business. Commercial Union, General Accident and the Union des Assurances de Paris (U.A.P.) are emblematic in this sense: they wish to remain essentially insurance companies, and always assume absolute control of the equity of any concern they buy or start up in whatever country they have decided to establish themselves. A 50:50 joint venture in a market, on the other hand, bears witness to a desire to combine certain strategically valuable resources brought by the partner (e.g. a distribution network, particularly well-qualified personnel, a particularly interesting client portfolio, etc.) with their own. This was so for Winterthur, for example, which, in most of the Far East countries, operates in partnership with Norwich Union. Even Alstate, started up in Japan in 1876, is in partnership with a mass distribution firm. Lastly, a minority participation is occasionally accepted; the aim of this is to set up a business experimentally—to gain experience, in other words, or else simply to have a convenient currency to bargain with in negotiating other types of business.

These motivations hold for some transactions recently effected by the Hartford Group, which forms the financial insurance nucleus of the vast ITT empire. As far as (capital-oriented) control over the associates or subsidiaries is concerned, this may be direct or else arranged via a 'third country' finance company. Lastly, control by a local finance company may prove to be a convenient way of getting round (to a certain extent) limitations imposed by local legislation on business expansion (moving from the insurance business, for example, into the field of financial intermediation). Legal & General for example, has, in some cases, put this kind of control structure into effect.

Human Resources

The personnel obviously provide the means of guiding and controlling operations abroad. A simple list of the problems which usually crop up in this area brings out the following questions:

☆ Should the foreign subsidiary's top management be local or come from Head Office? Several different orientations emerged during the course of our analysis: assignment of only local personnel to top positions occurs on the condition that these become well-versed in and integrated into the 'corporate culture'; in the case of U.A.P. or Skandia, as in the case of Chubb & Son, foreign operations are directed by placing in the topmost positions of the associated firm only men originating from head office or who, at the very least, come from within the corporation.

☆ Which positions should be covered by insiders? As far as American corporations are concerned, the tendency is to assign their own managing director and controller to the foreign subsidiary.

☆ How should top managers working abroad be paid, considering the fact that they may predictably be moved about from country to country?

☆ How can they be trained and integrated into the corporate 'culture'?

As for the above, a general trend emerging from the survey consisted of laying on centralized training programmes. These not only provide an important opportunity for the transmission of knowledge and experience, but are also a significant aid to cultural integration and a chance for top management from head office to do some co-opting. Amongst the European firms surveyed, the Zurich Group and General Accident seem to endow the training programmes with special significance; amongst other things, these two companies maintain permanent training centres located near Chicago and in Scotland respectively. In the U.S.A., the attitude taken by the Prudential, Cigna, Aetna and the Hartford group was of particular interest, as these corporations pour vast sums of money into the training of the middle-management personnel destined to assume responsibility for foreign activities.

Services Provided by the Holding Company
The policy of offering services to the foreign subsidiaries may permit the quality of their management systems to be improved and, furthermore, function as a catalyst for the integration process.[9] The services normally offered are:

☆ EDP services

☆ technical assistance

☆ documentation

☆ assistance with financial problems

☆ information concerning the development of innovations (of products or processes).

The general tendency was to provide technical assistance to the subsidiaries, especially while the business was starting up; subsidiaries were also strongly advised by head office to 'computerize', given the considerable implications that developments in informations science have for management and cost levels. Furthermore, it must be borne in mind that the electronic transfer of funds may allow the business to be expanded and may thus be strategically important.

Headquarters may thus be connected up with its associates operating in the various different countries by a close-knit network of relations (see Figure 4).

The strategic orientations and the reasons for developing their foreign activities which the insurance companies expressed, involve choosing some elements of this network and binding them more or less firmly together. Typical situations where the specificity of the means of control is coherent with the strategic orientation are given in the examples contained in Table 1.

General Models for Guidance and Control of Overseas Insurance Businesses

In this survey of insurance operations, we have attempted to set into focus the relationships between the various levels and the methods used in guidance and control, the motivations operating in the overseas market, and the basic forms their presence can take. Three general models have emerged, and these are described below. The models can characterize the behaviour of the companies in each individual market because the specific market penetration strategies and market profile aims can be changed to suit each new set of circumstances. Therefore the models do not necessarily provide a faithful description of the overall approach of the company in all markets.[10]

The 'opportunistic' model is frequently to be found

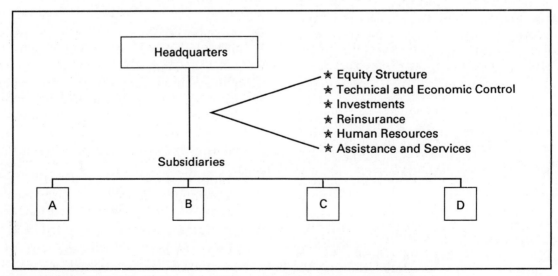

Figure 4. Techniques for the guidance and control of overseas activities

Table 1. Strategy and control for an overseas insurance business

	Strategic goal	Plan of operation	Capital structure	Responsibility for management	Aim of control	Reporting structure	Services and assistance
Case 1	Trading currency availability	Buy	Relative control (51%)	Former owner	Profit	Schematic	–
Case 2	Acquire important market position	Make	Absolute control (100%)	Managing director and controller from holding company	Market share Investments	Extensive and detailed	Technical assistance EDP Product innovation

wherever the reasons for a firm's presence in a given market are as follows.

The need to explore the true potential of the market and the wish, for example, to test the reactions of clients to the introduction of a new line of insurance services.

The goal of 'planting' an insurance business so that it can later be used as a 'trading currency' to acquire other operations, in line with whatever basic corporate strategies have been chosen. This frequently occurs in multi-business groups (usually with a predominantly industrial structure).

The need to ensure the availability of an insurance business which may represent a 'bridgehead' to be developed, in time, into a wider range of activities (integrating, for example, insurance with the finance business). American Express has made various acquisitions of insurance companies in Europe and the Far East over the last 5 years in order either to complement the range of services it already provides or else to have a reliable base camp from which to set up its complete range of activities. Over the last few years, the approach of Alstate and Metropolitan Life outside the United States has seemingly been very similar.

The need to keep a place for itself within the insurance sector, which is, however, required mainly for the development of the reinsurance business in the country in question. In this case, 'a creaming-off' operation is usually carried out in the market, exclusively via the intermediation of brokers; this typically has the aim of ensuring that the company involved obtains a well-appointed place for itself in the industrial risk reinsurance sector. The company's presence, in keeping with these motivations, seems to be somewhat limited, both from the market share viewpoint and as regards the thickness of its portfolio. It does not, moreover, appear to be permanent, in the sense that it may easily be modified over time, or even wiped out.

As far as means of control are concerned, normally:

☆ head office exercises control over the capital or owns a majority share of it (while operating in partnership with another organization);

☆ from the human resources viewpoint, the responsibility for directing the company is entrusted to one or two faithful persons from head office, who undertake to function rather like gatekeepers;

☆ the reporting system stresses the essentially economic–financial aspects of the business;

☆ the subsidiary is not offered any special services, but much importance is given to the circulation of information which is vital to the running and development of the business;

☆ lastly, reinsurance may play a very substantial role, and in this case it is not intended as a control device but, on the contrary, its role becomes that of an autonomous business, which often takes priority over normal insurance activities.

Generally speaking, this model characterizes the presence abroad of those firms which belong to a large-scale multi-business group or which, from the insurance viewpoint, have especially developed the life assurance branch, which is generally acknowledged to be remarkably open to diversification and to integration with financial business.

An 'organic' model can be found whenever the 'mission' of the company wishing to expand abroad is essentially to provide insurance; that is to say that the long term objectives of the firm do not foresee development in a given market overlapping the boundaries of the insurance business.[11] This basic orientation may gradually be specified to:

☆ investing steadily to increase market share, or

☆ angling the supply towards specific segments of clientele and consequently offering specialized services (niche strategies);

☆ developing campaigns to concentrate existing activities and improve the efficiency of them—streamlining, for example, the structures of the distribution network or the claims adjustment service;

☆ making acquisitions with the primary aim of complementing the range of services supplied and, in any case, to consolidate the existing position in the market. Here, a market profile which remains steady over time is to be expected, with continuous reinvestment of incoming revenue and a substantial market share, both in the absolute sense of the term and as related to individual market segments.

The guidance and control system usually involves:

☆ Absolute control by head office of corporate capital.

☆ The presence of key men in the associate company who are strongly integrated in the corporate culture; significant investments, in the form of training, are generally made to ensure this level of integration. In the most important operations, carefully worked-out management development plans and manpower planning systems can be detected; these aim to ensure that the business is constantly protected by particularly highly trained personnel.

☆ The marketing intelligence system is very extensive and reports are made several times a year. Reports do not merely contain items of economic interest, but also information on the technical–actuarial trends in the insurance field and news on the evolution of the market.

☆ Reinsurance is largely seen as a control device.

☆ From the services viewpoint, a considerable amount of technical assistance is provided towards product development. In cases where this model has been most thoroughly adopted (e.g. Winterthur, Chubb & Son, Prudential), the assistance given to the foreign holdings tends to underscore their knowledge and experience in the direction of 'critical factors' for success (supplying, for example, computer software for claims adjustment purposes, or for working out procedures concerned with cost-saving programmes or even, lastly, providing technical assistance in the phase of introduction of a new product which has already been tested out in some other market).[12]

☆ Finally, precise guidelines are provided for investments, which are, quite rightly, considered to be a fundamental means of consolidating and developing the insurance business.

Local Collaboration

Some of the approaches analysed suggest that there is in operation a model of guidance and control through local collaboration. This is typical of firms which, in their strategy for penetrating foreign markets, use collaboration with other organizations. The basic aim is to develop the firm along with others in the market, at least initially. The need for collaboration is due, in particular, to cultural-type barriers (as in the case of the joint ventures undertaken over the last 5 years in Japan by Alstate, together with local firms) or to the need for sufficient resources to bypass the 'barriers to entry' erected by companies which already have a significant weight in the market. We are dealing here with operations which are—as experience has proved—highly complex to carry out, operations which involve, in particular, painstaking evaluation of the objectives one expects to reach and of the complementary resources of both partners involved. In fact, as a rule, these joint ventures are successful only when the two firms have, for other reasons, already been collaborating profitably for many years. The guidance and control system which corresponds to these strategic orientations appears to be arranged as follows:

☆ the capital is obviously shared;

☆ from the human resources point of view, a few key men are assigned to the joint venture—besides managing the business, part of their function is to learn;

☆ the reporting system seems to be on the extensive side and contains a mix of technical and economic information as well as news on the current market situation;

☆ the services provided derive from the specific competence and experience acquired by the partners;

☆ reinsurance is seen not only as a business opportunity, but also as a means of controlling both economic viability and insurance procedures.

Conclusions

Insurance companies are, with ever-increasing frequency, driven into taking steps towards internationalization; the reasons for this stem from the fact that services (insurance and financial services amongst them) are increasingly becoming a means of competing amongst industrial concerns which operate at an international level. Moreover, complex organizations are becoming more vulnerable, and new risks must today be faced in the evolution of the industrial system (pollution risks, civil reponsibility for products etc.). Furthermore, the insurance business is particularly attractive to multinational firms because it offers substantial cash availability and appears to be strictly complementary to the finance business.

It was basically for these reasons that the author was persuaded to carry out a survey on guidance and control systems in the foreign operations adopted by 18 international-level American and European insurance companies. The hypothesis underlying this piece of research is that there exist different guidance and control systems which are related to the various different motivations and strategies for penetrating the markets. Indeed, analysis of the data has highlighted the fact that the possible areas for guidance and control (capital structure, human resources, reinsurance, cash investments, technical–economic control and services) may be differently combined and made use of to different extents, strictly depending on which strategic orientations guide the running of the organization. Substantially, three different models ('opportunistic', 'organic' and 'conditioned development' can be identified; these have been analytically described above.

References

(1) B. Berliner, *Limits of Insuperabilty of Risks,* Prentice–Hall, Englewood Cliffs, NJ (1982).

(2) O. Fiarini, *The Emerging Service Economy,* Pergamon, London (1987).

(3) H. Bohman, Reinsurance, profitability, insurability, *Geneva Papers,* **11** (39), (1986).

(4) F. C. Doyle, Corporate reserving and growth models, in J. D. Cummins (Ed.), *Strategic Planning and Propelling in Property-Liability Insurance,* Kluwer Nighoff Publishing, Boston (1985).

(5) F. Padoa, *L'Assicurazione internazionale,* Hoepli, Milan (1984).

(6) A. Kraus and S. A. Ross, The determination of four profits for the prosperity-liability insurance firm, *Journal of Finance,* **37,** 101–115, September (1982).

(7) P. B. Walker, Building a winning strategy, *Best's Review* (Property–Casualty Edition), **80,** April (1980).

(8) *Corporate Planning in the Insurance Industry,* Insurance Institute of London, London (1982).

(9) *Corporate Planning in the Insurance Industry,* Advanced Study Group No. 213, Chartered Insurance Institute, London (1982).

(10) E. Kirkby Warren, Perspectives on planning: trends and changes, *Risk Management,* **28,** 34–40, March (1981).

(11) John Willox, Formulating an operation plan for a large company, *The Interpreter,* 26–28, November (1976).

(12) Robert B. Nicholas, A newcomer's viewpoint of planning in the insurance industry, *Best's Review* (Property–Casualty Edition), **24,** February (1973).

Towards 1992: A Strategy for Training

Derek Day

1992 is now 3 years away and much is now being spoken and written on the free market within Europe following the magic date. The need for businesses to think about a strategy for training to equip their staff to take advantage of the new opportunities is ever more important. Training has historically lived under the 'stop-go' policy. When business is good, we can afford training; when business is bad, training is the first to suffer. The author has tried to formulate a strategic approach to ensure people become conscious of the necessity of management involvement and commitment in training. The 1990s offer great potential to companies who direct activities to these opportunities, and those who meet the threat will be winners.

These days we all seem to be suffering from an acute overdose of 1992. The date appears to have acquired a mystical quality and is used for a range of purposes from selling consultancy services to gaining the ear of otherwise inaccessible managing directors to present topics they would not have given a hearing without the 'magic tag!' However, the implications, of 1992 are critical to us all. One important message is the need for organizations to develop a clear training strategy to deal with the challenges of the 1990s.

Using the 1990s generally rather than 1992 specifically is quite intentional. It appears to me that 1992 and the movement to a single European market is part of a wider process of the globalization of business. In fact in no sector is the world market trend more noticeable than in the financial sector. The reality of this was made painfully clear on 19 October 1987—Black Monday.

It is within the context of this globalization that we should consider the requirements of a training strategy for 1992 and beyond Inevitably we will

---

Derek Day is a Managing Director of Alexander Howden Ltd. He has responsibility for Human Relations and elements of Strategic Planning and he works closely with his U.S. colleagues on global HRD issues.

need to consider some specific aspects of 1992 in establishing our requirements.

1992—The Issues

Without moving into a detailed examination of the processes and changes associated with 1992 it is important to identify some of the key issues which will impact on business and hence requirements for a training strategy.

1992 is not a single event. It is the code name for a process designed to create a single European market. In some sectors that process is well underway already (e.g. Aerospace), whilst in others, the process will continue well beyond 1992. The financial and insurance sector have started the process. 1992 is concerned with deregulation. The regulation surrounding the European insurance markets is extensive and complex. It will take a long time to be unwound and replaced with what will certainly be a complex single market structure.

(1) *Urgency*
Urgency perhaps represents the first issue to flow from 1992 for trainers. There is a need to establish a sense of urgency and develop plans without knowing, in detail, the legislative framework within which we will be operating.

(2) *Legislation*
The second issue for trainers is that there will be much new, detailed, legislative knowledge for people to acquire. We need to plan to help them acquire this knowledge and at the same time ensure that focusing on technical training does not detract from the equally important need to develop business marketing and people skills to compete in the new markets.

(3) *Languages*
Europe offers enormous potential. Taking advantage of opportunities presents the third issue. We

need to consider what action, as managers we need to be taking to equip our people to take advantage of opportunities. This immediately leads to consideration of developing language skills. If we wish to conduct business in a market we really will need to speak the language of the market.

(4) *Investing in Training*

1992 is generally promoted in terms of the opportunities presented. However, it is a two-way trade. We also face competition and threats not only in attacking new markets but also in defending our established markets. We need to ensure that our people are better equipped than our competitors. Here we face some major challenges. In a recent article on Training and Development, Lord Young, (former Secretary of State for Trade and Industry), addressed this issue and pointed out that:

☆ 'In Germany 5 times as many people gain vocational qualifications as in the U.K.'

☆ In France 10 times as many people are trained to perform intermediate level office work as in the U.K.

☆ In France just under 10 times as many people are trained in selling as in the U.K.

☆ In both France and Germany far more emphasis is placed on post-school language training than in the U.K.

This points to a competitive training gap that we must close.

(5) *Understanding Cultural and Market Differences*

The move to a single European market can be a misleading concept. We need to help people understand the real nature of the markets in which they will be operating. The single European market will not be like the model provided by the U.S.A. There will be wide variation in national taste, preferences and practices. In product development, marketing and selling, people will need to understand and be sensitive to cultural differences and to possess linguistic skills.

(6) *Mobility*

An important aspect of the deregulation process associated with 1992 relates to common acceptance of professional qualifications. Clearly we are going to face a further increase in the mobility of professional and technical staff. This will, no doubt, lead to greater competition for skilled people. Our training strategy must both help us to improve our ability to develop skills and offer long term growth and developmental opportunities to help us retain our key players.

From this overview we can see six major issues flowing directly from 1992, that a training strategy must address. In summary these are:

(1) Maintaining a sense of urgency.

(2) Developing understanding of legislative frameworks.

(3) Developing linguistic skills.

(4) Investing more in training our staff, and being better at it than our competitors.

(5) Understanding cultural/market differences.

(6) Increased mobility of qualified staff.

Issues relating to 1992 and Europe may be clearly identified, but there are a range of additional issues which any strategy needs to address. These are issues we face in our current domestic market which we will also face in the European and, to a large extent, in world markets.

(1) *Demographic Changes*

The first of these issues relates to demographics. Throughout much of the developed world we face an ageing population structure. People are living longer, fewer are being born and young people are spending longer periods in full-time education. The economic implications of this trend are considerable and will impact on our businesses. However, in terms of training strategy we face some significant decisions. Clearly the competition for good young people will increase dramatically. To cope with this challenge we may have to consider reducing our entry standards. If we do make such a move then we must develop means of training lower level entrants to meet performance requirements more rapidly. We must also review our thinking on career development and structures to take account of a different mix of entrants.

At the other end of the scale perhaps our training and development strategy will have to be modified to ensure that we make better use of the skills of older people. New thinking on career structures and recruitment criteria will have to occur to enable us to tap into the older portion of the population.

(2) *Changing Values and Expectations*

Closely linked with demographics is the second general issue. This is concerned with 'changing motivation patterns' in the developed world. It is recognized that the expectations and values of young people joining organizations today are significantly different from those encountered 20 years ago. Training and development strategy must take account of values, expectations and motivations. In a move towards global markets we must also take account of regional and cultural variations.

A recent survey conducted by Henley Management College showed considerable variation in motivation structures within the U.K. For example, the most important factor in a job varied between three regions as follows:

NORTH EAST: Good Communications

SOUTH EAST: Further Education
MIDLANDS: Recognition

If we encounter this degree of variation within the U.K. how much greater will it be in the whole of Europe.

Changes in Industry Structure

The key question in any strategic planning process is to ask what business are we in? The insurance and financial sectors are undergoing a process of rapid and fundamental change. Traditional lines of demarcation are disappearing. It is increasingly difficult in the U.K. to define the practical differences between banks and building societies.

Banks throughout Europe are becoming involved in the insurance business through acquisitions establishment of subsidiaries or marketing as intermediaries. In the life and personal lines market distribution capacity is becoming a critical success factor. For example in France banks entered the life assurance market only 5 years ago and now have a 30 per cent market share. In Spain, it is estimated that banks will in the near future control around 70 per cent of the rapidly evolving pensions market.

There is a need to train people to develop broader business skills to meet this competition. At the strategic level it is financial protection and at a training level it means a training strategy will have to encompass the building of new skills. In any event it must address broader market understanding and the development of creative and innovative thinking.

In addition to the six 1992 specific issues then, there are a further three general issues to address in a training strategy. In summary, these are:

☆ Changing demographics.

☆ Changes and variations in motivation patterns, expectations and values.

☆ A broader view of the nature of our business stemming from a unification of financial markets.

Having identified the key issues relating to training and development for the 1990s, what of the strategy for addressing them?

A Training and Development Strategy

Throughout this article I have quite deliberately referred to a training and development strategy. The issues raised in looking to 1992 and beyond are fundamental and complex and they have training implications which must be addressed within a strategic framework.

In practice this model would be used to deal with a specific organization's strategy. Whilst we clearly cannot come out with a specific strategy for training for 1992 and beyond, it is possible to identify some of the major components of such a strategy which in turn will be relevant to individual business.

Strengths and Weaknesses

The historical role of training has been concerned with the provision of technical training. This has resulted from a highly technical view of the nature and management of our business.

In reviewing strengths and weaknesses we must identify a major strength as being development of technical knowledge and skills. Another strength which training has had has been in identifying what action beyond technical training is needed to improve business performance. Unfortunately, a major weakness in training performance has been the inability to secure top management commitment to resource action to meet the non-technical needs.

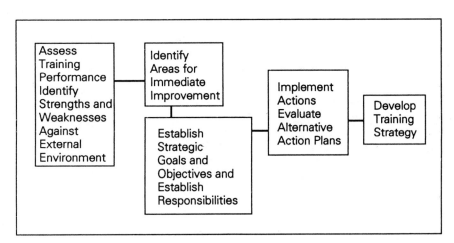

Figure 1. Developing a strategy for training and development

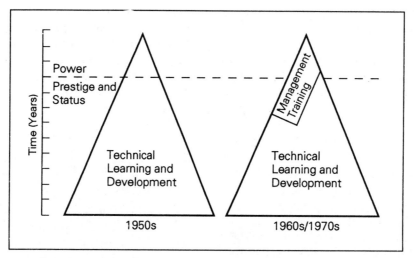

Figure 2. Past development frameworks

A second and related weakness of training has been that the planning of training has not been sufficiently (if at all) integrated with business planning.

Further weaknesses include:

☆ Failure to exploit technology

☆ Inability to identify potential, relate current skills to future job requirements and systematically develop people to meet future business needs.

This analysis seems negative. However, in training, we have been good in developing the skills which top management perceived as important and were prepared to support with resources. We have a further strength in that the methods employed are often innovative and effective.

In the first part of this article we have reviewed the external environment but we should of course consider the current national environment as well as the international situation.

Within the U.K. market organizations are faced with increasing volatility and competition. This brings with it a need to support technical skills and excellence with an increased understanding of business and market issues and personal skills in the areas of selling, marketing, planning and communication.

We are already facing skill shortages and fierce competition for existing experienced staff and good calibre new entrants. There is a need in such an environment to develop programmes:

☆ to attract and retain good people

☆ to review the whole range of talent and potential available and to develop these resources.

Opportunities and Threats

We can also analyse the external environment in terms of the *Opportunities* and *Threats* which it

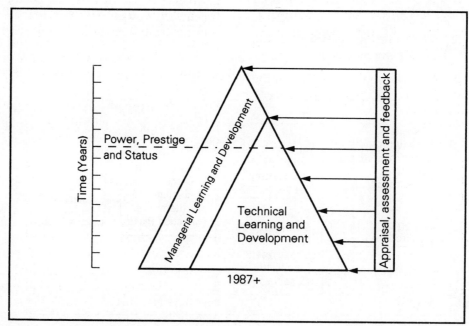

Figure 3. A development framework for the future

presents in the context both of the business and the training strategy.

The opportunities presented from a business viewpoint relate to the scope for growth and development in an expanding market. From the viewpoint of training strategy the major opportunity presented is that the environment is underpinning the role of human resources as a critical success factor for the business. This creates the opportunity to discuss training and development strategy at the most senior level and ensure that it becomes integrated with business planning.

A major threat presented by the environment to the business relates to competition. Intensification of competition will inevitably further squeeze margins. If the competition is not effectively tackled then business will face decline or take over (given the high propensity to grow by acquisition dominant in Europe).

Another threat from a training viewpoint is that competitive pressures will lead to a further reduction in training budgets. So any training strategy will have to be clearly positioned as being relevant to business needs and business performance.

Immediate Action

Reviewing strengths and weaknesses together with the external environment leads to the conclusion that, in terms of training and development, there are a number of areas where immediate action is required.

These would appear to be:

☆ Development of training plans to become more closely wedded to business planning.

☆ Audit of current people to identify full range of existing and potential skills, talents and abilities.

☆ Broadening scope of training to include the development of key non-technical skills.

☆ Examination of methodologies to determine ways of increasing the coverage and cost effectiveness of training.

In addition to these areas perhaps the most important action point is to 'sell' the value and contribution of training and development to senior management. These messages which have to be put over are clear:

☆ Training has to broaden beyond technical skills.

☆ Training and development expenditure is not 'icing'—it is an investment which if properly managed is core to the continued growth and success of the business.

Perhaps this carries with it a further immediate action point for training and development managers. *They must understand their company's business.* In future, they will require this understanding in order to be able to identify and 'sell' the vital contribution which they can make to the performance of the business.

The analysis of needs which drive the training and development strategy will lead to the formulation of clear strategic goals and objectives. In a general treatment of the subject we cannot identify specific goals and objectives. However, in applying this framework to industry, we can identify the major areas in which such goals and objectives must be developed.

Strategic Goals and Objectives

Examination of current and past performance contrasted with the issues raised by the changing environment indicates that strategic goals and objectives in training and development must be concerned with:

☆ Underpinning the performance of industry and contributing to the development of competitive edge.

☆ Ensuring the optimum development, use and performance of people.

☆ Equipping industry and its people to cope with change and develop innovative and flexible solutions to problems.

☆ Ensuring that training and development is inexorably linked to business needs and business planning.

☆ Contributing to excellence in performance by excellence in the analysis, design and delivery of training.

☆ Building the commitment of talented people by recognizing their expectations and values and ensuring that their training and development is handled in a way which causes them to value it and the company providing it.

From these broad goals and objectives a range of specific objectives would be developed to reflect the requirements and needs of each organization.

Establish Responsibilities

Having identified that training and development needs to be driven by and integrated with the business plan it is critical that the message is reinforced in considering the allocation of responsibilities. Training and development will only become an integral part of a business when responsibility for it is accepted and fulfilled as an integral part of line managers' functions.

At the end of the day it is a managerial responsibility to determine:

☆ Who requires training and when it is needed,

☆ What training is required,

☆ How training is to be provided, and

☆ How effectively training is impacting on individual, group and corporate performance.

The Training and Development Specialist's role is to support line management in fulfilling their accountabilities for training.

Following this line through it is evident that senior management are accountable for an organization's training and development strategy. The training specialist can provide input to the strategy and assist line management in its formulation.

The most important responsibility of the training specialist is to persuade senior management to acknowledge, accept and fulfil their accountability for training and development strategy. Once this has been achieved then commitment will be obtained through recognition of the business value of such a strategy and involvement in its formulation.

Produce Action Plans

Senior line management having agreed on and become committed to the strategic goals and objectives for training and development will need to agree on courses of action likely to lead to achievement of these objectives.

The input of the training specialist at this stage is important. It is also important in considering action plans to think broadly and innovatively in terms of methodology.

Secondments, projects and action learning are every bit as important as training courses, seminars and workshops.

In this article, it is not possible to cover the wide range of considerations that can arise at this stage in the planning process. It is, however, worth highlighting a few of the current and future areas for consideration which include:

☆ *Technology*—the extent to which training and learning might be more widely and effectively distributed is influenced by the application of technology to training situations.

☆ *Assessment*—training and development action plans will increasingly need to use techniques of individual and group assessment in order to cost effectively target action, improve people job matching and make cost effective use of resources.

☆ *Performance*—performance review and management techniques will grow in importance in both the identification of training needs and the evaluation of training effectiveness.

☆ *Career Paths*—the career paths that will need to exist to meet future business needs will impact on development planning as well as recruitment and promotion criteria. Action plans will need to take account of both constraints and opportunities presented by current and future career paths and business health.

The Training Strategy

From the overall analysis to date of the strategy for training for 1992 and beyond, it is clear that any action plans will most certainly need to address:

☆ Linguistic skills

☆ Marketing and selling skills

☆ New legislation

☆ Interpersonal skills

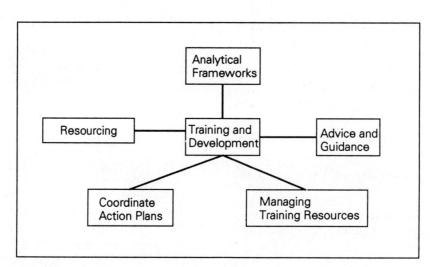

Figure 4. The training and development specialist's role

☆ People management skills

☆ Technical skills/Computer 'linkage' training

The process described will be pulled together to form a clear training and development strategy. This strategy will, if developed as described, carry the support and commitment of senior management. Specific and measurable objectives will be supported by clear allocation of resources and responsibilities.

If properly tied to the business needs and evolved through the exercise of managerial responsibility, the training strategy will be implemented by line management in much the same way as overall business strategy.

Co-operation and Co-ordination

So far I have developed two themes:

☆ The issues raised, in terms of training and development, by 1992 and associated developments.

☆ The adoption of a strategic approach to training and development in the light of these developments.

It is necessary to develop a third and final theme. This is one of industry-wide co-operation and co-ordination and one particularly pertinent in the light of 1992.

It is clear that the advent of 1992 and associated developments has sparked a rush of activity in most industries in the U.K. (and indeed throughout the rest of the community). It is equally clear that the main thrust, at this stage, is concerned with research, information gathering and attempting to clarify and interpret trends, developments and projected changes.

A large amount of effort on an individual company basis is going into these activities, and there is likely to be an enormous amount of duplication of effort and research. Within industry, there must be considerable scope for co-operation and co-ordination. Whilst recognizing the need of individual companies to develop and retain competitive positions, we do have a mutual interest in developing a strong competitive edge over our European competitors.

There is scope for, and value in, establishing a process for the exchange of information relating to 1992 and associated developments. The advantages of such co-operation would appear to be:

☆ Saving time—and in planning terms 1992 is not far away.

☆ Saving money—duplication of effort is always expensive.

☆ Avoiding the need to re-invent the wheel—capitalizing on the experience of others can also save time, effort and money.

Summary

In summary, this paper has set out to review the implications for training of 1992 and considerations to be taken into account in formulating a strategy for training to deal with needs relating to 1992 and beyond.

In looking at the implication of 1992, it is important to be clear that it is a process we are considering and not a single event. The process is one of de-regulation, and is part of a much wider trend towards globalization of markets. In examining 1992 and associated trends and developments the following major issues with training and development implications emerge:

☆ The need to maintain a sense of urgency

☆ Understanding legislative frameworks

☆ Increasing our investment in training in all sectors, technical skills or Management Development, including computerization and/information technology.

☆ Understanding cultural and market differences

☆ Mobility of qualified staff

☆ Changing demographics

☆ Expectations and values of people and businesses

☆ Unification of financial markets.

Tackling these issues will be important to the future success of businesses. Training and development associated with the issues should be formulated using a strategic model.

The strategic approach to training and development enables the process to become wedded to the needs of the business and, by ensuring line management involvement, increases support and investment in training and developing people.

The issues surrounding 1992 and associated strategic approaches to training can become complex and confusing. Whilst much effort is being invested by companies in this area, there is scope for industry-wide co-operation and a forum for this should be developed.

The 1990s offer tremendous opportunities and exciting challenges. They also offer real threats. Those companies that ensure all activities are directed towards realizing opportunities and meeting threats will be the winners. All activities will include training and to contribute effectively trainers must espouse and sell the strategic approach.

PART THREE

Experiences from the Public Sector

Corporate Strategic Planning in a University

Professor Raymond Thomas, University of Bath School of Management

This paper reviews the relevance of key constituents in modern corporate strategic planning to policy determination in universities. The emphasis is on corporate policy making at the level of the individual institution, not the universities or higher education as a whole. From the outset it is assumed that a university has a measure of autonomy within a wider negotiated environment of which the universities, as a group, are a sector for negotiating purposes. There are therefore important elements in the working of any university that are bound not only by general laws and customs but by specific standard policies, practices and conditions applicable to all universities within a country, e.g. salary and wage-scales.

First the environment of universities is examined to ascertain the relevance of such an approach to their problems before passing to an appreciation of their unique features in terms of decision-taking and adaptability. Only in the light of this survey is an attempt then made to concentrate on the particular issues which a university may have to resolve and to which such longer term planning can make a contribution.

Inevitably this paper is coloured by the experiences and observations of the author when involved in two U.K. institutions that have undergone rapid growth and change at a pace previously unprecedented in the history of higher education in the United Kingdom. This experience has been shared by many universities and replicated in other higher educational institutions such as polytechnics.

Scope and Purpose

Given the changed scale and context of higher education, whatever their future scale of operations, universities and other semi-autonomous institutions each need to make their own choices as to future activities and uses of resources, whatever the negotiating frameworks through which these choices have to be implemented. The turbulence of the environment is, in no small degree, the direct result of the contribution of universities to change, both social and technical, and that turbulence, far from abating, shows every sign of compounding itself. In any

business or public organization having so long a lead-time in any change in its operations corporate planning and strategic decision taking would be axiomatic.

Furthermore, given the deeply entrenched suspicion of academics of 'academic managers' and still more of administrators a vital point is the relationship of the processes of corporate planning to the central political direction by those senior academics who constitute the inner councils of most universities. To many academics who truly inhabit ivory-towers the idea of any accountability—except to themselves—or of any corporate strategy may appear to be anathema. Yet that very attitude is a policy. What is now being challenged is whether it is a viable one for survival in the real world that universities have done so much to create.

Essence of Corporate Strategic Management

The essential features of an autonomous enterprise are its freedom to select (i) its main types of activity, (ii) its key decision-making bodies or posts and those who are to occupy them, and (iii) its broad policy or style of operation. All three interact to give each enterprise a particular 'ethos' within a wider ethos of comparable institutions which, in turn, operate within and at least partially reflect the 'culture' of society. They also interact through (ii), the key influential leader(s) and decision-taker(s) to give a 'style' of operation. The enterprise is never wholly autonomous as it has to operate within the laws and customs of a nation-state. Furthermore it may act collectively with others in the same 'industry' as with common collective bargaining and employment arrangements.

Subject to the foregoing each enterprise or institution has to adapt to a continually changing environment externally and composition or membership internally. This poses a need for different types of decision, one of which we term 'strategic'.

At the outset therefore the nature of strategic issues has

The author is Professor of Business Administration at the University of Bath.

93

to be established. The decisions required for the continued operation of enterprise or institution can be defined as operating, administrative and strategic. Operating decisions are within an existing established framework of both systems/procedures and policy objectives. They are required continually to enable the organization to continue to function. In university situations they cover admissions, examinations, the organization of teaching and research activities and the supportive activities so often described as 'administration'. The systems and procedures used stem from more fundamental decisions on the methods of resource allocation and control, the general policies on examinations and assessment of research, and the need for standard procedures for the appointment, promotion and removal of staff. These in turn are subordinate to, though closely interconnected with decisions on more fundamental policy. Such policy choices concern whether or not to seek to enter some new field of teaching and research, whether to change radically the basis of admission of students or the appointment of staff, or what balance of activities to seek to maintain.

The essence throughout is change external to the enterprise. This may be the general level of economic activity or the specific place in their life-cycles of its various products. The latter may depend on changes in population or in consumer preferences, notably as between the products not just of competing firms in one industry but of alternative products and activities.

A key question is the extent to which such changes, the origin of which is outside the control of those managing any one enterprise, can first be foreseen, second be taken into decision-taking so as to meet or offset their effects, and third used to the advantage of the enterprise and its members. Many situations arise where firms and institutions are carried along in movements which they do not fully comprehend and to which they can only react by following the trend. The distinction of the well-directed enterprise is its ability to forecast and then act in such a way that it, at least accommodates if not benefits from the changes with which it has no option but to contend.

Only in such a way can the enterprise hope to achieve any degree of independence or insulation from the adverse effects of change around it, whether by new initiatives and pursuit of opportunities or greater reserves upon which to fall back. This is not to claim that all changes are predictable in such a way as to be wholly manageable. On the contrary sudden 'discontinuities' whether in the nature or only the timing or scale of changes are not so predictable. Thus political decisions, often on a massive scale, may impart savage jolts to an otherwise evolving situation, even to the point of producing crises which then test the management process in its entirety.

But to embark on any remedial action it is essential to establish what are the strengths and weaknesses of the existing enterprise, and to select which courses of action to follow bearing in mind both the costs of dropping existing activities and of entry into new activities.

Choices here have to be evaluated before proceeding and just as there has to be an analysis of strengths and weaknesses at a moment in time so there has also to be an analysis of threats and opportunities to which the enterprise is exposed.

The starting point of the corporate strategic policy approach to the management of any enterprise is that the identification and continual up-dating of a long-term strategy is conducive to handling all forms of environmental turbulence and the evaluation of specific short-term policy decisions, and thereby to survival on terms that are consistent with the objectives of its stakeholders as interpreted by one of them, namely the top management.

For any organization having such long lead-times as a university such a review is not only essential, it is also something that the nature of the institution should facilitate if only because so much of its research is anticipating the turbulence of the world at large for a long period ahead. The lead-times for the impact of that turbulence may even be a multiple of those of the university's own internal decisions but the university has the potential to engage in speculation as to future scenarios as to its own environment. This however poses rather fundamental questions about the balance in any such review between what may be described conventionally as 'top-down' and 'bottom-up' planning, and the way in which they reflect the continuing review of objectives, responsibilities and constraints.

Relevance to Universities

At first it may be thought that none of these are university problems but a moment's reflection should dispel this. Universities have latterly shown a dramatic flexibility in a massive expansion at a speed unprecedented in university history and involving institutions of a social and managerial complexity that makes them relatively large units measured by numbers of persons involved when compared to the general run of industry or commerce. This expansion of their teaching function at the behest of society has gone ahead at a time of increasing turbulence in both patterns of student demand and employment opportunities. At the same time pressure for economy in resources and greater accountability for their deployment has coincided with a resurgence of demands for greater vocational relevance in their courses and immediate practical application of their research.

Individual universities have therefore been faced with questions of basic objectives and priorities. These have ranged from the balance of teaching and research or of undergraduate and postgraduate activities to those of growth, scale and diversity of interests. The environment within which such issues have had to be resolved has been one of increasing central direction of resources, especially for activities that are either capital-intensive or new fields of provision such as management studies. The outcome is the emergence of two levels of planning. First there is overall 'indicative' planning of higher education in general and the university sector in particular. Their former has been concerned with overall government resources to be allocated whereas the latter has sought to influence the decisions of specific institutions. Second, the pressure on resources, the long lead-times associated with so much of university activity and the need to allow for the impact of governmental economic and social policies on the operations of public sector, if not all enterprises, has created a need for strategic planning at the level of the individual institution.

While the legal basis of the university is that it is a charitable foundation in practice it depends for both capital and revenue on what governments choose to provide. It may be argued that this dependence has now proceeded to the point at which individual universities are absolved from any need for strategic planning but surely this is not so as long as there is any semblance of negotiation of targets and activities.

On the contrary for four reasons each institution has to formulate its own plans. The first is that planning is a mixture of 'top-down' planning of aggregate expenditure, both capital and current, with only a limited central planning of specific branches of activity: even here 'bottom-up' initiatives are considered whatever the suspicions that may exist as to how far allocations have been pre-empted. The second is the flexibility in the use of resources within an institution which extends beyond

the 'block grant' that it receives to the 'private' funds it may build up, notably by research and private donations, and to this then is added the third factor, namely the extent to which success in so doing enhances reputations and thereby influences favourably the next 'block' allocation. Lastly the points of initiative in both research and teaching are such as to emphasize 'bottom-up' planning, and the consequent pressures on resources the disposition of which is in the gift of the individual university.

Even the use of higher tuition fees, whether met privately or by a charge on public funds, at least enables a modified market mechanism to operate. This applies a student consumer pressure on one hand which may have no common ground with that of research funding agencies. Furthermore the complex negotiating processes for funding new developments, coupled to the turbulence in the demand for different offerings when set alongside the fixed resources in plant and specialized personnel, create a need for long term strategic capability.

Hitherto however, this has taken place against a prospect of continuing growth based on a combination of rising birth rates and/or rising demand for higher education in general. But it is now necessary to consider how currently known population trends are to be met in university planning when there is the prospect not only of a 'bulge' in potential university recruitment but then of absolute decline in the numbers coming forward (Figure 1).

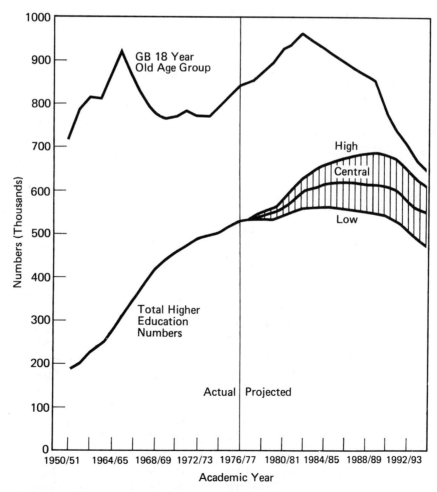

Figure 1. Student population predictions   DES discussion document

Universities as Autonomous Enterprises

At the outset there is the extent of their dependence on central government for funds and the way in which their affairs are planned or dictated by government through whatever ministry is responsible for higher education. This therefore poses very major questions of public policy on the scale, form and funding of higher education.

On the one extreme it is possible to conceive a highly centralized system in which not only the size of university provision is to be determined by government but there is an attempt to plan provision by subjects in accordance with some overall policy. Such a policy may range from one in which an attempt at manpower planning in relation to economic planning yields a 'product-mix' attuned to the vocational requirements of the state or the economy to the Robbins policy of opportunity to go to university for a given proportion of the relevant age groups with choice of study being related to 'customer preference' on the part of the students among the range offered by universities, whatever the basis of that range as internally decided within universities. Such a policy may also provide for a clear separation of the teaching and research roles of universities or it may assume that these are linked to teaching either on the centrally planned or the locally determined basis. The key constraint for all the alternatives so far enumerated is that the funds for them are wholly provided by government which can therefore determine both the scale and conditions of provision. Fluctuations in preferences, however determined, are only resolved either by differing levels of competition for places in various disciplines —where these are allowed to be restricted—or by the examining processes and study conditions that obtain where no such restriction is operative.

The opposite extreme, at least in theory, would be one where the balances of supply and demand were resolved by the price mechanism operating through a tuition fee-based financing of operations. But it would be one that, at anything approaching current costs of provision in plant and personnel, would require such a higher level of fees that unless these were largely abated by state grants and/or tax reliefs the resulting scale of university operations would be very much smaller than that currently available.

In practice almost every state regards universities as a long-term public investment in education and research. However apparently distasteful it may be to many academics, it is the trained manpower needs of society and therefore the teaching function, that it is dominant in the consideration of university funding by governments, but, especially in advanced industrial countries, their role as sources of research and advice, not least to government itself, is an important second function.

The question is then one of the extent to which individual institutions are free to determine the scale and

pattern of their activities, and in practice this is dominated by their teaching function. Such domination is not only a question of the balance as between their forms of income and especially that part which is directly related to student numbers, but also there is the problem of the terms upon which a university engages in other activities, notably research. It can be shown that, impressive as many research funds are, they all too often do not represent even the true marginal cost of the activity, being unable to 'contribute' to fixed costs that are funded from teaching or launching donations.

The outcome is that negotiation and attainment of student numbers within the constraints of a given financing arrangement becomes a key element in university strategy since so much else depends upon success in doing so. Obviously the more a university is able to attract private funds, whether for general purposes or for designated activities, the greater its freedom to determine what it wishes to do.

The initiative for such private funding and also for securing research funding is, however, divided in a way which immediately distinguishes a university from a conventional business firm. Already it appears that the latter analogy is hard to sustain; an individual university though having the turnover, manpower and capitalization of a medium-sized company is at most one of a group of such firms. But where the analogy with the company group structure breaks down is in the ability first of the individual university and then of the individuals or units within it to obtain outside funds to supplement and extend their activities. When this is coupled to the degree of independence of the tenured-academic staff member then a unique source of dispersed initiative appears which poses fascinating questions for strategic planning.

Thus, the success of an institution is seen as only partially dependent on decisions as to the allocation of centrally controlled funds. Success by a professor in a line of enquiry not only may attract funds and researchers; it sets up demands on the institution and at the same time offers possibilities of not only developing new teaching activities but of enhancing the institution's standing and thereby its ability to attract both students and funds— whether for teaching or research.

The university is therefore faced with demands for resources to launch or support activities which may be partially supported externally and with the consequences of successful initiatives. It is therefore naturally disposed to a 'bottom-up' planning sequence even before allowance is made for its 'industrial democracy'. At the same time the extent of governmental finance plus the pressures implicit in private funding, especially of the 'pump priming' variety, create external pressure points which may lead to 'top-down' planning.

At this point however, the process of government has to be brought into this review. Universities are partial industrial democracies. The most common U.K. model provides for an operational governing body, usually known as the Council, which exercises overall financial control but acts only on the advice of Senate on any matter of academic policy. Council though largely outside or 'lay' in membership has a significant minority of members appointed by Senate and usually nowadays some student representation. Only non-academic staff are not represented and their trades unions are now seeking representation. Senate, in turn, is wholly academic, with representatives of professors, other academic staff and students in that order of weighting. Any policy proposal has therefore to be brought to Senate, either from the centre by the Vice-Chancellor—direct or via a committee—or from below through School, Faculty or similar boards having academic staff membership and student participation.

Initiatives may be introduced by an individual at an accessible point or by a department/school/faculty or at the centre. These have then to be related to such basic necessities as space, funds, equipment and personnel. This is usually seen to be a function of 'central administration'. This prepares the papers required by the relevant central committee or body which proceeds to review them and make recommendations to Senate and/or Council both of the latter being usually too large, to undertake detailed examination. Among the checks that are applied at this stage, apart from physical space etc. is the relation of any proposal to long-term policy, whatever that means in the particular university.

As in a business firm, proposals may well involve competing demands for limited resources; a priority has to be established and a recommendation made to the relevant body for approval. In this there is likely to be a political bargaining process between conflicting interests but this argument has also to take place in the knowledge first of the resources available for allocation and second, of whatever longer term development on overall policy is being followed, whether explicitly or implicitly—as between the general ethos of those involved and their appreciation of the pressures and resource constraints/opportunities within which the university must work.

There has therefore to be, explicitly or implicitly, a continual monitoring of trends in finance, student numbers and preferences, space and equipment needs, internal and external initiatives and trends. This may involve one or more administrative officers and perhaps a small senior committee advisory to the Vice-Chancellor, which acts as a long-term planning/review body on a rolling programme basis.

Where it differs from a business is in the need for open debate and for approval by representative bodies in which many, if not all main interests may have membership. It is therefore more difficult to carry through particular policy decisions where these involve changes in resources or the success or failure of particular proposals for new initiatives. But it has hitherto been relatively easy to operate such processes as universities have experienced either rapid growth or intervening periods of a total freeze on developments and appointments. What is now in prospect is much more difficult.

It is at most a steady state, yet having a need to continually redistribute resources internally. Indeed, for a university having the levelling-off and contraction of the system as a future scenario the question had become one of how to be in a strong position when that levelling-off or downturn occurs. To do this it is submitted that conventional strategic planning can be of value, and can be readily adapted to a university context.

Strategic Planning in Practice

The starting point must be the type of institution a given university seeks to be or to become, in terms of (a) the balance between undergraduate teaching, postgraduate study and research, and other activities e.g. adult education; (b) the balance and emphasis among its activities, notably as between science, technology, medicine, the social sciences and the arts/humanities; and (c) the type of academic community it seeks to maintain. All these, especially the last, are partly a function of size, and the dominant element here is the undergraduate population. Whatever the origin and history of the institution, there remain critical questions of overall objectives, quite apart from the content of their offerings. At one end of the spectrum are hallowed establishments enjoying relatively less overwhelming dependence on governmental funds and having collegiate organizations which further disperse both initiative and decision permitting diversity and innovation within a strong corporate ethos. At the other extreme are the many new foundations having diverse origins, and each seeking to attain a distinctive place in the total system.

Each has therefore to assess its position not only overall but in terms of its respective offerings. Thus its undergraduate courses have to be viewed in relation both to overall demand for the types of study and the resulting level of competition for places. Given the existence of limitations on the numbers to be admitted the entry price is the average academic standard attained by those admitted. Such performance data reflect both the institution as a whole, its reputation, facilities and setting, and the popularity of its courses whether viewed for their esteem or their track record as avenues to employment! Changes in demand, both overall and by discipline, are therefore of fundamental significance to policy-makers (Figure 2).

Thus the expansion of the U.K. universities after 1950 not only increased their total capacity but did so on the assumption of a change of balance in favour of science and technology derived from a view of national need. When this capacity came 'on stream' neither the demand from students nor the take-up from industry were there to justify the full extent of the swing in places in favour of science and technology, and it was halted and even reversed. Now in 1980 there is strong evidence of a swing back, notably towards engineering, against a background of widespread concern as to the relevance to industry of so much of university output (Figure 3).

In planning and in resource allocation, potential undergraduate intakes have to be reconciled with the parallel

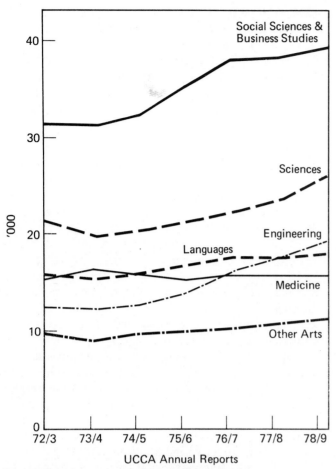

Figure 2. University applications (national)   UCCA/
University

problems in research. Given the basic tenet of the inter-dependence of teaching and research, and allowing for the consequent tendency for specific research funding not to cover the full costs of research projects, universities are faced with comparable allocation/priority problems in what they chose to underwrite. Normally whatever the initial basis for a new activity it will be seen as contributing to both research and teaching.

But both are seen as being carried on within an 'academic community' which therefore has at least three levels of 'critical mass' as understood in business terms. The first is the minimum group required to launch a particular activity, and here there is almost certainly going to be a minimum group not only within a given discipline, but for each discipline that is involved in any multi- or inter-disciplinary activity. Furthermore, the leadership of any new discipline at a given institution, calls for a professorial or at least a senior staff appointment, thereby adding to the minimum launching cost.

The second is the minimum mix of disciplines that is acceptable for such an academic community. The notion that the individual institutions have to be broadly based, covering arts, science, social science and technology, if not also medicine and professional studies such as architecture, has been largely dropped if only because of the supporting buildings, plant and library costs, at least in key areas such as medicine and law. The former requires linkage to a teaching hospital; the latter involves particularly heavy library investment and running costs.

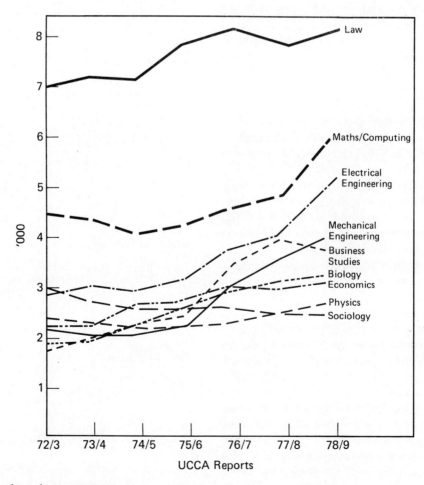

Figure 3. Demand by disciplines   UCCA

The third is the minimum size of university which is regarded as 'viable' in terms of common user facilities such as libraries and other support systems. This consideration has led to progressively larger 'minimum viable' sizes being deemed appropriate on economic grounds.

As in any other organization, ability to launch new activities is dependent, in part, on both 'organizational slack' and the opportunities for 'synergy', that is the creation of new activities by new combinations with existing resources. These are partly dependent upon previous activities.

So far, however, the argument has avoided the really hard choices that arise when growth stops or even switches into decline. First, let us consider the effect of a major decline in demand for a given teaching activity e.g. teacher training. The alternatives for a commercial undertaking would be to seek to reverse the process if it is only confined to one firm's market share by a combination of product improvement, cost and price reduction, or new marketing approaches. If the decline appears longer term and wider than just the one firm, then either new activities have to be developed and tried, or contraction must follow.

A university faced with such a situation may seek to compensate by expansion elsewhere or by new activities involving some of the now under-utilized resources; otherwise the institution as a whole has to slowly redistribute resources with periods of staff recruitment embargoes, and similar constraints. Clearly it would be preferable to avoid being caught in such a situation and this means close monitoring of trends, not only in overall numbers, but for each discipline or specialization. This should also involve close attention to the pressure on available places with entrance standards acting as a pricing mechanism.

Performance on a comparative basis—a form of inter-firm comparison—may also be helpful in establishing the strength of demand for a particular discipline at a given university. The discipline and the institution are interactive here; individual disciplines may acquire a strong reputation which reflects on the institution as a whole. The location, facilities and conduct of the institution are, in turn, factors which can favour or hinder recruitment. The term 'conduct' here refers to the general 'style' of the institution, including its reputation in 'student conflict' terms.

This leads to a major phase in strategic planning, namely strengths and weaknesses analysis. This involves identifying activities/departments that are strong, as reflected in student and research support as opposed to those that are weak in one or both respects. Furthermore, it then requires acceptance of a deliberate switch of resources by an institution within whose governmental processes political power may not reflect activity-based power! This may lead to glaring anomalies as key posts in 'low demand' subjects go on being filled, whole 'high demand' activities are either held back or under-resourced. 'Natural wastage' may be a humane basis of redeploy-

ment of resources, but it may be so long drawn-out as to restrict severely the progress that can be made.

The university that wants to assess the alternatives in an increasingly turbulent future needs to:

(i) consider the internal and external evidence and predictions of likely trends in both total and specific (sector or discipline) environments for at least 10 years ahead;

(ii) review and evaluate its own total and sector performance over recent years, and the immediate indicators for 2–4 years ahead;

(iii) prepare from the records available a forecast of resources available, notably manpower, including prospective natural wastage (retirement etc.);

(iv) seek and review proposals for developments that are anticipated up to 5 years ahead.

From these two analyses can then be made, one of current strengths and weaknesses, the other of prospective threats and opportunities. A forecast can then be made of gaps that may arise as well as of resources that become redeployable. Against this background, alternative courses of action can then be evaluated, whether they arise centrally or from initiatives dispersed across the university.

In assessing strengths and weaknesses it is necessary to identify those activities which are likely to develop not only on the basis of current or prospective demand already evident, but in terms of new areas or branches of study where research already gives indications of future applications. Whereas many long-established disciplines may show little change over time, many more, especially in science, technology and social science are often radically different in content and approach from even a decade ago. This continually evolving 'product' is not wholly contained within an evolutionary process. Periodically sharp changes of emphasis and of resource requirements call for substantial capital investment. The revolution in computer use and provision is an obvious example and the emergence of highly sophisticated and expensive equipment, such as electron microscopes, is another. Capital investment budgeting, as in business, has to be related to overall policy and the recognition of areas of strength in research and teaching.

The corollary is the recognition that there may be areas of weakness. The question is then as to its nature. If it is performance weakness in an otherwise sufficiently demanded activity then remedial action may be required having resource implications. If it is a case of static or declining demand then resources may not be renewed and the activity contracted, even abandoned altogether. This is likely to be fiercely resisted by those directly involved; yet there may be a case for 'restructuring' by combining the activity concerned with a similar one in an adjacent institution.

Here, as elsewhere in the planning process, at least three ingredients are necessary. The assessment of measurable trends and of academic strengths/weaknesses has to be related to resources available or to be sought. It is neither a purely administrative nor a solely academic appraisal, but a combination of both to which the third additional ingredient is a view of opportunities, whether arising from existing developments within the institution or foreseen externally.

In both situations, internal and external, a fundamental necessity is the fullest possible dissemination of information. Internally this means going behind the annual report with its list of publications that have at last won through the delays of academic publishing to the ideas as to future prospects, over several planning horizons, that those in each discipline currently project as having implications for the nature and scale of their future activities. Externally it means combining a similar type of exercise for each major sector of activities with a totally different appreciation of likely political, economic and social pressures that might have a bearing on the university's fortunes, if not in isolation then within the total tertiary system.

A university ought to be better placed than almost any other institution to engage in, and profit by, such wide-ranging speculation. The question is one of whether and how this can be achieved, given systems of organization and government which appear better designed to maintain a status quo than provide for dynamic renewal. Yet the very anarchy which sometimes appears to be the state of university government could be one way of ensuring some form of dynamism, at least among those who 'can do their own thing'. However, the sheer scale of operations, the rising costs of support facilities and the capital intensive nature of more activities, compel us to develop alternative resolution of our problems.

Taking a view of the types of forward strategy that may then result, it is possible to identify at least four policy decisions:

(a) The degree of concentration/diversification of activities within one university.

(b) Possible new groupings/joint ventures within a given university.

(c) Restructuring with joint activities with another institution or transfer to or from it to achieve a single viable unit.

(d) More fundamental longer term changes to replace declining conventional undergraduate numbers by 'continuing education' of adults, a major change of policy having extensive implications for the character of, as well as the methods used in, university teaching.

The planning horizon for such a review as that just described is likely to be not less than 3, more likely 5 years ahead, with notional perspectives beyond that time where considered significant. Such a planning horizon is clearly related to that of the funding of the university system; one current U.K. problem is the difficulty of regaining the old quinquennial basis of planning, following a bout of annual planning in which allocations only become finally well known into the year to which they applied!

The academic plan, so arrived at, has to be set in the context of physical resources—buildings, plant—and manpower—both academic and non-academic. The collation of data on most of these is an administrator's task, but the policies to be pursued in relation to each have to involve both academics and administrators. In parallel there has to be a continual monitoring of the disposition of resources and at some point, usually the Vice-Chancellor or Director, with an Advisory or Deans' Committee; the academic development plan, the physical development plan in terms of buildings and facilities, the equipment programme and manpower plan, have to be brought together. It is the task of the Vice-Chancellor, from time to time, assisted by or through such a steering committee of Senate both to propose the overall policy, and then to secure confirmation from council through its Finance and General Purposes Committee. It is then possible for proposals, as they arise, to be examined, not only in terms of resource implications, but against the academic development policy which should be monitored regularly, with more extensive reviews not less than every 2 or 3 years.

The process so far described, therefore, involves both academics and administrators. The academics involved, act in two roles; a few act as members of the planning committee, but many more are involved in consultations with it and the reports that are produced are for debate at Senate. Ideally, however, such a review process is needed from time to time in each main unit of the institution. Fortunately, in the U.K. the combination of quinquennial visits to each university both by the UGC and by its subject committees, and parallel visits by the research councils, ensure that such reviews occur besides performing a valuable 'learning' function by comparison and discussion with colleagues and peers in the system as a whole.

At 'top-level', the 'top-down' planning may indicate broad sectors of potential development or disengagement. It may, in some situations, propose quite specific developments, but, in the main, it is likely to rely on those internal initiatives that combine promise in academic terms and compatability with overall policy objectives. There is therefore a heavy reliance on 'bottom-up' initiatives amongst which a selection is then made. For such initiatives to occur in the first place, and for them to arise in preferred forms or directions, then becomes a matter of influence and incentive.

As for incentives, those that are the most likely to be effective are concerned with resource allocation. Once it becomes evident from the fate of internal applications for funds 'which way the wind is blowing', future applications and operational decisions begin to reflect the policy being pursued. Whether the source of change—as of funds—is internal or external, the enterprising and innovative members of the academic staff may be expected to react surprisingly strongly.

Such an outcome is easier to achieve where external and internal pressures are in line with each other. If, however, a university seeks to adhere to an internally set policy to favour sections which find difficulty in securing external support, while freezing those who are in a strong external support situation, then it must (a) recognize the strategic significance of what is being pursued, and (b) have to cope with continual pressure for a change of policy from those who it is deliberately restraining. This is a common problem where new developments grow rapidly, but there is resistance to them by the 'established' disciplines, especially where the latter are 'politically' powerful through representation on committees and Senate.

In short, there is a strong internal political dimension to the integrated use of the central committees and decision processes. This may find expression in the emergence of *ad hoc* decision-making bodies which 'pre-plan' the proposals and data with which the formal bodies are then presented. The difficulty of handling detailed resource allocation decisions in large 'legislative' bodies forces their reference to smaller 'inner councils'. The test is then in the compatability of policies across these.

A 'co-ordinated' approach involving the Head of the institution, a slowly changing core group of senior academics and the senior administrators, is consistent with the encouragement of initiative of a wide range of individual academics without whose independence of specialized insight and search the options open for overall development would be very much poorer. Indeed, the sense that those at the centre have a grip on affairs and a willingness to support innovation is a self-reinforcing factor.

Conclusions

The implications for future university development confirm neither the pessimistic view of planning represented by 'muddling through' nor the over-optimistic centralized planning dreams of a later wave of enthusiasts. Rather they challenge those in leading roles in universities by suggesting that the strategically adaptable 'environment oriented organization' of the future should display many of the characteristics which university staffs might regard as applicable to their activities. Thus the 'culture' of the university might be 'exploring/creative', its power structure seen as 'decentralized' and the main sources of constraint as being external, usually with those who hold the purse-strings. But is this a true reflection, and would they also accept 'strong strategic' management, whether centralized or dispersed?

The first implication is that there has to be a long-term policy review body concerned with academic development, and that the academics must make the dominant contribution to this. Side by side is the resource planning aspect and here the administrators have a major part to play, but not an exclusive one. Such resource planning has to be comprehensive and anticipatory.

The second is that universities already demonstrate, if more by accident than design, the need for a longer term appraisal of their own activities, yielding a planning process which is often of far greater value than any single plan. It becomes an attitude of mind shared in the organization, and providing a means for reconciling and optimizing the diversities of strengths and interests of academics in the interests of the institution and the community it serves.

The third is the need to develop and sustain these processes at several levels in the institution, and thereby involve staff and students in discussions on future developments in its work. The question here is how far this is done at departmental, school or other unit level. If there is to be 'organizational' development then one feature is fuller discussion of all aspects, academic and resources, at lower levels in order to achieve greater understanding, and indirectly, promote initiatives.

Lastly, the external environment has not only to be monitored but influenced by advice and continual interaction given the negotiated corporate state into which we have all drifted, whether we like or are aware of the fact.

To deny a practical significance to strategic institutional planning is to invite our own destruction as environment oriented organizations of value to our societies through our collective individual independence of exploration, instruction and advice.

Participative Planning for a Public Service

Timothy Grewe, James Marshall and Daniel E. O'Toole

This article aims to provide managers in public administration with information about strategic planning as a tool for promoting adaptation in a changing environment. The authors' collective experience with strategic planning in the public sector includes facilitating creation of strategic plans for state and local government and non-profit agencies, and their experience has provided the data on which the conclusions drawn are based. They believe in the participative approach to planning and that this approach has benefits for the participants which are as important as the contents of the plan.

In public administration, strategic planning continues to receive increasing attention.[1] A number of factors contribute to this growing interest. Strategic planning focuses on long-recognized crucial management concerns—the need to understand the organization's environment, examine the future, and adapt the agency accordingly. Many public managers realize that if they do not accommodate their agency to a changing environment, organizational change will be based on someone else's plan. The widespread use of strategic planning in the private sector confirms that it is both a feasible and valuable tool for promoting adaptation.

For many public organizations there is an urgent need to adapt. They face continuing fiscal stringency accompanied by unabated if not expanding service demands. Figure 1 depicts the impact of this condition on a public agency. The organization's inability to maintain its revenue base creates greater pressure for increased productivity and reinforces the need to reconsider agency goal(s) and to discern how to accommodate it to this environment. Strategic planning promotes examination of both the fit between agency goals and the environment and potential improvements. In addition, the tool can be used to foster a participative consideration of these areas. The Japanese experience demonstrates

The authors are members of the Graduate Programme in Public Administration at Portland State University.

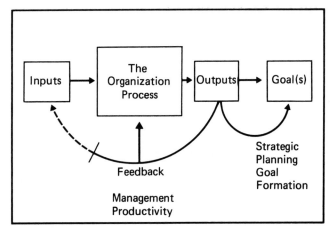

Figure 1. The impact of fiscal stringency on a public agency

the efficacy of a participative management approach, particularly in a resource scarce environment.

Public managers who look to public administration literature for information about this tool find that it does not yet include an in-depth consideration of how to *manage* a strategic planning process, particularly one that involves the participation of more than just the top managers. Only the steps in developing a strategic plan receive attention. How to accomplish the steps is not discussed.[2] Yet this concern is vital to the success of a strategic planning project. A belief in the value of participative strategic planning is not enough. It must be reflected in careful attention to the preparation, design and facilitation of the process.

This article seeks to fill this gap in the literature. The authors' collective experience with strategic planning in the public sector includes facilitating creation of strategic plans for state and local government and non-profit agencies in the Pacific Northwest as well as training managers of several state agencies in how to do strategic planning. One of these projects involved 35 participants in developing the strategic plan. This collective experience has provided us with data about managing and facilitating a strategic planning process. We believe much of this data is pertinent to managing other group process endeavours.

Preparation

Strategic planning entails the creation of a strategic plan—a long-term, co-ordinated plan for meeting goals based on explicit assumptions as well as an investigation of past, present and future conditions. The plan ranges anywhere from 3 to 10 years in length and focuses on the organization's target population, its service area, and potential technological advancements and service modifications necessary to meet the changing needs of its service clientele.

Figure 2 is an example of a strategic plan outline. It indicates the general directions the Portland (Oregon) Fire Bureau will pursue in order to attain its strategic goals by 1990 (the end of the time frame) and the year work begins on each direction. This outline is the Bureau's action agenda (in general, conceptual terms) for the future. Top management can use this outline to oversee the planning and managing of a more specific set of action plans (i.e. tactical actions) that will implement the directions.

A fully developed strategic plan contains both the strategic directions and the tactical actions. It pinpoints specific objectives and action steps to attain the organization's goals through a specified date. It identifies what is to be done, by whom, and in what order, to adjust the agency to its probable future environment(s) and attain its goals by the end of the plan's time frame. This plan can lead to the assignment of responsibilities and completion dates and to monitoring progress. Careful consideration of a number of factors prior to the start of the strategic planning process can help achieve such a plan.

PORTLAND FIRE BUREAU

1984–1985 1985–1988 1986–1987 1987–1988 1988–1989 1989–1990

1. **More** Emphasis on Emergency Medical Services
2. **More** Emphasis on Hazardous Materials
3. **More** Emphasis on Training
4. **More** Emphasis on Resource Management
5. **More** Emphasis on Prevention
6. **More** Emphasis on Interagency Coordination of Emergency Service Delivery Systems
7. **More** Emphasis on Alternative Financing
8. **More** Emphasis on Public Relations
9. **More** Emphasis on Minority Recruitment
10. **More** Emphasis on Strategic and Other Planning
11. **More** Emphasis on Public Education
12. **More** Emphasis on Legal Affairs
13. **More** Emphasis on Productivity
14. **More** Emphasis on Technological Advances
15. **Same** Emphasis on Fire Suppression
16. **Same** Emphasis on Planning for Annexation and/or Consolidation
17. **Same** Emphasis on Public Services: Non-emergency
18. **Same** Emphasis on Labour–Management Relations
19. **Same** Emphasis on Bureau Re-organization
20. **Same** Emphasis on Decision-making
21. **New** Activity: Leadership Role in Regional Disaster Planning and Emergency Services
22. **New** Activity: Exercise of Political Influence
23. **New** Activity: Establish Critical Staffing Levels

Figure 2. Strategic plan for 1990

The Facilitator's Role

We have found that the complexity of participative strategic planning warrants the involvement of a facilitator who is knowledgeable about strategic planning and skilful in fostering group processes. Establishment and clarification of the facilitator's role is an important initial step. While we consider the various facets of this role throughout this article, some comments about its general features are pertinent here.

The facilitator plays a key part in preparing for as well as managing the strategic planning process. In the preparation phase this role includes ensuring that top management understands strategic planning and the implications of its use and helping devise a design for the process of developing the strategic plan. During the strategic planning process the facilitator's responsibility centres on implementing the design and managing the process participants to go through to create *their* plan. The facilitator does not participate in specifying the plan's contents and must resist the impulse to do so and sometimes, the pressure from participants to 'give us the plan'. This approach and participant perception of the facilitator as a 'neutral' concerning the project, i.e. viewed as not having an agenda regarding the outcome, promote their involvement in the process and focus on the task and their ownership of the final product.

Top Management Risk

Top management needs to be aware at the beginning that strategic planning is a risk for the organization and its management. The participants in the process and others in the organization assume that its final product will lead to action. This action involves top management pursuit of the directions indicated by the strategic planning process. Hence, this tool's viability depends upon top management's willingness and ability to risk acting on the basis of the plan. Strategic planning should not be under-taken without top management's recognition and acceptance of this risk.

Another initial issue top management faces concerns the potential threat strategic planning poses for participants' jobs. Participants may be less open and honest about sensing the environment and identifying appropriate organizational adaptations if they feel the results may jeopardize their jobs. Any steps top management can take at the beginning to enhance participant job security can help avoid the tendency to 'play safe'.

The Procedures Followed

Careful preparation includes creating an appropriate design of the process for developing the strategic plan. The major purpose of the design is to have the plan emerge logically and consistently from the process. Creation of the design involves both the facilitators and top management. The facilitators present a model of the process. The final design is the result of the modifications and fine tuning made by both parties to adapt the facilitators' model to the needs of the particular situation.

A number of model designs for developing a strategic plan are available.[3] Figure 3 depicts an overview of the model we have found useful. The specific steps the participants follow in order to move through the process are:

(1) Setting the time frame for the strategic plan (e.g. 1984–1990).
(2) Identification of the organization's *existing* mission, goals and organizational structure.
(3) Specifying the values that underlie the agency's operation (e.g. loyalty to the public and fiscal responsibility).
(4) Conducting the 'futures research' necessary to identify and consider key levers/elements in the agency's future environment (e.g. an expenditure or tax limitation).

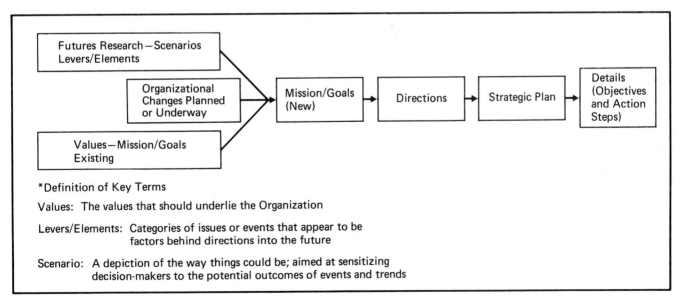

Figure 3. An overview of the strategic planning process

(5) Formulating the scenarios the agency will face at the end of the time frame.

(6) Identifying new or substantially modified goals derived from the scenarios and/or stated values.

(7) Identifying general activities/directions (current and new) needed to adjust the organization to the scenario(s) (e.g. what we need more/the same/less of).

(8) Identifying opportunities in the scenario(s) the agency can use to achieve its mission and goals.

(9) Identifying problems in the scenarios the agency must manage, avoid, and/or solve.

(10) Noting any proposed efforts to change elements in the scenarios.

(11) Listing specific actions derived from this analysis. Decide on the basis of steps 7–10 the organization's specific future activities.

(12) Sequence the proposed activities during the time frame of the strategic plan.

The Time Span

Completion of the strategic planning process requires approximately 4 to 6 full-day sessions. The variance in the number of sessions needed is due to the nature of the group developing the plan (size and cohesiveness) and the amount of detail desired in the final product. The actual time span can vary considerably. Among the possible arrangements for these sessions are:

☆ A short period—completion of the plan within 1–2 weeks.

☆ A medium period—plan completion within 1–2 months. Sessions are about 1 week apart.

☆ A long period—completion of the plan requires at least 4 months. Sessions are approximately 1 month apart.

We prefer the medium period. It allows enough time to obtain additional data for futures research; affords participants time to digest what is going on and share their experience with and receive input from other organization members; and still avoids problems that may arise with a long period (participants forgetting and losing interest). Also the plan is ready in a reasonable amount of time.

Selection and Preparation of Participants

Participant selection is a key element of preparing for the strategic planning process. It gives top management an opportunity to develop a participative approach toward environmental sensing and organizational adaptation. Use of such an approach enhances the acceptability of both the tool and its final product in the organization. If only top management participates, then others may view strategic planning as a control device.

One participation issue concerns the role of the top manager. The most appropriate role for the top manager may not always include active involvement in developing the plan. In one strategic planning process the top manager did not directly participate because he believed it would impede others from freely participating. However, he did play an essential role throughout the process—a strong advocate and active supporter of strategic planning.

We try to prepare participants so that they are ready to work when the first session begins. This preparation entails providing them with the following prior to the first session:

☆ A communication from the top manager that notes their selection as a participant and the significance of the strategic planning process and its final product;

☆ A project schedule that contains session dates and activities;

☆ A brief description and overview of the strategic planning process, including definitions of key terms and a flow chart of the steps involved; and

☆ An article that describes the process.[4]

However, undue burdens or disincentives on participants should be avoided. Participants may feel punished if too much preparation is required outside the sessions.

Location and Materials

Two prominent features of our strategic planning processes are participant interaction in various types and sizes of groups and the use of graphics to depict information pertaining to the process and to record and illustrate the participants' tentative and final products. The group processes we use receive attention in a later section of this article. The use of graphics helps in communication and results in a faster decision-making process.[5] Other studies of the use of graphics support our findings.[6]

Both features influence the type of physical setting that is appropriate for a strategic planning process. Moveable chairs and tables permit various group configurations. Blank wall space allows the posting of charts. The graphics approach also requires chart paper, 5 × 8 in. cards, marking pens, and masking tape. The importance of the physical setting and materials and supplies is more evident when they are not suitable.

Data Base for 'Futures Research'

During the preparation phase the facilitators must develop a set of relevant information participants will use early in the strategic planning process as a basis for doing 'futures research'. This data base is an important ingredient. The scenarios and the eventual plan emerge from the data. It is essential for testing participants' assumptions and possible predetermined scenarios.

The creation of an appropriate data base can be

difficult. At this point all the data needs may not be evident. One virtue of doing strategic planning is that the process will indicate the kinds of information the organization should collect and analyse. Part of the plan's final product is an identification of key data needs. Even if facilitators know what information is necessary, it may not be available.

The participative approach helps with these problems. The inclusion of the 'experts' in the process means that the participants already possess some of the relevant data. Hence, there is less call for voluminous information. The facilitators can be more selective in developing the data base. The participants can also help determine data needs. During the 'futures research' step they may want additional data. The facilitators and planning specialists in the organization can try to obtain information for the participants if there is sufficient time between sessions.

The First Session

The first session sets the tone for the entire strategic planning process. Hence, a principal goal for this session is to start the process well. This involves taking a few initial steps that will launch the process in the right direction and help keep it on track until its completion.

An introduction by the top manager is the first step. The top manager's stated support for strategic planning, and commitment to use the final product reinforces the earlier letter sent to the participants and emphasizes the project's importance. The facilitators follow with an overview of the strategic planning process and a discussion of the project's goals. This procedure enables the participants to check and clarify the impressions of strategic planning and the task they obtained from the preparatory material.

The final initial step consists of setting ground rules for participant behaviour during the strategic planning process. These rules are intended as a pre-emptive strike to limit potential disruption. They help manage behaviour by establishing at the beginning what is appropriate and inappropriate. They also strengthen the desire of the majority of the group to get the job done.

A collaborative process involving the facilitators and the participants produces the rules. The participants reach a consensus on a final set after considering the facilitators' suggested rules. Figure 4 contains the rules adopted for a recent strategic planning project. Among other considerations are attendance, interruptions and smoking. The collaborative approach to setting the rules expedites their use during the process. Participants pick them up. For instance, during one project they posted a sign on the door leading out of our meeting room that read,

- Be Serious About the Task—Emphasize "Task" and "Maintenance" (process) behaviour and avoid "Self-oriented" behaviour.

- Avoid Competition for "Air Time"—Speaking for the sake of being noticed.

- Avoid Other Agendas—Such as setting your social calendar.

- Maintain a Low-risk Climate or Environment

- Play Appropriate Roles

Figure 4. Session rules for a strategic planning project

'Now leaving low-risk environment'. Participants engage in self-policing behaviour by telling members when they are violating a rule. This behaviour indicates that facilitators and participants share responsibility for rule enforcement.

Development of the Plan

Management of the strategic planning process to maximize the effective use of participants' time is a key aspect of a successful project. It helps participant involvement and interest in the process and reduces the time and cost needed for project completion. Both factors promote a positive attitude toward the tool and its continued use.

Some features of the process design and preparation discussed earlier facilitate the plan's creation. For instance, the presence of the overview of the strategic planning process (Figure 3) and the accompanying steps on a wall give participants a general sense of direction (an overall framework) and the discrete and more manageable segments of this large, complex task. This enhances the perceived feasibility of the project by providing a clear agenda and desired outcome for each segment of the process.

This example also suggests the value of graphics for managing the process. Charts and movable cards play an important role in the application of a number of tools.[7] In strategic planning we use charts to depict information pertaining to the process and charts and movable cards to record and illustrate the participants' tentative and final products. The flexibility of the movable cards expedites the identification of levers and elements (one element per card) and the selection of the most important ones. They are also useful for developing relationships between components of the plan over time (i.e. constructing a time line that displays scheduled activities). The cards and charts focus participants' attention on the task at hand and how it fits into the overall process. They also help document the process and confirm what participants have already accomplished. The plan is the sum of the products created during the process.

The contribution of the overall process design and graphics to managing the strategic planning process is substantial but insufficient by itself to secure an optimal final product. Accomplishment of each step in the process requires the facilitators' constant attention. They must be prepared to deal with attitudes and behaviours that inhibit development of a strategic plan. The rules mentioned earlier help. Nevertheless, a participant may still attempt to disrupt the process, particularly at the end (e.g. 'Why are we doing this?'). Other pitfalls that may appear include consideration of only the status quo, avoidance of tough issues, unfounded assumptions, predetermined scenarios and hidden agendas. Anticipation of these problems and dealing with them quickly and firmly, often by referring to the overall process design and the accompanying instructions and rules, usually removes them. We have found that peer pressure in favour of the process usually nips such problems in the bud.

The facilitators must continuously attend to the process for developing the strategic plan, for it is always idiosyncratic and evolutionary in nature. Each application is unique. A process 'formula' does not work equally well for all situations. This is due, at least in part, to the nature of the group working on the plan. For instance, large groups (at least 20 participants) require a more complex process to achieve participatory decisions on each segment of the plan. Groups often differ in their members' experience and effectiveness in group problem-solving. Less experienced groups generally need more help and structure. The facilitators must also respond to particular concerns of the group. For example, during one recent project some participants became worried that the final product could end up in the 'wrong hands' and be used against their organization. The facilitators took care in working on this concern with the participants. The group's adoption of the facilitators' suggestion to stamp 'DRAFT—NOT FOR CITATION' on each page of the final product alleviated their apprehension. The participants viewed the stamp as reinforcing the idea that their plan is for the agency's internal use and is dynamic.

These factors suggest that the group process for each step emerges as the process continues. While planning for the process before it begins is important, facilitators must also be prepared to adjust and change their initial plan as their knowledge about the task, the situation and the participants increases (e.g. the number of scenarios required?). Especially with large groups, the facilitators create some of the processes as the project unfolds. These aspects of implementing the plan also indicate why having two facilitators for the process is helpful. The use of two facilitators increases the attention paid to diagnosing the situation. Development of the

process as it unfolds benefits from their shared diagnosis and resulting collaboration on an appropriate design for completing each part of the plan.

The importance of diagnosing the situation and integrating the findings into the structure of the process as it unfolds is a key to effectively managing the idiosyncratic and evolutionary nature of developing a strategic plan. The facilitators' task here is to devise and implement an optimal group arrangement that fosters completion of each step in the overall process. Two considerations guide these decisions: The nature of the step and the desire for an effective participatory process. The group arrangement must promote accomplishment of the task *through* participation. This approach reflects a belief that participation is a 'good' in itself as well as leading to better decisions and outcomes. It requires the facilitators to find ways to foster, structure and manage effective participation. They must continuously structure and channel participation to avoid boredom, meaningless tasks, cliques and the continuation of unproductive small groups; promote the exchange of ideas and perspectives; and stay on target. Consequently, the facilitators are constantly reconstituting groups during the strategic planning process.

Group Processes
The frequent reformulation of groups involves the use of various group process arrangements and configurations. Two examples of these arrangements and their specific applications to steps in developing a strategic plan are below:

Example 1: The intramural exercise. Figure 5 depicts the structure of an exercise we have found useful for formulating a group composite view of the values that underlie their agency's operation. The facilitators provide an example of a 'Values' list (one produced by a different organization) and instruct the participants to individually prepare their own lists. The process consists of developing a single list of 'Values' in successively larger groups. For the project that contained 35 participants the procedure moved from individual lists to a list for each group of three then to one for each group of eight or nine

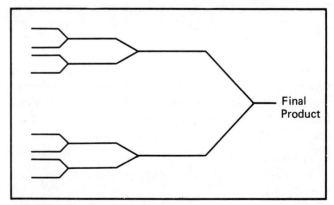

Figure 5. Formulating a group view of values in successively larger groups

and finally to a composite list composed by a task force of representatives from each of the four larger groups. The task force presented the list to the entire group for their adoption.

Example 2: Futures research. Categories of issues or events (levers) provide the structure for performing 'futures research'. Participants receive a list of these levers (social, technological, environmental, political, economic and agency resources) and examples of the issues and events (elements) each one contains.[8] Each lever becomes the focus of one small group, whose membership is determined on the basis of interest and expertise. Each small group identifies elements of the lever that pertain to the agency's environment and selects and further details each *key* element on a 5 × 8 in. card (i.e. whether and how the element will change and its impact on the agency). A chart for each lever that contains the finished cards for the selected elements in that category is posted on the wall. An ensuing plenary session that includes a report by each small group of its findings and a review of the list by other participants for questions and possible changes or additions to it, completes the 'futures research' step.

The participative approach can alter the roles of the facilitators and the participants during the strategic planning process. Participants may at some point begin to take interest in process concerns (i.e. how various tasks should be accomplished). This development often occurs when the process 'jells' and becomes more 'theirs'. Facilitators must be prepared for this possibility and encourage it by moving to a more collaborative approach with participants regarding the process. This feature of the participative approach reflects the facilitators' interest in promoting growth in group problem-solving capabilities as well as task completion.

The Final Product

The approach discussed in this article produces a strategic plan by the end of the final session. There is little 'lag' time between the final session and when the plan is available. The charts that display the final products of the participants' work constitute the plan. Figure 2 is an example. The transfer of the plan from the charts to a publishable form and its subsequent dissemination to the participants and others requires only a short time.

The strategic plan's value is not limited to helping the organization adapt to a changing environment. Among other potential benefits a strategic plan offers are:

☆ A plan to head off someone else's plan that may be imposed on the organization from the outside;

☆ Assistance for overcoming some problems that often accompany management turnover; and

☆ A guide for restructuring the agency, making budget decisions, choosing personnel, deploying capital improvements, etc.

However, the availability of a plan does not mean it will be used.

Others have noted the difficulty of implementing strategic plans.[9] Among the problems that often impede effective execution of a plan are limited integration of it into other agency decision processes, lack of staff commitment, an ineffective monitoring system, and a tendency to view the plan as an immutable strategy. We have found the following helpful in overcoming these problems and facilitating implementation:

☆ Disseminate the final product to the participants and others as soon as possible. This step is an important part of the participative approach. It fosters participant advocacy for the plan and its execution, thus increasing the impetus for implementing the plan.

☆ A statement by the agency's top person shortly after completion of the process that acknowledges creation of the plan, details how its implementation will occur, and assigns responsibility for its implementation to a co-ordinator. This statement should confirm top management's commitment to the plan and its implementation.

☆ Present the plan to the agency's governing body. This step should increase commitment to its implementation.

☆ Integrate the strategic plan into the organization's annual budget preparation process. It increases the likelihood that the plan is a major part of the 'data' upon which decisions are made.

☆ Design the final product to be the basis for monitoring progress on achieving the objectives of the plan.

☆ Have the agency institute an annual review and update of its strategic plan. This procedure insures the plan's continued utility and emphasizes that it is always subject to change if the assumptions underlying it change significantly.

Strategic Thinking

Our experience with strategic planning in public organizations has yielded a number of insights. First, strategic planning underscores the importance of the conceptual skill area for managers. This skill area focuses on a manager's, 'ability to understand the complexities of the overall organization and where one's own operation fits into the organization'.[10] The need to think conceptually; to see things from different perspectives; and the ability to consider beyond the status quo (i.e. what the organization currently does and the way it is done) are components of this area. They are essential for adapting the organization to a dynamic environment. Everyday management concerns and problems can drive out conceptual thinking. Strategic planning provides a forum for it and helps to cultivate 'strategic thinking' in the organization's line managers.

We have found that some characteristics of public organizations present particular concerns or issues for the application of strategic planning. For instance, their 'publicness' raises the consideration of who should participate in developing the plan (e.g. the role of the public?). This characteristic also affects the final product. Issuing the plan probably makes it public information. This factor can benefit strategic planning efforts by promoting public input to the plan and accountability for its results, adding impetus to its implementation, and fostering its use by an agency as a marketing tool. However, it also increases the possibility that the plan can end up in the 'wrong hands' and be used against the agency. As we noted earlier, some participants in one process became worried about this possibility. Use of the stamp 'DRAFT—NOT FOR CITATION' on each page of the final product helped alleviate this concern. Finally, the vagueness and/or difficulty of quantifying goals for many public organizations requires the strategic planning process to spend more time on this area. This characteristic indicates why examining existing organizational goals is an important step.

The participative approach highlights the significance of the process dimension of strategic planning. It reflects Marshall McLuhan's idea that 'the medium is the message'.[11] Participation in the process may be at least as important as the contents of the plan. It promotes the following among participants:

☆ *A common vision of the future and its implications for the organization, including any necessary changes.* Especially for middle managers, there may be no other opportunity to participate in this type of discussion during the year.

☆ *More effective group problem-solving skills.* These skills carry over to other decision making situations as well as to future strategic planning iterations.

☆ *Recognition that continuous planning is a management necessity.*

References

(1) For example, see Douglas C. Eadie, Putting a powerful tool to practical use: the application of strategic planning in the public sector, *Public Administration Review*, **43** (5), 447–452, September/October (1983), and Barry Selberg, Strategic planning and energy management, *Public Management*, **64** (4), 6–7, April (1982).

(2) John B. Olsen and Douglas C. Eadie, *The Game Plan: Governance with Foresight*, Studies in Governance, Vol. 1, The Council of State Planning Agencies, Washington, DC (1982) is an exception. It contains a few suggestions for handling the process.

(3) For instance, see Robert E. Linneman and John D. Kennell, Shirt-sleeve approach to long range plans, *Harvard Business Review*, **55** (2), 141–150, March/April (1977) and Olsen and Eadie, *The Game Plan*.

(4) We have used Linneman and Kennell, Shirt-sleeve approach to long range plans.

(5) See James Marshall, Daniel E. O'Toole and Francis Sargant, A visual approach to training plan development, *Public Administration Review*, **43** (2), 166–175, March/April (1983).

(6) Futures Research Division, Security Pacific National Bank, *Future Scan*, No. 362, p. 3, 16 January (1984) cites a study by the Wharton Applied Research Center that found that meetings are 28% shorter when information is presented in graphic form.

(7) For example, see Cortus T. Koehler, Product planning and management technique, *Public Administration Review*, **43** (5), 459–466, September/October (1983).

(8) The levers/elements draw upon material developed by the Futures Research Division of the Security Pacific National Bank of California.

(9) For instance, see Walter Kiechel III, Corporate strategists under fire, *Fortune*, **106** (13), 34–39, 27 December (1982); Richard T. Pascale, Our curious addiction to corporate grand strategy, *Fortune*, **105** (2), 115–116, 25 January (1982); and Research spotlight, *Management Review*, **72** (6), 55–56, June (1983).

(10) Paul Hersey and Kenneth H. Blanchard, *Management of Organizational Behavior: Utilizing Human Resources*, p. 5, 4th edn, Prentice-Hall, Englewood Cliffs, NJ (1982).

(11) See Marshall McLuhan, *Understanding Media: The Extensions of Man*, McGraw-Hill, New York (1964).

A Strategic Planning Process for Public and Non-profit Organizations

John M. Bryson

A pragmatic approach to strategic planning is presented for use by public and non-profit organizations. Benefits of the process are outlined and two examples of its application are presented—one involving a city government and the other a public health nursing service. Requirements for strategic planning success are discussed. Several conclusions are drawn, namely that: (1) strategic planning is likely to become part of the repertoire of public and non-profit planners; (2) planners must be very careful how they apply strategic planning to specific situations; (3) it makes sense to think of decision makers as strategic planners and strategic planners as facilitators of decision making across levels and functions; and (4) there are a number of theoretical and practical issues that still need to be explored.

I skate to where I think the puck will be.
                                        Wayne Gretzky

Men, I want you to stand and fight vigorously and then run. And as I am a little bit lame, I'm going to start running now.
                                    General George Stedman
                                    U.S. Army in the Civil War

Not all of the readers of *Long Range Planning* may be familiar with either Wayne Gretzky or George Stedman, but their two quotes capture the essence of strategic planning (often called corporate planning in Britain). Wayne Gretzky is perhaps the world's greatest offensive player in professional ice hockey. He holds the single-season scoring record for players in the National Hockey League—by such a wide margin that many consider him the greatest offensive player of all time. His quote emphasizes that *strategic thinking and acting,* not strategic planning *per se,* are most important. He does not skate around with a thick strategic plan in his back pocket. What

he does is to think and act strategically every minute of the game, in keeping with a simple game plan worked out with his coaches and key teammates in advance.

Let us explore Gretzky's statement further. What must one know and be able to do in order to make—and act on—a comment like Gretsky's? One obviously needs to know the purpose and rules of the game, the strengths and weakneses of one's own team, the opportunities and threats posed by the other team, the game plan, the arena, the officials, and so on. One also needs to be a well-equipped, superbly conditioned, strong and able hockey player—and it does not hurt to play for a very good team. In other words, anyone who can assert confidently that he or she 'skates to where the puck will be' knows basically everything there is to know about strategic thinking and acting in hockey games.

Wayne Gretzky is respected primarily for his extraordinary offensive scoring ability. But defensive abilities obviously are important, too. Whereas Gretzky is a great offensive strategist, General George Stedman of the U.S. Army in the Civil War was an experienced defensive strategist. At one point he and his men were badly outnumbered by Confederate soldiers. A hasty retreat was in order, but it made sense to give the lame and wounded —and the General, too!—a chance to put some distance between themselves and the enemy before a full-scale retreat was called. The General and his men then would be in a position to fight another day.

Stedman had no thick strategic plan in his back pocket, either. At most he probably had a general battle plan worked out with his fellow officers and recorded in pencil on a map. Again, strategic

John M. Bryson is Associate Professor of Planning and Public Affairs in the Hubert H. Humphrey Institute of Public Affairs and Associate Director of the Strategic Management Research Center at the University of Minnesota, MN 55455, U.S.A.

thinking and acting were what mattered, not any particular planning process.

How does this relate to public and non-profit organizations today? The answer is that strategic thought and action are increasingly important to the continued viability and effectiveness of governments, public agencies and non-profit organizations of all sorts. Without strategic planning it is unlikely that these organizations will be able to meet successfully the numerous challenges that face them.

The environments of public and non-profit organizations have changed dramatically in the last 10 years—as a result of oil crises, demographic shifts, changing values, taxing limits, privatization, centralization or decentralization of responsibilities, moves toward information and service-based economies, volatile macroeconomic performance, and so on. As a result, traditional sources of revenue for most governments are stable at best or highly unpredictable or declining at worst. Further, while the public may be against higher taxes, and while transfers of money from central to local governments are typically stable or declining, the public continues to demand a high level of government services. Non-profit organizations often are called on to take up the slack in the system left by the departure of public organizations or services, but may be hard-pressed to do so.

To cope with these various pressures, public and non-profit organizations must do at least three things. First, these organizations need to exercise as much discretion as they can in the areas under their control to ensure responsiveness to their stakeholders. Second, these organizations need to develop good strategies to deal with their changed circumstances. And third, they need to develop a coherent and defensible basis for decision making.

What is Strategic Planning?

Strategic planning is designed to help public and non-profit organizations (and communities) respond effectively to their new situations. It is *a disciplined effort to produce fundamental decisions and actions shaping the nature and direction of an organization's (or other entity's) activities within legal bounds.*[1] These decisions typically concern the organization's mandates, mission and product or service level and mix, cost, financing, management or organizational design. (Strategic planning was designed originally for use by *organizations*. In this article we will concentrate on its applicability to public and non-profit organizations. Strategic planning of course can be, and has been, applied to projects, functions —such as transportation, health care or education —and communities.)

What does strategic planning look like? Its most basic formal requirement is a series of discussions and decisions among key decision makers and managers about what is *truly* important for the organization. And those discussions are the *big* innovation that strategic planning brings to most organizations, because in most organizations key decision makers and managers from different levels and functions almost *never* get together to talk about what is truly important. They may come together periodically at staff meetings, but usually to discuss nothing more important than, for example, alternatives to the organization's sick leave policy. Or they may attend the same social functions, but there, too, it is rare to have sustained discussions of organizationally relevant topics.

Usually key decision makers need a reasonably structured process to help them identify and resolve the most important issues their organizations face. One such process that has proved effective in practice is outlined in Figure 1. The process consists of the following eight steps:

1. *Development of an initial agreement concerning the strategic planning effort.* The agreement should cover: the purpose of the effort; preferred steps in the process; the form and timing of reports; the role, functions and membership of a strategic planning coordinating committee; the role, functions and membership of the strategic planning team; and commitment of necessary resource to proceed with the effort.

2. *Identification and clarification of mandates.* The purpose of this step is to identify and clarify the externally imposed formal and informal mandates placed on the organization. These are the *musts* confronting the organization. For most public and non-profit organizations these mandates will be contained legislation, articles of incorporation or charters, regulations, and so on. Unless mandates are identified and clarified two difficulties are likely to arise: the mandates are unlikely to be met, and the organization is unlikely to know what pursuits are allowed and not allowed.

3. *Development and clarification of mission and values.* The third step is the development and clarification of the organization's mission and values. An organization's mission—in tandem with its mandates—provides its *raison d'être*, the social justification for its existence.

Prior to development of a mission statement, an organization should complete a stakeholder analysis. A *stakeholder* is defined as any person, group or organization that can place a claim on an organization's attention, resources or output, or is affected by that output. Examples of a government's stakeholders are citizens, taxpayers, service recipients, the governing body, employees, unions, interest groups, political parties, the financial community and other governments.

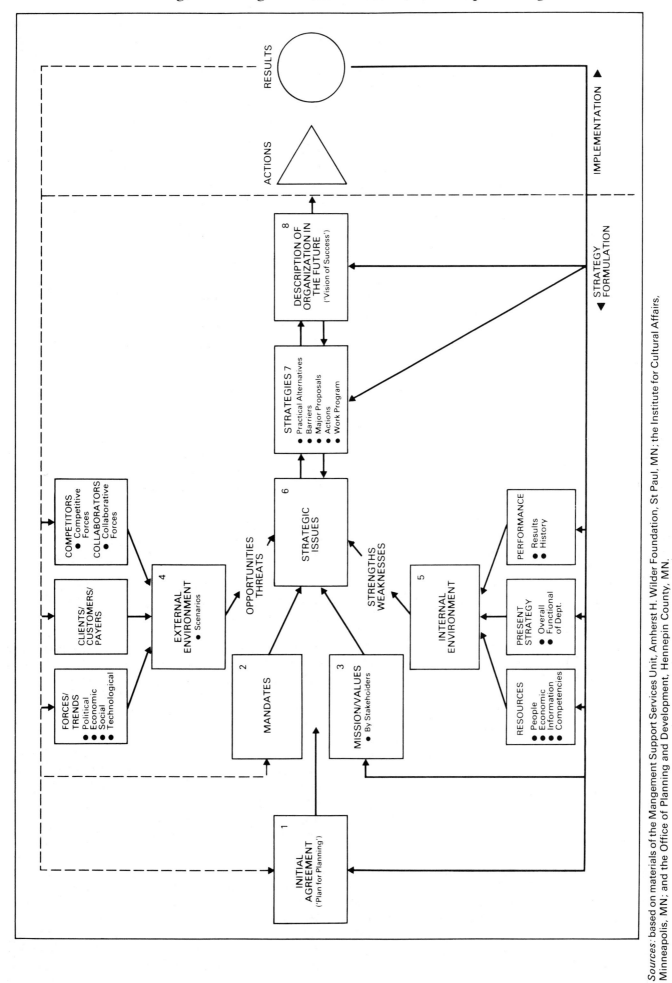

Sources: based on materials of the Mangement Support Services Unit, Amherst H. Wilder Foundation, St Paul, MN; the Institute for Cultural Affairs, Minneapolis, MN; and the Office of Planning and Development, Hennepin County, MN.

Figure 1. Strategic planning process

In the simplest form of stakeholder analysis, the organization identifies its stakeholders and their 'stakes' in the organization, along with the stakeholders' criteria for judging the performance of the organization. The organization also explores how well it does against the stakeholders' criteria. Once a stakeholder analysis is completed, the organization can develop a mission statement that takes key stakeholder interests into account.

4. *External environmental assessment.* The fourth step is exploration of the environment outside the organization in order to identify the opportunities and threats the organization faces. Political, economic, social and technological trends and events might be assessed, along with the nature and status of various stakeholder groups, such as the organization's customers, clients or users, and actual or potential competitors or collaborators.

5. *Internal environmental assessment.* The next step is an assessment of the organization itself in order to identify its strengths and weaknesses. Three assessment categories include—following a simple systems model—organizational resources (inputs), present strategy (process) and performance (outputs). Unfortunately, most organizations can tell you a great deal about the resources they have, much less about their current strategy, and even less about how well they perform. The nature of accountability is changing, however, in that public and nonprofit organizations are increasingly held accountable for their outputs as well as their inputs. A stakeholder analysis can help organizations adapt to this changed nature of accountability, because the analysis forces organizations to focus on the criteria stakeholders use to judge organizational performance. Those criteria are typically related to output. For example, stakeholders are increasingly concerned with whether or not state-financed schools are producing educated citizens. In many states in the United States, the ability of public schools to garner public financing is becoming contingent on the schools' ability to demonstrate that they do an effective job of educating their students.

The identification of strengths, weaknesses, opportunities and threats—or SWOT analysis—in Steps 4 and 5 is very important because every effective strategy will build on strengths and take advantage of opportunities, while it overcomes or minimizes weaknesses and threats.

6. *Strategic issue identification.* Together the first five elements of the process lead to the sixth, the identification of strategic issues. *Strategic issues* are fundamental policy questions affecting the organization's mandates; mission and values; product or service level and mix, clients, users or payers, cost, financing, management or organizational design. Usually, it is vital that strategic issues be dealt with expeditiously and effectively if the organization is to survive and prosper. An organization that does not

address a strategic issue may be unable to head off a threat, unable to capitalize on an important opportunity, or both.

Strategic issues—virtually by definition—embody conflicts. The conflicts may be over ends (what); means (how); philosophy (why); location (where); timing (when); and who might be helped or hurt by different ways of resolving the issue (who). In order for the issues to be raised and resolved effectively, the organization must be prepared to deal with such conflicts.

A statement of a strategic issue should contain three elements. First, the issue should be described succinctly, preferably in a single paragraph. The issue itself should be framed as a question the organization can do something about. If the organization cannot do anything about it, it is not an issue—at least for the organization. An organization's attention is limited enough without wasting it on issues it cannot resolve.

Second, the factors that make the issue a fundamental policy question should be listed. In particular, what is it about mandates, mission, values or internal strengths and weaknesses and external opportunities and threats that make this a strategic issue? Listing these factors will become useful in the next step, strategy development.

Finally, the planning team should state the consequences of failure to address the issue. A review of the consequences will inform judgments of just how strategic, or important, various issues are. The strategic issue identification step therefore focuses organizational attention on what is truly important for the survival, prosperity and effectiveness of the organization—and provides useful advice on how to achieve these aims.

There are three basic approaches to the identification of strategic issues: the direct approach, the goals approach and the scenario approach.[2] The *direct approach*—in which strategic planners go straight from a view of mandates, mission and SWOTs to the identification of strategic issues—probably will work best for most governments and public agencies. The direct approach is best when one or more of the following conditions prevail: (1) there is no agreement on goals, or the goals on which there is agreement are too abstract to be useful; (2) there is no pre-existing vision of success and developing a consensually based vision will be difficult; (3) there is no hierarchical authority that can impose goals on the other stakeholders; or (4) the environment is so turbulent that development of goals or visions seems unwise, and partial actions in response to immediate, important issues seem most prudent. The direct approach, in other words, can work in the pluralistic, partisan, politicized and relatively fragmented worlds of most public organizations—as long as there is a 'dominant coalition'[3] strong enough and interested enough to make it work.

The *goals approach* is more in line with conventional planning theory which stipulates that an organization should establish goals and objectives for itself and then develop strategies to achieve those goals and objectives. The approach can work if there is fairly broad and deep agreement on the organization's goals and objectives—and if those goals and objectives themselves are detailed and specific enough to guide the identification of issues and development of strategies. This approach also is more likely to work in organizations with hierarchical authority structures where key decision makers can impose goals on others affected by the planning exercise. The approach, in other words, is more likely to work in public or non-profit organizations that are hierarchically organized, pursue narrowly defined missions and have few powerful stakeholders than it is in organizations with broad agendas and numerous powerful stakeholders.

Finally, there is the *scenario*—or 'vision of success'[4]—*approach*, whereby the organization develops a 'best' or 'ideal' picture of itself in the future as it successfully fulfills its mission and achieves success. The strategic issues then concern how the organization should move from the way it is now to how it would look and behave according to its vision. The vision of success approach is most useful if the organization will have difficulty identifying strategic issues directly; if no detailed and specific agreed-upon goals and objectives exist and will be difficult to develop; and if drastic change is likely to be necessary. As conception precedes perception[5] development of a vision can provide the concepts that enable organizational members to see necessary changes. This approach is more likely to work in a non-profit organization than in a public-sector organization because public organizations are more likely to be tightly constrained by mandates.

7. *Strategy development.* In this step, strategies are developed to deal with the issues identified in the previous step. A *strategy* is a *pattern* of purposes, policies, programmes, actions, decisions and/or resource allocations that define what an organization is, what it does and why it does it. Strategies can vary by level, function and time frame.

This definition is purposely broad, in order to focus attention on the creation of consistency across *rhetoric* (what people say), *choices* (what people decide and are willing to pay for) and *actions* (what people do). Effective strategy formulation and implementation processes will link rhetoric, choices and actions into a coherent and consistent pattern across levels, functions and time.[6]

The author favours a five-part strategy development process (to which he was first introduced by the Institute for Cultural Affairs in Minneapolis).

Strategy development begins with identification of practical alternatives, dreams or visions for resolving the strategic issues. It is of course important to be practical, but if the organization is unwilling to entertain at least *some* 'dreams' or 'visions' for resolving its strategic issues, it probably should not be engaged in strategic planning.

Next, the planning team should enumerate the barriers to achieving those alternatives, dreams or visions, and not focus directly on their achievement. A focus on barriers at this point is not typical of most strategic planning processes. But doing so is one way of assuring that strategies deal with implementation difficulties directly rather than haphazardly.

Once alternatives, dreams and visions, along with barriers to their realization, are listed, the team should prepare or request major proposals for achieving the alternatives, dreams or visions directly, or else indirectly through overcoming the barriers. For example, a major city government did not begin to work on strategies to achieve its major ambitions until it had overhauled its archaic civil service system. That system clearly was a barrier that had to be confronted before the city government could have any hope of achieving its more important objectives.

After the strategic planning team prepares or receives major proposals, two final tasks must be completed. The team must identify the actions needed over the next one to two years to implement the major proposals. And finally, the team must spell out a detailed work programme, covering the next 6 months to a year, to implement the actions.

An effective strategy must meet several criteria. It must be technically workable, politically acceptable to key stakeholders, and must accord with the organization's philosophy and core values. It must also be ethical, moral and legal.

8. *Description of the organization in the future.* In the final (and not always necessary) step in the process the organization describes what it should look like as it successfully implements its strategies and achieves its full potential. This description is the organization's 'vision of success'. Few organizations have such a description or vision, yet the importance of such descriptions has long been recognized by well-managed companies and organizational psychologists.[7] Typically included in such descriptions are the organization's mission, its basic strategies, its performance criteria, some important decision rules, and the ethical standards expected of all employees.

These eight steps complete the strategy formulation process. Next come actions and decisions to implement the strategies, and, finally, the evaluation of results. Although the steps are laid out in a linear, sequential manner, it must be emphasized that the process is iterative. Groups often have to repeat steps before satisfactory decisions can be reached and actions taken. Furthermore, implementation typically should not wait until the eight steps have been completed. As noted earlier, strategic thinking *and* acting are important, and all of the thinking does not have to occur before any actions are taken.

To return to Wayne Gretzky and George Stedman, one can easily imagine them zooming almost intuitively through the eight steps—while already on the move—in a rapid series of discussions, decisions and actions. The eight steps merely make the process of strategic thinking and acting more orderly and allow more people to participate in the process.

The process might be applied across levels and functions in an organization as outlined in Figure 2. The application is based on the system used by the 3M Corporation.[8] In the system's first cycle, there is 'bottom up' development of strategic plans within a framework established at the top, followed by reviews and reconciliations at each succeeding level. In the second cycle, operating plans are developed to implement the strategic plans. Depending on the situation, decisions at the top of the organizational hierarchy may or not require policy board approval, which explains why the line depicting the process flow diverges at the top.

The Benefits of Strategic Planning

What are the benefits of strategic planning? Government and non-profit organizations in the United States are finding that strategic planning can help them:

☆ think strategically;

☆ clarify future direction;

☆ make today's decisions in light of their future consequences;

☆ develop a coherent and defensible basis for decision making;

☆ exercise maximum discretion in the areas under organizational control;

☆ solve major organizational problems;

☆ improve performance;

☆ deal effectively with rapidly changing circumstances;

☆ build teamwork and expertise.

While there is no guarantee that strategic planning will produce these benefits, there are an increasing number of case example and studies that indicate it can help as long as key leaders and decision makers want it to work, and are willing to invest the time,

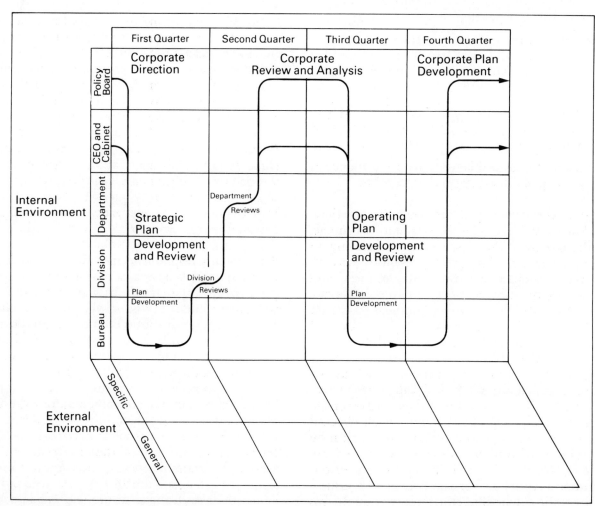

Figure 2. Annual strategic planning process

attention and resources necessary to make it work.[9] In the next two sections we will turn to two cases in which the strategic planning process outlined above produced desirable results. The author served as a strategic planning consultant in each case.

Case No. 1—Suburban City

Suburban City is an older, middle-class, 'first ring' suburb of a major metropolitan city in the American Midwest. Suburban City is regarded among city management professionals as one of the best-managed cities in the state. The city has 227 employees and an annual budget of $25·6m. The assistant city manager was the leader of the strategic planning team. The city manager was a strong supporter and member of the team. The team performed a stakeholder analysis, developed a mission statement, identified strategic issues, and developed strategies to deal with its most important issues. They are now implementing their strategies.

The following strategic issues were identified:

☆ What should the city do to enhance and improve its vehicular and pedestrian movements throughout its hierarchy of transportation facilities?

☆ What should the city do to improve its image as a place to live and work?

☆ What should the city do to attract high quality housing that meets the needs of a changing population and maintains the integrity of the existing housing stock?

☆ What should the city do to maintain its physical facilities while responding to changing demands for public services?

☆ What should the city do to restore confidence in its water quality and supply?

Strategies were developed to deal with all these issues, but we will consider the strategies stemming from the last two. The first step in responding to changing demands for public services was to undertake a major survey of households and businesses in the city to uncover preferences for services. Now that the survey is complete, city staff are rearranging and reorganizing services and delivery mechanisms to respond effectively.

Suburban City residents became worried, to the point of panic, when the city's water supply was found to be contaminated by uncontrolled seepage from a creosote plant. The city immediately closed down the affected wells and began a major cleanup effort. The water *quality* problem was cleared up, but the public *perception* that the city had a serious water quality problem persisted. City staff undertook a public education effort to deal with this misperception, and another effort was undertaken to deal with the remaining—and real, not just perceived—problem of a water *quantity*.

The strategic planning team did not go on to draft a 'vision of success' for the city. One reason why this was not done was that the team had had real difficulty developing a mission statement that all could support. The difficulty was not over content, interestingly enough, but over style. The city manager felt that a mission statement should give a person 'goose bumps', and the team had trouble drafting a mission statement that did. Finally, the city manager relented and supported a mission statement that had less of a physiological effect.

An interesting result of the city's strategic planning effort has been the recognition by members of the city council that they have not been an effective policy-making board. As a result, they hired a nationally known consultant on effective governance to help them become better policymakers. The city manager and assistant city manager are convinced that as the council becomes more effective, strategic planning for the city also will become more effective.

Case No. 2—Public Health Nursing Service

Public Health Nursing Service (Nursing Service) is a unit of the government of a large, urban county in the same state as Suburban City. The county executive director decided to explore the utility of strategic planning for the county by asking several units of county government, including Nursing Service, to undertake strategic planning.

Nursing Service is required by statute to control communicable diseases, and it also provides a variety of public health services at its clinics throughout the county. In 1984 Nursing Service had over 80 staff members and a budget of approximately $3·5m.

The strategic planning team was led by the director of the service, who was a major supporter of the process. Other sponsors, though not strong supporters, included the county's executive director and the director of the department of public health, of which Nursing Service is a part. The department's health planner was an active and dedicated promoter of the process.

The director, deputy director and staff of Nursing Service saw strategic planning as an opportunity to rethink the service's mission and strategies in light of the rapidly changing health care environment. They were concerned, however, that they had been selected as 'guinea pigs' for the executive director's experiment in strategic planning. Nursing Service has always lived with the fear that it would be taken over, put out of business or otherwise circumvented by the county government's huge medical centre, a famous hospital that was considering entering the home health care field (Nursing Service's main 'business') at the same time that Nursing Service began its strategic planning process. Nursing Service was afraid that any information or arguments it created as part of its process might be used against it by the executive director and county board to benefit the medical centre. A number of reasssurances from the executive director were necessary before Nursing Service would believe it was not being 'set up'.

As a result of the process, Nursing Service identified a number of strategic issues. The principal issue was what the mission of Nursing Service should be given the changing health care environment. After rethinking their mission, the Nursing Service team rethought their first set of strategic issues. The team identified a new set of strategic issues concerning how the new mission could be pursued. Those issues were:

☆ What is the role of Nursing Service in ensuring the health of the citizens of the county?

☆ How should Nursing Service deal with the growing health care needs for which there is inadequate or no reimbursement of services?

☆ What is the role of Nursing Service (and the county) in ensuring quality in community-based health care?

☆ What is the role of Nursing Service (and the county) in ensuring community health planning and health system development?

Nursing Service went on to develop a set of strategies designed to deal with these issues. The set includes:

☆ Differentiation and clarification of line and staff functions of Nursing Service's supervisors and administrators.

☆ Development of a process for programme development and change.

☆ Development of an organizational structure which will allow the agency to respond most effectively and efficiently to the needs of communities as well as individuals and families.

By the end of 1987 these strategies should be fully implemented. The strategies do not necessarily deal with the strategic issues directly. Instead, they focus primarily on overcoming the barriers to dealing with the issues. Once the agency is organized properly and has programme development and change procedures in place, it will be better able to address the health care needs of the citizens of the county.

Nursing Service also developed a 'vision of success'

for itself. The Service's idealized scenario of itself envisages an agency thoroughly responsive to community, family and individual health care needs.

Ironically, it was Nursing Service's strategic planning efforts that in part forced strategic planning on the county board. Nursing Service prepared its strategic issues and then was asked to make a presentation to the county board on the issues and desirable strategies to address them. The issues ultimately concerned the county government's role in the health care field and the board's willingness to pay for meeting the health care needs of the county's residents. County board members realized they were completely unprepared to deal with the issues raised by Nursing Service. The board also realized that they might soon be faced with similar vexing issues by other departments engaged in strategic planning. The board felt a need to think about the county government as a whole, and about how to establish priorities, before they were presented with any more policy questions for which they had no answers. The board decided to go on a retreat in order to clarify the county government's mission, to identify strategic issues and to agree on a process for resolving the issues. They identified eight key issues, including issues prompted by Nursing Service's questions concerning the county's role in health care.

Also ironically, partway through Nursing Service's planning efforts, the county board forced the county's executive director to resign. Nursing Service then saw the strategic planning process as a real opportunity to think through its position so that it could have the most impact on the thinking of the new executive director.

What it Takes to Initiate and Succeed with Strategic Planning

The two case histories and the growing body of literature on strategic planning for the public and non-profit sectors help us draw some conclusions about what appears to be necessary to initiate an effective strategic planning process. At a minimum, any organization that wishes to engage in strategic planning should have: (1) a process sponsor(s) in a position of power to legitimize the process; (2) a 'champion' to push the process along;[10] (3) a strategic planning team; (4) an expectation that there will be disruptions and delays; (5) a willingness to be flexible about what constitutes a strategic plan; (6) an ability to pull information and people together at key points for important discussions and decisions; and (7) a willingness to construct and consider arguments geared to very different evaluative criteria.

The criteria for judging the effectiveness of strategic planning for governments and public agencies probably should differ from those used to judge effectiveness in the private sector. The nature of the public sector prevents exact duplication of private sector practice.[11] The more numerous stakeholders, the conflicting criteria they often use to judge governmental performance, the presssures for public accountability and the idea that the public sector is meant to do what the private sector cannot, all militate against holding government strategic planning practice to private-sector standards. Until governments and public agencies (as well as non-profit organizations) gain more experience with strategic planning, it seems best to judge their strategic planning efforts according to the extent to which they: (1) focus the attention of key decision makers on what it important for their organizations, (2) help set priorities for action, and (3) generate those actions.

Conclusions

Strategic planning for public and non-profit organizations is important and probably will become part of the standard repertoire of public and non-profit planners. It is important, of course, for planners to be very careful about how they engage in strategic planning, since every situation is at least somewhat different and since planning can be effective only if it is tailored to the specific situation in which it is used.[12] The process outlined in this article, in other words, represents a generic guide to strategic thought and action, and must be adapted with care and understanding to be useful in any given situation.

To assert that strategic planning will increase in importance raises the question of who the strategic planners are. It is likely that within the organization they may not hold job titles that include the word 'planner'; instead, they may be in policy making or line management positions.[13] Since strategic planning tends to fuse planning and decision making, it makes sense to think of decision makers as strategic planners and to think of strategic planners as facilitators of decision making across levels and functions in organizations (and communities). The specific blend of technical knowledge and process expertise that the persons with the formal job title of planner should bring to strategic planning exercises, of course, will vary in different situations. The more the key decision makers already have the necessary technical knowledge, the more the planners will be relied upon to facilitate the process than to provide technical knowledge.

Finally, research must explore a number of theoretical and practical issues in order to advance the knowledge and practice of strategic planning for governments, public agencies and non-profit organizations. In particular, more detailed strategic planning models should specify key situational factors governing their use; provide specific advice on how to formulate and implement strategies in different situations; be explicitly political; indicate how to deal with plural, ambiguous or conflicting goals or objectives; link content and process; indicate how collaboration as well as competition should be handled; and specify roles for the strategic planner. Progress has been made on all of those fronts[14] (to which, it is hoped, this article and the book from which it is drawn attest), but more is necessary if strategic planning is to help governments, public agencies and non-profit organizations, as well as communities and functions, fulfill their missions and serve their stakeholders effectively, efficiently and responsibly.

Acknowledgement—This article is based on a chapter in John M. Bryson, *Strategic Planning for Public and Nonprofit Organisations*, Jossey-Bass, San Francisco (1988).

References

(1) J. B. Olsen and D. C. Eadie, *The Game Plan: Governance With Foresight*, p. 4, Council of State Planning Agencies, Washington, D.C. (1982).

(2) B. Barry, *The Strategic Planning Workbook for Nonprofit Organizations*, The Amherst H. Wilder Foundation, St Paul, MN (1986).

(3) J. D. Thompson, *Organizations in Action*, McGraw-Hill, New York (1967).

(4) B. Taylor, Strategic planning—which style do you need?, *Long Range Planning* **17**, 51–62 (1984).

(5) R. May, *Love and Will*, Norton, New York (1969).

(6) P. Bromiley, Personal communication (1986).

(7) T. J. Peters and R. H. Waterman, Jr, *In Search of Excellence: Lessons from America's Best-Run Companies*, Harper & Row, New York (1982); E. A. Locke, K. W. Shaw, L. M. Saari and G. P. Latham, Goal setting and task performance: 1969–1980, *Psychological Bulletin* **90**, 125–152 (1981).

(8) M. A. Tita and R. J. Allio, 3M's strategy system—planning in an innovative organization, *Planning Review*, September, pp.10–15 (1984).

(9) J. M. Bryson and R. C. Einsweiler (Eds), *Strategic Planning for Public Purposes—Concepts, Tools and Cases*, The Planners' Press of the American Planning Association, Chicago, IL and Washington, D.C. (1988).

(10) P. Kotler, *Marketing Management*, p. 200, Prentice-Hall, Englewood Cliffs, N.J.; R. M. Kanter (1976), *The Changemasters*, p. 296, Simon & Schuster, New York (1983).

(11) P. S. Ring and J. L. Perry, Strategic management in public and private organizations: implications and distinctive contexts and constraints, *Academy of Management Review* **10**, 276–286 (1985).

(12) J. M. Bryson and A. L. Delbecq, A contingent approach to strategy and tactics in project planning, *Journal of the American Planning Association* **45**, 167–179 (1979); K. S. Christensen, Coping with uncertainty in planning, *Journal of the American Planning Association* **51**, 63–73 (1985).

(13) J. M. Bryson, A. H. Van de Ven and W. D. Roering, Strategic planning and the revitalization of the public service, in R. B. Denhardt and E. T. Jennings, Jr (Eds), *The Revitalization of the Public Service*, pp. 55–75, Extension Publications, University of Missouri, Columbia, MO (1987).

(14) B. Checkoway (Ed.), *Strategic Perspectives on Planning Practice*, Lexington Books, Lexington, MA (1986).

Performance Review: Key to Effective Planning

Stan J. Berry*

Performance Review can be one of the most important of strategies used by corporate planners. The author sees it as a communications process in which people in the organization rationalize their aspirations in the context of the goals of the organization and its working out in relation to a school system is described.

I am personally committed to the concept that we can influence the direction of our futures; and that with good planning and input from all parts of our communities it is possible, within the framework of agreed aims and objectives, to plan and make choices among alternatives that will move the educational process along a chosen path to a preferred future. It makes sense to go through a process of setting out our aims and objectives and developing strategies to put us in the right direction. Without this process, we are like a ship in a stormy sea with no tools of navigation—running our engines at full speed and going nowhere. One such process organizations can use is Performance Review.

The Performance Review process, used positively, can be one of the most 'important 'planning' strategies adopted by corporate managers. It can be a process which allows us to express individual and corporate expectations, or goals, and then, later, to measure how well we have fared, and go on to establish further goals based on that experience.

The words 'Performance Review' conjure up many different ideas to different people. Some see performance review as a way of ensuring that subordinates are doing their job, through regular 'check-ups' by superiors—like putting a car through a car clinic to see how well everything is working. Some view it as an accounting procedure stressing the negative and highlighting character or performance weakness. Those using a method based on these attitudes will obtain some type of evaluation of their personnel, but will not tap the potential benefits to be obtained by organizations and staff alike from a well designed true performance review system.

Performance Review as I perceive it can be defined as follows:

> Performance Review is a disciplined communications process, relying heavily on the interview process, in which people in the organization co-operatively express their hopes and aspirations for a stated period, and rationalize them within the context of the overall goals of the corporation as stated by the Trustees (or Board of Directors or whatever).

In Table 1 comparison of what Performance Review is, and is not, expresses the definition in more pragmatic terms.

Performance Review is not a static process; it undergoes revisions and refinements as we learn more about its influence on people and organizations as people adapt to the concept, and as we adapt to the everchanging social, political and financial environment around us.

To give you a clue as to how Performance Review has evolved and is working to the benefit of one particular school system, I will review briefly our experience in Carleton over the best part of a decade.

The 'Performance Review' process has been a feature of the Carleton Board of Education's organizational structure since 1970. Initially it resulted from a series of meetings between myself and our very energetic first Chairman. I must admit that some Trustees viewed the initial attempts very much in the 'negative' mode, that is purely as a vehicle to ensure that senior staff were doing their jobs. Some of the senior staff felt threatened by this new process, but I viewed it as a very positive move which would force me to sit down at regularly scheduled intervals with my senior staff colleagues on one hand, and Trustees on the other, to develop a consensus about where we were headed as a collectivity, and where our personal career plans fitted into the overall scheme of things.

Since its inception, Performance Review has undergone several modifications to adapt it to changed conditions and as we have matured in our use of this goal setting/evaluation device.

*The author is Director of Education, Carleton Board of Education, 133 Greenbank Road, Repean, Ontario K2H 6L3.

Table 1

What *it is*	What *it is not*
A clean statement of the *major features* of the job. Set as a first process, by the individual with his superior	Based on out-of-date job descriptions or misconceptions
A *discipline* that creates an occasion where a view of progress and next steps can be made--built on natural continuous reviews	An annual or semi-annual *special ceremony* where everyone is ill-at ease and where people are surprised to find things that went wrong—5 months ago
A *co-operative* effort. Where the person being reviewed is not threatened and participates in an open and frank discussion of goals achieved and goals missed	A process where the reviewer comes close to a violation of the integrity of personality—*judging* personal worth of individual
A commitment through *participation,* where the individual is able to rationalize his own career expectations with goals of the organization	Perfunctory interviews or formal discussions, where the individual is *told* by his superior the goals he is to reach
A process where the goal setter is an *active* agent	A process where the goal setter is a *passive* object
A commitment for *future* action that will improve performance result	Review of *past* failures with directed solutions from the interviewer—not an occasion to prove individual guilty of some omission
Measure of *current performance*	Measurement of *potential*
Participation in controlled *freedom*	*Authoritative* management
Stresses *analysis* vs appraisal. Implies a more positive approach	An accounting that stresses the *negative* and emphasizes weaknesses
A tool of *accountability* and potent way to motivate people—superior a helper—encourages innovation, creativity and initiative	A superior sitting in judgment of the subordinate. *Autocratic* management
Based on belief that each individual knows his own capabilities better than anyone else—therefore self-appraisal with guidance of superior	Belief that individuals are motivated through fear, etc.
A process that considers the *development of human resources* a primary means of achieving the objectives of the organization	Stress *organizational patterns* as primary means of ensuring productivity of the system

The most significant change has been the evolution from a strictly individual goal setting process, to one in which the individuals set goals within the context of the objectives of the total management team. We have gone through several stages to reach this point, including a rather elaborate system of 'Plans of Action'. The Trustees became involved initially through the Director's Review Committee and its successor, the Chairman's Committee, but only in a 'monitoring' reactive mode.

The other significant change has been the expansion of the principles of Performance Review to the classroom through the vehicle of Results-Oriented Supervision. Beginning with its initial meeting in November 1973, the Director's Committee on Supervision (composed mainly of in-school personnel) worked for over 2 years and recommended in 1975 that a co-operative goal setting process known locally as 'positive supervision' be adopted by teachers in our schools. Subsequent to Board approval and with the strong leadership of Carleton principals, this concept has gradually spread across the jurisdiction.

In 1971, the Board adopted a series of aims and objectives which set the overall tone of the organizations. However, it was not until 1977 that the Board as a whole set for the first time system-wide annual corporate goals. In reality, these goals were the product of meetings of the Superintendents' Council with limited influence by the Board. At that time, it was stressed that in future we hoped that Trustees would be involved in the corporate goal setting process in a more dynamic fashion.

A cycle of performance review and goal setting has emerged in Carleton which ensures that the 'Field' managers (school superintendents in co-operation with principals) have priority input into the corporate goal setting process, and that central office managers respond to the needs of the schools (and not the other way around!). The Board of Trustees, as elected representatives of the wider community we serve, establishes overall goals of the system for the ensuing 12 months, cognizant of the hopes and aspirations of the various parts of the organization.

The initial stage for this yearly cycle was set when the Board approved corporate goals last fall. We were on the cycle in 'pure' form as of last May when the Field Managers began their goal setting processes. Once we are genuinely into the cycle, Field Managers will be key influencers within the organization in the establishment of corporate goals. These corporate goals set the parameters within which the general objectives of the two main branches within our organization are formulated as well as goals of the Directorate and individual staff member. The personal goals of the Chief Executive Officer—the Director of Education—are set in support of the total enterprise.

To show how all of this translates into action, Annex I and Annex II show our current corporate goals, and my personal goals.

The cycle, together with the actual goals and objectives,

Directorate's 1978 Objectives

Director's leadership commitment		
1978 Objectives—field services	**1978 Corporate goals**	**1978 Objectives—central services**
(1.1) To assist in public discussions on budgetary and program limitations through personal and delegated participation	**(1)** The Carleton Board of Education to make efforts to impress upon its total community (both staff and general public) the fiscal constraints facing it in 1978, and therefore limited resources available for the support of the system	**(1.1)** To develop a document to explain the 1978 budget so that both staff and general public better understand the fiscal constraints of 1978
(1.2) To maintain a flow of communication among Field Services staff on major developments in the budgetary process in order to ensure an appreciation and understanding of the budgetary restraints		**(1.2)** To develop a policy respecting French Language special grants
(1.3) Through close monitoring of expenditures throughout the Field Services, to support fiscal restraints		
(2.1) To make recommendations in concert with the Program Department concerning the 'extended' component of the CEL program for the 1978/1979 year	**(2)** To identify the long-term implications of the French-As-A-Second Language (FL2) programs in respect to: Staff recruiting and deployment Staff development School organization Program development	**(2.1)** To develop a 5-year staffing projection to provide a base for personnel and financial planning, including FL2
(2.2) To identify the impact that will be felt on regular programs and on teacher/supervisor requirements, as the FL2 program expands through the intermediate and secondary school levels		**(2.2)** To determine the most effective procedure for the recruitment and assignment to schools of FL2 staff
(2.3) To co-operate with the Personnel Department in developing the interview and hiring process of French Language Teachers		**(2.3)** To prepare a report on the 'extended' component of the CEL program emphasizing equity of application, optionality and staffing implications
(2.4) To encourage supervisory staff to improve their bilingual capability by making opportunities available through courses or programs		**(2.4)** To prepare the FL2 component of the Multi-Year Plan for Curriculum Development and begin to integrate English and French program content
(2.5) Through the Program Liaison Council, to analyze the implications for school organizations in FL2 program proposals		**(2.5)** To establish closer liaison with French Departments at universities and colleges with a view to arriving at a continuum of FL2 programs
(3.1) To advise and co-operate through the Program Liaison Council, in developing effective policy proposals on program evaluation	**(3)** To develop a comprehensive evaluation policy supported by an increased ability to assess the effectiveness of school programs	**(3.1)** To analyze and, if appropriate, propose revisions to the present methods of evaluating work performance
(3.2) To analyze the implications for the Results-Oriented Supervision Program of an improved ability to evaluate school programs		**(3.2)** To prepare the policy proposals on program evaluation and support activities
(3.3) In concert with the Program Liaison Council, to promote leadership at the school level in the knowledge and skill in the evaluation of school programs through systems initiatives		**(3.3)** To develop in teachers an increased awareness of program evaluation and skill in the use of the techniques involved
		(3.4) To install a procedure for the identification of system evaluation priorities
(4.1) To work in co-operation with the Personnel Department to maintain relationships with the Federations by means of informal meetings and discussions with their executives, and provide for the opportunity for ongoing day-to-day discussions	**(4)** To ensure that carefully negotiated collective agreements are administered consistently and recognized as the basis of good Board/Federation communication and co-operation	**(4.1)** To prepare detailed back-up data before the 1978 salary negotiations begin, and to provide support to the Personnel Committee during the negotiation process
(4.2) To ensure, on a day-to-day basis, that the management rights of the Board are sustained without infringing on the negotiated perogatives of the teachers		**(4.2)** To prepare, through the Personnel Liaison Council, a plan for ensuring the consistent administration of the new collective agreements
(4.3) Through the Personnel Liaison Council to make recommendations for the improvement in personnel policies and procedures		**(4.3)** To maintain channels of co-operation and communication with the Federation's executives

Yearly Cycle for Management Objective Setting and Review

School Year Cycle — Field Services	Month	Events Significant to the Board	Month	Calender Year Cycle — Central Services
	January	1 January — Fiscal Year Begins Corporate Goals in Effect	January	1 January — Annual Objectives of Directorate and Central Supts. in Effect
Supts'. of Schools Hold Mid-Year review of Principals' Objectives for the Current Year — Chief Supt. A/O Holds Mid-Year Review of Supts'. of Schools' Objectives for Current Year	February		February	IMPLEMENTATION
IMPLEMENTATION	March	1 March — Budget Approved	March	
	April		April	
Supts. of Schools Hold Annual Review of Principals Objectives for Current Year	May		May	
Chief Supt. A/O Holds Annual Review Supts'. Objectives For Current Year — Principals Set Own Objectives for Next School Year	June	Chairman's Cttee. Holds Mid-Year Review of Directorate's Objectives for Current Year / 30 June — School Year Ends	June	Chief Supt.— C/S Holds Mid-Year Review of Central Supts'. Objectives for Current Year
Field Services prepare a synthesis of Principals' Objectives	July		July	IMPLEMENTATION
Supts. of School Set Own Objectives for Next Year	August		August	
1 September — Annual Objectives of Supts'.of School and Principals in Effect	September	1 September — School Year Begins	September	
IMPLEMENTATION	October	Board Holds Annual Review of Corporate Goals for Current Year / Board Sets Corporate Goals for Next Year	October	
	November	Mid-November Election Year-Election / Chairman's Cttee. Holds Annual Review of Directorate's Objectives for Current Year	November	Chief Supt. C/S Holds Annual Review of Central Supts. Objectives for Current Year / Central Supts'. Set Own Objectives for Next Calendar year
	December	1 December — New Board Year Begins / New Chairman's Cttee. Confirms Directorate's Objectives for Next Calender Year	December	Directorate Sets Own Objectives for Next Calendar Year

Figure 1

reflect the changes which have taken place in the organization of our staff, and in the Board itself, since last summer. They also reflect the changing role of the Chief Executive Officer as more of the 'internal' systems goals are taken over by Chief Superintendents and the branches they represent. This has allowed the Director of Education to spend more time and energy in the fulfillment of his personal goals in support of the Board of Trustees, and as a professional leader in the wider educational community.

Performance Review is very much an art involving high level skills, such as the ability to write measurable and acceptable goals, and the techniques of the co-operative

1978 Personal goals—Director of Education

Support the Board and its policy and decision-making process	Liaison and co-operation in the education community
(1) Provide professional leadership and give administrative support to any possible re-organization of the delivery of public educational services in Ottawa–Carleton	(1) As Chairman of the Ottawa Valley Education Liaison Council, promote its role as an effective professional voice for secondary and tertiary level institutions in the Ottawa Valley
(2) Support the interboard liaison committee in strengthening present areas of co-operation with area boards as well as identifying new possibilities	(2) Take advantage of our recent contacts with the leaders of Ottawa–Carleton municipalities to develop a closer on-going liaison
(3) Provide leadership for Carleton staff in learning to live with restraint as well as helping them understand all the implications of such a policy	(3) Promote the establishment of parent advisory committees at the local school level in Carleton
(4) To continue to monitor the efficiency and effectiveness of the re-organization of central staff (August 1977) and make an evaluation report to the Chairman's committee in June	(4) Maintain a schedule of bi-monthly meetings of the Directors of Education in Ottawa–Carleton
(5) To stand ready to assist the Board in June in assessing the effectiveness of its own Board organization	(5) Make more deliberate attempts to increase personal contacts with Ministry of Education officials
	(6) As former Chairman, act as an advisor to the Ontario Council for Leadership in Educational Administration, and serve as a member of the OAEAO provincial committee studying supervisory officer regulations

interview. As these skills are developed, and with increasing familiarity, we find that the participants' comfort indices go up. Also, over the years, there is a definite shift away from emphasis on normal 'Job' commitments to higher order professional goals.

Like many other concepts, Performance Review cannot simply be 'plugged in' to a system and work perfectly from day one; it grows and changes as people and organization alike grow and change. In fact, in Carleton, policy in this field has always been formulated by staff and approved by the Board of Education as an attempt to regularize what has already become an accepted practice.

Fundamentally, it requires corporate and individual commitment, in an atmosphere of trust and co-operation, to collectively chart the waters ahead and pick the best course for all concerned.

Strategic Planning for the World Wildlife Fund

G. J. Medley

WWF United Kingdom introduced strategic planning in 1978. In the next 9 years, as a result of planned actions, cohesive team work and clear objectives, the organization increased net funds by a factor of 5 and productivity by a factor of 6. Careful analysis, on an annual basis, of the organization's strengths and weaknesses and the opportunities available in the marketplace, led to the development of major strategies. Action plans designed to achieve and implement these strategies concluded the process which is described in detail.

Introduction

The National Organization of the World Wildlife Fund operating in the United Kingdom (WWF U.K.), is a 'not for profit' organization registered as a charity. It was founded in 1961 with the object of promoting education and research on the conservation of world fauna and flora, water, soils and other natural resources. In its early years, it developed like the majority of 'not for profit' organizations using relatively low-paid staff who had a concern for the charity's objectives. By 1973 gross income had risen to around £750,000 per annum and it stayed in this region for the next 5 years.

In 1977 a new Chairman of Trustees, Sir Arthur Norman, was appointed who was, himself, chairman of a major British Corporation. He identified the necessity of bringing in sound business management to develop the charity and when the previous Chief Executive Officer (CEO) left in April 1977, he searched for a Senior Executive who had already demonstrated a sound and successful business career. The author took up appointment as CEO of WWF U.K. on 1 January 1978, arriving to a relatively demoralized staff who had been without direct leadership for 9 months.

Preparing for Change

The first task was to identify, from the existing staff of 70, those who would fit in with a sound business approach compared to those who were working because of their interest and dedication to conservation. Whilst there was a need for good conservationists in the project departments, those in the fundraising areas needed to be capable of taking a wholly professional and sound business approach to their work. A structural reorganization took place in September 1978 and coincided with the introduction of strategic planning based on a 'management by objectives' (MBO) process developed by the author in his previous assignment as CEO of the subsidiary of a large multi-national. This was the first time that WWF U.K. had taken a hard look at its operations and it turned out to be a most revealing exercise.

The management team consisting of the Heads of each of the organization's departments of Promotions, Membership, Regional, Information, Education, Finance and Administration under the Chairmanship of the Director, met for the strategic planning exercises for two days at the end of September 1978.

To help with these exercises we were very fortunate to have the late Ron Felstead, a member of the Urwick Orr Partnership, who had been a considerable assistance to the author in introducing MBO in his previous assignment. Ron's quiet, clear, concise and informative control of the discussions played a very substantial part in converting a somewhat sceptical management team to a realization that strategic planning was not only an essential to success but also a major annual therapy and a forum at which matters could be brought out into the open which, for the rest of the year, were difficult to address.

G. J. Medley is Director of the World Wildlife Fund United Kingdom.

Photo by courtesy of WWF and Behram Kapadia

Plate 1. Project 'Tiger'. WWF's first major conservation success. At the turn of the century there were 80,000 tigers in India which had declined to only 2000 by 1972. Today there are estimated to be over 4000 tigers in 11 nature reserves in India

Deciding on the Purpose

The first essential was deciding the purpose of WWF U.K. The purpose is the reference point which makes possible the formulation of clear and realistic objectives. Prior to the strategic planning exercise the general view was that WWF U.K. was a conservation organization. After some considerable discussion however, it was recognized that in fact WWF U.K. was a fundraising business but that it also had as its purpose the proper spending of the funds raised. In 1978 the team decided that the purpose was 'to raise the maximum funds possible from U.K. sources and to ensure that the funds are used wisely for the benefit of conservation of the natural environment and renewable natural resources with emphasis on endangered species and habitats'.

Key Areas

Having decided the purpose, attention was then turned to the result-influencing areas of the organization, specific areas in which success would contribute significantly to improve results or areas in which failure would have an adverse impact on results. The team were asked to give free range to their thinking and a list of some 60 possible areas emerged on the blackboard. Further analysis of these showed that many of them were in fact overlapping or similar and a final list of nine was chosen.

It is interesting to see that these nine can be matched to the more usual designations found when this process is followed in industry. 'Marketing' is the

Photo by courtesy of WWF and Woodward

Plate 2. The Arabian oryx. The Arabian oryx was hunted to extinction in the wild but fortunately a few animals were in captivity in San Diego, California. Selected individuals from this captive herd were re-introduced in Oman and in Jordan and are now thriving back in their natural habitat under the watchful eye of local tribesmen

same word. 'Public Awareness' and 'Fund Status' relate to customer and shareholder perceptions of a business. 'Innovation' is the same concept as research and development and, most importantly, 'Net Funds' is the same as profitability. The full list is shown in Figure 1.

1. Marketing
2. Public Awareness
3. Fund Status
4. Quality of Application
5. Use of Personal Resources
6. Use of Financial and Physical Resources
7. Administrative Control
8. Innovation
9. Net Funds

Figure 1. WWF U.K. key areas 1978

Each key area was then taken in turn and subjected to a strengths, weaknesses, opportunities and threats exercise. This systematic review identified the internal strengths and weaknesses of the organization and examined the external environment to identify the opportunities that might be available and the threats that might exist.

Photo by courtesy of WWF and Vollmar

Plate 3. Pére David's deer. A similar situation to that of the Arabian oryx affected Pére David's Deer which were re-introduced to their natural habitat in China in 1987

The marketing strengths of WWF U.K. in 1978 were seen largely to be its emotive and visually appealing message, its 'Panda' logo and the uniqueness of its work. It was weak in its lack of a large donor base, its poor record on innovation and its lack of marketing penetration.

The rising awareness of the need to conserve the earth's natural resources, the size of the market-place and the general increase in disposable income, all presented opportunities to be tapped. On the other hand, competitive charities were also growing and some legislation proposals threatened certain freedoms to fundraising in specific areas, notably national lotteries.

In the key area of fund status, WWF U.K.'s international connections and scientific authority were seen as strengths offset by the weakness that the organization was not itself active in conservation work nor was it campaigning.

A major effort to devise and publicize a strategy for world conservation was to be carried out in the near future by WWF's international scientific sister organization, The International Union for the Conservation of Nature and Natural Resources (IUCN) with the financial backing of WWF and the United Nations Environmental Programme (UNEP) and this was seen as a major opportunity to improve further the public perception of WWF U.K. A concomitant threat was the Government's disinterest in the environment and its reluctance to enhance existing legislation in this field.

The full lists of strengths, weaknesses, opportunities and threats in the areas of marketing and fund status are shown in Figures 2 and 3.

Agreeing Strategies

At this point in the exercise, comprehensive answers to questions such as: (a) Where are we now? (b) What do we think will happen in the future? and (c) Where do we want to go? had been determined.

It was now necessary to devise guidelines—termed strategies—which would be developed for all future actions—a strategy is a guide for action. Clearly the marketing strategies concentrated on improving those areas of fundraising that were perceived to be weaknesses. Thus the first strategy was to increase membership and the second to increase the number and yield effectiveness of WWF's volunteer supporter groups around the country. Business would be concentrated on through effective commercial promotions and licensing the 'panda' trade mark and increased efforts would be made to raise income from business and charitable trusts. As the donor list had been identified as a major weakness, significant efforts would be made to build these lists. At that time, the cleaned list yielded 12,000 members

Photo by courtesy of RAF Kinloss

Plate 4. Sea eagles. Sea eagles used to breed in Scotland but no breeding pairs had been sighted for many years until WWF collaborated with the Nature Conservancy Council to re-introduce them to the Island of Rhum. The RAF assisted in this project by flying a pair of eagles from Norway for the re-introduction programme

STRENGTHS	WEAKNESSES
Image	Image
Logo	Small Membership
Charity	Poor Lists
Emotive Appeal	Communications
Visual Appeal	Inadequate Intermediaries
Achievements	Transience of Fashion
Communications	Reference to Cost: Income Ratio
Schools Lecture Service	Conservatism
Flexible	Inadequacy of Follow Through
Technical Support	Lack of Innovation
Diverse	Lack of Physical Resources
In Fashion	Scientific Inflexibility
Cost: Income Ratio	Inadequate Market Penetration
Recognition of Need	No Active Conservation
Awareness of Market Research	No Audio-visual Equipment
Unique	Photographic Resources
Caravan	
OPPORTUNITIES	**THREATS**
£700m Given to Charity in 1977	Competition
Schools	Legislation
Legislation	Economic Climate
Better Positioning	
Current Events	
Economic Clinate	
Untapped Sources	
Growing Awareness of Conservation Importance	

Figure 2. WWF U.K. SWOT analysis: key area—marketing

STRENGTHS	WEAKNESSES
Achievements	Non-controversial
Clear Aims and Programmes	Snob Charity
Non-political	No Active Conservation
Practical	Lush Literature
Affiliate of Largest Most Effective Conservation Organization	Trading Company
Scientific Authority	
1001	
Elitism	
Good Financial Standing	
Management	
OPPORTUNITIES	THREATS
World Conservation Strategy	Possible Defeat by Government on Major Conservation Issue
Lack of Conservation Legislation	Adverse Publicity
Confused Conservation Ethics	
Global 2000	

Figure 3. WWF U.K. SWOT analysis: key area—fund status

together with a further 25,000 trading customers. The full strategies in the key area of marketing are shown in Figure 4.

This exercise covering all the nine key areas took 2 days, at the end of which WWF U.K. had a document setting out its clear objectives for the immediate and medium-term future.

The last key area—'net funds'—equates to a corporation's profitability. The achievement of the net funds objectives would show the progress of the organization. Net fund objectives were therefore agreed by the management team for the coming 3 years.

Action Plans

The next part of the process was to devise the actions needed to achieve the strategies. Each department was asked to take each of the strategies and write down the actions they proposed in the coming year to fulfil the strategy. Clearly a number of strategies were not applicable to all departments whereas others had impact across all departments. The final

1. We Will Increase Our Membership and Improve Services to Members
2. We Will Increase the Number and Yield Effectiveness of Supporters' Groups
3. We Will Undertake a Research Programme to Asertain the Best Marketing Opportunities in Schools and Will Then Increase Fundraising in This Sector
4. We Will Increase the Yield Effectiveness of Commercial Promotions and Licensing
5. We Will Liaise Closely With WWF International to Improve the Yield Effectiveness in the United Kingdom of International Promotions
6. We Will Make a Concerted Effort to Increase Substantially Our Income from Business and Charitable Trusts
7. We Will Improve the Profitability of Our Trading Operations and Will Search for New Wayes of Increasing Income from Trading Opportunities
8. We Will Ensure That We are Able to Take Advantage of Special Opportunities for Raising Funds
9. We Will Build Our Lists in Order to Maximize Fundraising
10. We Will Seek to Further Improve and Widen Our Market Image
11. We Will Build up Active Key Contacts in Show Business, Commerce, and Conservation and Programme Them Centrally
12. We Will Ensure That We Have Adequate and Effective Audio-visual Equipment
13. We Will Ensure That We Use the Caravan to the Greatest Advantage
14. We Will Ensure That WWF Photographic Material is Made More Readily Available for Fundraising Purposes
15. We Will Encourage Donations in Covenant Form
16. We Will Increase Our Share of the Legacy Market

Figure 4. WWF U.K. strategies: key area—marketing

Plate 5. Grey seals. The United Kingdom is home to more than a quarter of the world's population of grey seals. These seals were being hunted for their pelts and were threatened with a severe decline in population. Harnessing public opinion, legislation and Parliament, WWF were able to ensure a ban on the hunting of these seals until population levels were restored

action plans from each department were amalgamated into a single document and this became the working forward plans for WWF U.K.

Budgeting to Meet Objectives

At the end of this strategic planning exercise, written documentation existed to show what WWF U.K. was hoping to achieve in all the key areas and how each department was going to take action to fulfil these strategies. At this stage however, there were no financial figures determined. The second part of the planning process involved the compilation of departmental budgets designed to achieve the strategies. Each department produced both income and expenditure budgets for the coming year and forecasts for the next 2 years. The departmental budgets were then consolidated to produce the budget for WWF U.K. It was a surprise to most members of the management team that

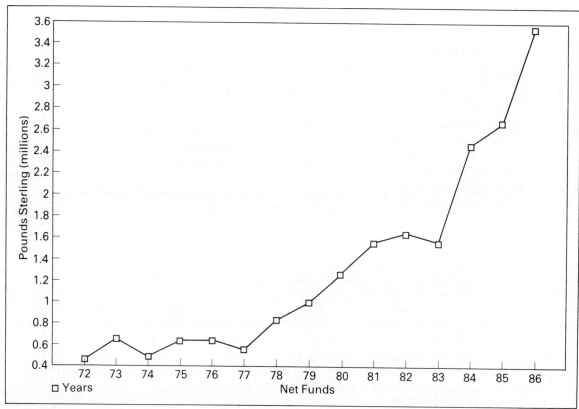

Figure 5. WWF U.K. net funds

Photo by courtesy of WWF and Paul Schauenberg

Plate 6. Tropical rainforests. Tropical rainforests are being destroyed at the rate of 100 acres every minute. Not only are the forests part of the world's natural heritage but they contain over 50 per cent of all known plant species, many of which have not yet been described to science. Destruction of the forest could therefore be destroying plants that might have the potential for considerable benefit to mankind. Forty per cent of prescription drugs come from plant origins and most of the world's major food crops rely on wild relatives for cross-breeding.
WWF has campaigned internationally to bring the plight of the tropical forests to the attention of Governments, industry and the general public with the result that a number of large areas of forest have been set aside as reserves, a more responsible attitude to forest products is emerging and the International Timber Trade Organization has recognized the necessity of using forest products only on a sustainable basis. The Korup Forest in the Cameroon is a project taken over and managed by WWF U.K. in 1987

when the departmental budgets were amalgamated the overall net fund projected for the budget year was extremely close to the objective net fund set in September as the final stage in the strategic planning exercise. This came as no surprise to the author because in his experience in the subsidiary of a major multi-national, the management team setting itself objectives with considerable 'stretch' produced budgets which met those objectives, and more importantly produced results which came within a

very few percentage points of achieving the budgets.

The setting of objectives in a strategic planning process and the compiling of budgets to achieve those objectives, are of no use without adequate factual information to show progress and achievement. WWF U.K.'s financial management was strengthened and systems set up to provide quarterly reporting by department against budget. At the end of each quarter departmental performance was assessed and where necessary corrective action was taken although the disciplines of budget and assessment of performance against budget led very rapidly to excellent control of expenditure.

The strategic planning exercises have been carried out each year in WWF U.K. and it is interesting to see how the process has evolved. The basic structure has remained unchanged but over the years, a number of key areas have been identified and a number dropped. For example, regional activities became important but when the problems within the regional area were resolved, that area no longer merited the microscopic examination of the planning process. It is also interesting to look at three measures of success and to see how the planning process has helped in the achievement of these successes.

Measures of Success

Net funds is the best measure of success. Net funds remained static between 1972 and 1977 at £400,000–£600,000. After the introduction of strategic planning in 1978, net funds grew steadily although there was a slight decline in 1983 due to an unexpected and unexplainable drop of significant proportions in income from legacies that year. The upward trend was resumed in 1984 and the last 2 years have been exceptional. Figure 5 shows the growth of net funds from 1972 to 1986.

Productivity in WWF U.K. is measured in terms of both gross and net income per employee. Staff numbers at 70 remained fairly constant from 1972 through to 1980 but since then marginal increases have occurred giving staff numbers at the end of 1986 of 85. With the growth in net funds by a factor of some eight times, it is clear that productivity will have increased substantially, as is shown in Figure 6.

At each annual strategic planning meeting net funds are projected forwards for the next budget year and the two following forecast years. Plotting each year's projections produces a matrix and adding to that matrix the actual achieved for each year gives an interesting diagram showing the fluctuations in objectives year on year set by the management team compared to actual achievement.

In the first 3 years, 1978–1980, actuals were remark-

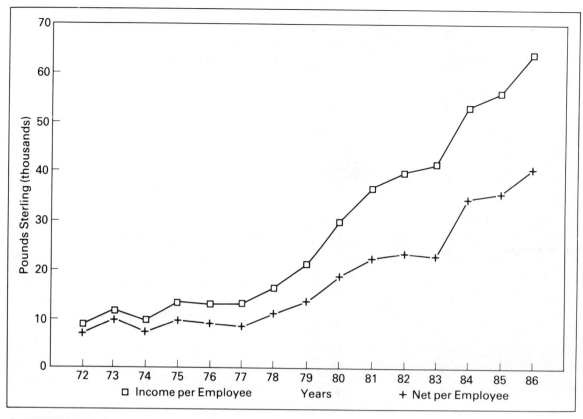

Figure 6. WWF U.K. income per employee–productivity

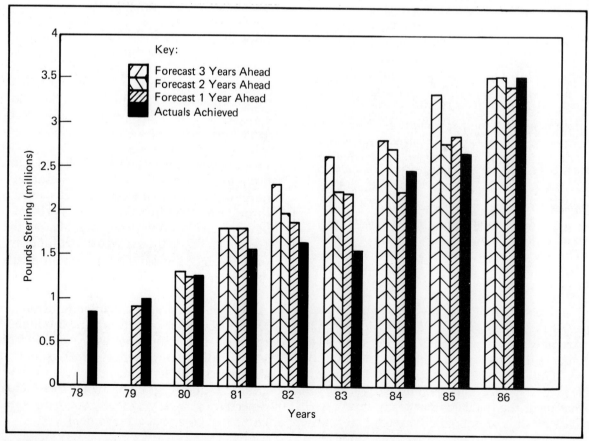

Figure 7. WWF U.K. forecast net funds vs actuals

1978

'To Raise the Maximum Funds Possible from U.K. Sources and to Ensure that the Funds are Used Wisely for the Benefit of Conservation of Renewable Natural Resources, with Emphasis on Endangered Species and Habitats.'

1986

'To Raise the Maximum Net Funds Possible from U.K. Sources and to Ensure that these Funds are Used Wisely for the Benefit of Conservation of Renewable Natural Resources, in Accordance with the Principles of the World Conservation Strategy.'

Figure 8. Statements of purpose compared

1. Marketing	1. Fund-raising
2. Public awareness	2. Reputation
3. Fund Status	3. Implementation of World Conservation Strategy
4. Quality of Application	
5. Use of Personnel Resources	4. Use of Personnel and Physical Resources
6. Use of Financial and Physical Resources	5. Communications
7. Administrative Control	6. Education
8. Innovation	7. Management
9. Net Funds	8. Lists
	9. Leverage
	10. Net Funds

Figure 9. A comparison of key areas

ably close to projections but in the following period, there were considerable shortfalls against projections which have been corrected in the last 2 years. Actuals now appear to be running ahead of projections which perhaps indicates that inadequate 'stretch' is being placed in the objectives, even though growth in the last 2 years has been considerable. This is clearly seen in Figure 7.

One other measure of success is the growth in the size of the donor list. At the end of 1986, WWF U.K. had 110,000 members and a donor list of 450,000 names. This compares with the 12,000 and 25,000 in 1978.

The purpose of the organization has changed but little and for comparison Figure 8 shows the 1978 purpose and underneath the 1986 purpose. Figure 9 shows the 1978 key areas alongside the 1986 key areas.

Conclusion

When strategic planning was first suggested for WWF U.K. there was a considerable degree of scepticism coupled with a willingness to try a new business method which might bring good results for the organization. After the first year it became clear to the whole management team that the exercise was invaluable, giving an opportunity for the whole team to participate in the forward planning resulting in a feeling of commitment by the whole team to the objectives that had been agreed after full and open discussion. This commitment seemed to transfer itself to other staff members giving the whole organization a sense of purpose and of drive which, coupled with team work, produced the outstanding results that the organization has achieved. It is now inconceivable to think of WWF U.K. working without an annual strategic planning exercise, developing clear strategies in key areas with action plans to achieve those strategies. The success of this method of management by objectives must be seen in the light of WWF U.K.'s performance in the last few years.

Reference

World Conservation Strategy, IUCN, Gland, Switzerland (1980).